Reminiscences Of Oxford

William Tuckwell

In the interest of creating a more extensive selection of rare historical book reprints, we have chosen to reproduce this title even though it may possibly have occasional imperfections such as missing and blurred pages, missing text, poor pictures, markings, dark backgrounds and other reproduction issues beyond our control. Because this work is culturally important, we have made it available as a part of our commitment to protecting, preserving and promoting the world's literature. Thank you for your understanding.

REMINISCENCES OF OXFORD

BY THE
REV. W. TUCKWELL, M.A.
LATE FELLOW OF NEW COLLEGE
AUTHOR OF "TONGUES IN TREES," "WINCHESTER FIFTY YEARS AGO,"
"REMINISCENCES OF A RADICAL PARSON," ETC. ETC.

WITH 16 ILLUSTRATIONS

SECOND EDITION

NEW YORK
E. P. DUTTON & COMPANY
31 WEST TWENTY-THIRD STREET
1908

O Thought, that wrote all that I met,
And in the tresorie it set
Of my braine, now shall men see
If any vertue in thee bee.
Now kith thy engine and thy might.
—CHAUCER, *House of Fame*, ii. 18.

PRINTED IN GREAT BRITAIN

REMINISCENCES OF OXFORD

THE VICE-CHANCELLOR ENTERING ST. MARY'S

The "Vice," Dr. Cotton, Provost of Worcester, is followed by his Pro-Vice-Chancellor Plumptre, Master of University, and "Ben" Symons, Warden of Wadham

PREFACE

MUCH of the additional matter in this Edition has appeared at different times in the Oxford *Magazine*. Extracts are also inserted, by kind permission of the Editor, from some of my Oxford Articles in the *Athenæum*. Fresh chapters are given to Trinity and Corpus. Names newly introduced are those of Baden Powell, Hungerford Pollen, T. H. Green, Hext of Corpus, Monsignor Patterson, Henry Coxe, Vaughan Thomas, Meyrick of Trinity, F. D. Maurice, Dean Lake, Archbishop Temple, Isaac Williams, Warden Sewell of New College, "Tommy" Short. The notices of Pusey, Newman, Sir H. Acland, Provost Hawkins, Mark Pattison, are enlarged. The brilliant squib of 1849, called "The Grand University Logic Stakes," now very scarce, appears, with a *Notularum Spicilegium*, in the Appendix.

CONTENTS

CHAP.		PAGE
I.	OXFORD IN THE THIRTIES	1
II.	ORIGINAL CHARACTERS	11
III.	PRESCIENTIFIC SCIENCE	32
IV.	SCIENTIFIC SCIENCE	45
V.	ÆSCULAPIUS IN THE THIRTIES	62
VI.	CALLIOPE IN THE THIRTIES	71
VII.	UNDERGRADUATES IN THE THIRTIES	83
VIII.	MORE ABOUT UNDERGRADUATES	104
IX.	SUMMA PAPAVERUM CAPITA. CHRISTCHURCH	122
X.	MAGDALEN AND NEW COLLEGE	158
XI.	ORIEL	179
XII.	BALLIOL	200
XIII.	TRINITY	223
XIV.	CORPUS	239
XV.	PATTISON — MAURICE — THOMSON — GOULBURN — SEWELL	252
XVI.	WALK ABOUT ZION	282
	APPENDICES	299
	INDEX	339

LIST OF ILLUSTRATIONS

1. The Vice-Chancellor entering St. Mary's. The "Vice," Dr. Cotton, Provost of Worcester, is followed by his Pro-Vice-Chancellor Plumptre, Master of University, and "Ben" Symons, Warden of Wadham. Photographed by Mrs. Frieda Girdlestone from a coloured drawing by the Rev. T. Woollam Smith . . . . *Frontispiece*
2. "Horse" Kett, from a portrait by Dighton . *To face page* 15
3. Dr. Daubeny, from a photograph, 1860 . . ,, 33
4. Dr. Buckland. The Ansdell portrait. Reproduced from Mrs. Gordon's "Life of Buckland," by kind permission of the authoress and of the publisher, Mr. John Murray . . . . ,, 41
5. Woodward, architect of the Museum. From a contemporary photograph . . . . ,, 51
6. Huxley, from a photograph taken at the Meeting of the British Association, 1860 . . . ,, 55
7. Tuckwell, from a water-colour drawing, 1883 . ,, 65
8. Charles Wordsworth, from Richmond's portrait . ,, 87
9. Pusey, from a pen-and-ink drawing of the Thirties, photographed by Mrs. Girdlestone . ,, 132
10. Sir Frederick Ouseley, from a photograph about 1856 . . . . ,, 148
11. Dr. Routh, from Pickersgill's portrait . . . ,, 159
12. J. H. Newman, from a pen-and-ink drawing 1841, photographed by Mrs. Girdlestone . . ,, 182
13. Mark Pattison, from a portrait in the possession of Miss Stirke . . . . ,, 252
14. John Gutch, engraved from a water-colour belonging to the family . . . . . ,, 289
15. Mother Louse, from the line engraving after Loggan . . . . ,, 290
16. Mother Goose, from a coloured lithograph by Dighton . . . . ,, 292

REMINISCENCES OF OXFORD

CHAPTER I

OXFORD IN THE THIRTIES

"καὶ μήν, ἦν δ' ἐγώ, ὦ Κέφαλε, χαίρω γε διαλεγόμενος τοῖς σφόδρα πρεσβύταις." "*To tell you the truth, Cephalus, I rejoice in conversing with very old persons.*" — PLATO, *Republic*, A. ii.

The Thirties—The Approach to Oxford—Coaching Celebrities—The Common Rooms—Then and Now—The Lost Art of Conversation—*Beaux Esprits* and *Belles*—Marshall Hacker — Miss Horseman.

THE evening of a prolonged life has its compensations and its duties. It has its compensations: the Elder, who, reverend like Shakespeare's Nestor for his outstretched life, has attained through old experience something of prophetic strain, reaps keen enjoyment from his personal familiarity with the days of yore, known to those around him roughly from the page of history or not at all. It has its duties: to hand on and to depict with the fascinating touch of first-hand recollection the incidents and action, the characteristics and the scenery, of that vanished past, which in the retired actor's memory still survives, but must scatter like the Sybil's leaves should he pass off the stage uncommunicative and unrecording.

REMINISCENCES OF OXFORD

The nineteenth century, in the second intention of the term, opens with the Thirties; its first two decades belong to and conclude an earlier epoch. The Thirties saw the birth of railroads and of the penny post; they invented lucifer matches; they witnessed Parliamentary and Municipal reform, the new Poor Law, the opening of London University; they hailed the accession of Victoria; in them Charles Dickens, Tennyson, Keble, Browning, John Henry Newman, began variously to influence the world; while with Scott, Crabbe, Coleridge, Lamb, Southey, all but a few patriarchs of the older school of literature passed away. Men now alive who were born, like myself, in the reign of George IV., recall and can describe an England as different from the England of our present century as monarchic France under the Capets differed from republican France to-day. Nowhere was the breach with the past more sundering than in Oxford. The University over which the Duke of Wellington was installed as Chancellor in 1834 owned undissolved continuity with the Oxford of Addison, Thomas Hearne, the Wartons, Bishop Lowth; the seeds of the changes which awaited it— of Church movements, Museums and Art Galleries, Local Examinations, Science Degrees, Extension Lectures, Women's Colleges—germinating unsuspected while the old warrior was emitting his genial false quantities in the Theatre, were to begin their transforming growth before the period which he adorned had found its close. The Oxford, then, of the Thirties, its scenery and habits, its humours and its characters, its gossip and its wit, shall be first among the dry bones in the valley of forgetfulness which I will try to clothe with flesh.

It was said in those days that the approach to Oxford by the Henley Road was the most beautiful in the world. Soon after passing Littlemore you came in sight of, and did not lose again, the sweet city with its dreaming spires, driven along a road now crowded and obscured with dwellings, open then to cornfields on the right, to uninclosed meadows on the left, with an unbroken view of the long line of towers, rising out of foliage less high and veiling than after seventy more years of growth to-day. At once, without suburban interval, you entered the finest quarter of the town, rolling under Magdalen Tower, and past the Magdalen elms, then in full unmutilated luxuriance, till the exquisite curves of the High Street opened on you, as you drew up at the Angel, or passed on to the Mitre and the Star. Along that road, or into Oxford by the St. Giles's entrance, lumbered at midnight Pickford's vast waggons with their six musically belled horses; sped stage-coaches all day long—Tantivy, Defiance, Rival, Regulator, Mazeppa, Telegraph, Rocket, "a fast coach, which performed the journey from Oxford to Birmingham in seven hours," Dart, Magnet, Blenheim, and some thirty more; heaped high with ponderous luggage and with cloaked passengers, thickly hung at Christmas time with turkeys, with pheasants in October; their guards, picked buglers, sending before them as they passed Magdalen Bridge the now forgotten strains of "Brignall Banks," "The Troubadour," "I'd be a Butterfly," "The Maid of Llangollen," or "Begone, Dull care"; on the box their queer old purple-faced many-caped drivers — Cheeseman, Steevens, Fowles, Charles Homes, Jack Adams, and Black Will. This last jehu, spending three nights of the week in Oxford, four in London, maintained in both a home, presided over by two several wives, with each of whom he had gone through the marriage ceremony; and had for many years—so distant was Oxford then from London—kept each partner ignorant of her sister's existence. The story came out at last; but the wives seem not to have objected, and it was the business of no one else; indeed, had he been indicted for bigamy, no Oxford jury could have been found to convict Black Will.

The coaches were horsed by Richard Costar, as great an original as any of his men; he lived in his picturesque house on the Cherwell, now converted into Magdalen School, just opposite Magdalen Turnpike, having two entrance gates, one on each side of the pike, so that he could always elude payment. I remember standing within his railings to see the procession of royal carriages which brought Queen Adelaide to Oxford in 1835. She drove about in semi-state, attending New College and Magdalen Chapels, lunching at Queen's, and holding a court at the Angel. Opposite to her in the carriage sat always the Duke of Wellington in his gold-tasselled cap, more cheered and regarded than the quiet, plain-looking, spotty-faced Queen. The Mayor of Oxford was an old Mr. Wootten, brewer, banker, and farmer, dressed always in blue brass-buttoned coat, cords, top-boots, and powdered hair. He was told that he must pay his respects to the Queen; so he drove to the Angel in his wonderful one-horse-chaise, a vehicle in which Mr. and Mrs. Bubb might have made their historic jaunt to Brighton, and was introduced to her Majesty by the Chamberlain, Lord Howe. She held out her hand to be kissed: the Mayor shook it heartily, with the salutation: "How d'ye do, marm; how's the King?" I saw Queen Victoria two years afterwards proclaimed at Carfax; and in the general election of 1837 I witnessed from the windows of Dr. Rowley, Master of University, the chairing of the successful candidates, Donald Maclean of Balliol, and William Erle of New College, afterwards Chief Justice of the Common Pleas. Erle rode in a fine open carriage with four white horses; Maclean was borne aloft, as was the custom, in a chair on four men's shoulders. Just as he passed University, I saw a man beneath me in the crowd fling at him a large stone. Maclean, a cricketer and athlete, saw it coming, caught it, dropped it, and took off his hat to the man, who disappeared from view in the onset made upon him by the mob; and, as Bunyan says of Neighbour Pliable, I saw him no more. Maclean was a very handsome man, owing his election, it was said, to his popularity among the wives of the electors; he died insolvent and in great poverty some years afterwards.

The University life was not without its brilliant social side. The Heads of Houses, with their families, formed a class apart, exchanging solemn dinners and consuming vasty deeps of port; but the abler resident Fellows, the younger Professors, and one or two notable outsiders, made up convivial sets, with whose wit, fun, frolic, there is no comparison in modern Oxford. The Common Rooms to-day, as I am informed, are swamped by shop; while general society, infinitely extended by the abolition of College celibacy, is correspondingly diluted. Tutors and Professors are choked with distinctions and redundant with educational activity; they lecture, they write, they edit, they investigate, they athleticise, they are scientific or theological or historical or linguistic; they fulfil presumably some wise end or ends. But one accomplishment of their forefathers has perished from among them — they no longer *talk*: the Ciceronian ideal of conversation, σπουδαῖον οὐδὲν, φιλόλογα multa, "Not a word on shop, much on literature," has perished from among them. In the Thirties, conversation was a fine art, a claim to social distinction: choice sprouts of the brain, epigram, anecdote, metaphor, now nursed carefully for the printer, were joyously lavished on one another by the men and women of those bibulous, pleasant days, who equipped themselves at leisure for the wit combats each late supper-party provoked, following on the piquet, quadrille, or whist, which was the serious business of the evening. Their talk ranged wide; their scholarship was not technical but monumental; they were no philologists, but they knew their authors—their authors, not classical only, but of mediæval, renaissant, modern, Europe. I remember how Christopher Erle, eccentric Fellow of New College, warmed with more than one glass of ruby Carbonel, would pour out Æschylus, Horace, Dante, by the yard. Staid Hammond of Merton, son to Canning's secretary and biographer, knew his Pope by heart, quoting him effectively and to the point. Edward Greswell of Corpus, whose quaint figure strode the streets always with stick in one hand and umbrella in the other, was a walking library of Greek and Latin inscriptions.

A select few ladies, frank spinsters and jovial matrons, added to the charm of these convivialities. Attired in short silk dresses—for Queen Addy, as Lady Granville calls her, was proud of her foot and ankle—sandal-shoes, lace tippets, hair dressed in crisp or flowing curls, they took their part in whist or at quadrille, this last a game I fear forgotten now, bearing their full share in the Attic supper-table till their sedan-chairs came to carry them away. There was gay old Mrs. Neve, belle of Oxford in her prime, living a widow now in Beam Hall, opposite Merton, with seven card-tables laid out sometimes in her not spacious drawing-room. Mrs. Foulkes, whose husband, the Principal of Jesus, walked the High Street always upon St. David's day with a large leek fastened in the tassel of his cap, piqued herself on the style and quality of her dress. She had a rival in Mrs. Pearse, a handsome widow living in St. Giles'; by the aid of Miss Boxall, the fashionable milliner, they vied with one another like Brunetta and Phyllis in the *Spectator*. Famous, not for dress, but for audacity and wit, was Rachel Burton,

"Jack" Burton as she was called, daughter to a Canon of Christchurch, whose flirtations with old Blucher, on the visit of the allied sovereigns, had amused a former generation, and who still survived to recall and propagate anecdotes not always fit for ears polite. Amongst her eccentricities she once won the Newdigate: the judges, agreed upon the poem which deserved the prize, broke the motto'd envelope to find within the card of Miss Rachel Burton. Her sister "Tom," married to Marshall Hacker, vicar of Iffley, I knew well; and I remember too the illustrious Jack, lodging in the corner house of what was then called Coach and Horse Lane, sunning herself on summer days without her wig and in wild dishabille on a small balcony overlooking the garden of a house in which I often visited. A wild story, which being absolutely untrue, does infinite credit to the inventive powers of the generation that originated it, explained in my time Mr. Marshall Hacker's double appellation. His name was said to have been Marshall; and he was by profession a surgeon. His intimate friend was injured while shooting, and Marshall amputated the wounded limb. The patient died, in consequence, he believed, of unskilful treatment under the knife. He bequeathed a fortune to the operator, on condition that he should at once take orders, becoming thereby precluded from professional practice, and that he should assume the surname of *Hacker*. It seemed to be one of those stories which, as Charles Kingsley used to say, are too good not to be true; but I am bound to destroy it: for I have learned that Mr. Marshall was never a surgeon, and that he took the name of Hacker on inheriting property descending to him from an ancestress, sister to Colonel Hacker the regicide, who married a Marshall in 1645.

Another of these vestals was Miss, or, as she liked to be called, Mrs. Horseman, dressy and made up, and posthumously juvenile, but retaining something of the beauty which had won the heart of Lord Holland's eldest son years before, when at Oxford with his tutor Shuttleworth, until her Ladyship took the alarm, swept down, and carried him off; and had attracted admiring notice from the Prince Regent in the Theatre, as she sat in the Ladies' Gallery with her lovely sister, Mrs. Nicholas. They came from Bath; I have always imagined their mother to be the "Mrs. Horseman, a very old, very little, very civil, very ancient-familied, good, quaint old lady," with whom Fanny Burney spent an evening in 1791.[1] Miss Horseman herself was a witty, well-bred, accomplished woman. Her memory was an inexhaustible treasure-house of all the apt sayings, comic incidents, memorable personages of the past thirty years, dispensed with gossip and green tea to her guests round the little drawing-room of her house in Skimmery Hall Lane, hung with valuable Claude engravings in their old black frames. She outlived her bright faculties, became childish, and wandered in her talk, but to the last shone forth in all the glaring impotence of dress, ever greeting me with cordial welcome, and pathetically iterative anecdote.

[1] Madame D'Arblay's "Diary," vol. v. p. 257.

She lies just outside St. Mary's Church; I see her grave through the railings as I pass along the street. That is the final record of all those charming antediluvians; "arl gone to churchyard," says Betty Maxworthy in "Lorna Doone." *La farce est jouée, tire le rideau;*—but it is something to recall and fix the *Manes Acheronte remissos.*

CHAPTER II

ORIGINAL CHARACTERS

"I am known to be a humorous patrician; hasty and tinder-like upon too trivial motion; what I think I utter, and spend my malice in my breath."—SHAKESPEARE.

Thomas Dunbar—Brasenose Ale—A famous Chess Club—Dunbar's Impromptus—"Horse" Kett of Trinity—Oriel Oddities—Copleston—Blanco White—Whately—Dr. Bull of Christchurch—The Various Species of Dons—The Senior Fellow—Some Venerable Waifs—Tom Davis—Dr. Ellerton of Magdalen—Rudd of Oriel—Edward Quicke of New College—Dr. Frowd of Corpus—His Vagaries as Preacher and Politician—A Brother Bedlamite—"Mo" Griffith of Merton—His Quips and Cranks.

READERS who, like supercilious Mr. Peter Magnus, are not fond of anything original, had better skip this chapter; if, with young Marlow in "She Stoops to Conquer," they can say more good-naturedly, "He's a character, and I'll humour him," let them persevere; for I shall recall not a few among the Oxford Characters of my early recollections. They were common enough in those days. Nature, after constructing an oddity, was wont to break the mould; and her more roguish experiments stood exceptional, numerous, distinct, and sharply defined. Nowadays, at Oxford, as elsewhere, men seem to me to be turned out by machinery; they think the same thoughts, wear the same dress, talk the same shop, in Parliament, or Bar, or Mess, or Common Room. Even in the Forties Characters were becoming rare; as the Senior Fellows of Corpus and of Merton, Frowd and Mo. Griffith—two oddities of whom I shall have something to say later on—were one day walking together round Christchurch Meadow, little Frowd was overheard lamenting that the strange Originals of their younger days seemed to have vanished from the skirts of Oxford knowledge; but was consoled by Griffith—"Does it not occur to you, Dr. Frowd, that you and I are the 'Characters' of to-day?"

First in my list shall come Thomas Dunbar, of Brasenose, keeper of the Ashmolean, poet, antiquary, conversationalist. Didbin, in his "Bibliographical Decameron," congratulates Oxford on Dunbar's appointment to the neglected museum, which he cleansed, smartened, rearranged, rescuing from dust and moths the splendid twelfth-century "Bestiarium" which Ashmole had placed in the collection. His poems, *vers de l'Université*, were handed about in manuscript, and are mostly lost. I possess an amusing squib on "Brasenose Ale," commemorating the else forgotten Brasenose dons and city wine merchants of the day;[1] with an ode composed by him as Poet Laureate to a famous chess club, whose minutes have passed from my bookshelves to swell the unrivalled collection of Mr. Madan, the accomplished Sub-Librarian at the Bodleian.[2] It was recited at an anniversary dinner, where sat as invited guests

[1] Appendix A.   [2] Appendix B.

ORIGINAL CHARACTERS 13

Mr. Markland, of Bath; Sir Christopher Pegge; porter-loving Dale of B.N.C. satirised in "Brasenose Ale"; with Henry Matthews, author of the "Diary of an Invalid."[1] "It was a sumptuous dinner," the minutes fondly record; it began at five o'clock, and must have continued till after nine; for "Old Tom is tolling" is written on the opposite page. The King's Arms, where it was held, still stands; but the delightful symposiasts, with their powdered hair and shirt-frills, their hessians or silk stockings, their sirloins and eighteenth-century port, are gone to what Dunbar's poem calls the Mansion of Hades. His, too, was the lampoon on the two corpulent brothers, whose names I will not draw from their dread abode. Respectively a physician and a divine, they were lazy and incapable in either function. This is Dunbar's friendly estimate of the pair:—

> Here D.D. toddles, M.D. rolls,
>   Were ever such a brace of noddies?
> D.D. has the cure of souls,
>   M.D. has the care of bodies.
>
> Between them both what treatment rare
>   Our bodies and our souls endure;
> One has the cure without the care,
>   And one the care without the cure.[2]

---

[1] Appendix C.
[2] One of my critics claims these lines for Horace Smith, of the "Rejected Addresses." They were ascribed to Dunbar in my time; are perhaps more likely to be by a man not known beyond Oxford, than to one amongst those of wider fame on whom at that time every unauthentic *jeu d'esprit* was fathered.

But his most brilliant reputation was colloquial; sparkling with apt quotations and with pointed well-placed anecdotes, he was especially happy in his impromptus. Leaving England for the East, the Club accredit him with a Latin letter, penned by Gilbert, afterwards Bishop of Chichester, to the Prince of the Faithful, as Grand Master of Oriental chess-craft. He returns thanks in "a warm and impressive Latin oration"; and suddenly perceiving that the seal appended to the commendatory epistle is enclosed in an oyster shell, he exclaims, "Et in Græcia Ostracismum Aristidi ostendam!" One of the Heads of Houses had four daughters—Mary, a don; Lucy, a blue-stocking; Susan, a simpleton; Fanny, a sweet unaffected girl. Asked by Lucy the meaning of the word *alliteration*, with scarcely a pause he replied :—

> Minerva-like majestic Mary moves;
> Law, Latin, logic, learned Lucy loves;
> Serenely silent, Susan's smiles surprise;
> From fops, from flatterers, fairest Fanny flies.

The "toast" of the day was a beautiful Miss Charlotte Ness. She asked Dunbar the force of the words *abstract* and *concrete*, which she had heard in a University sermon. A few moments' silence produced the following :—

> Say, what is Abstract? what Concrete?
> Their difference define.—
> They both in one fair form unite,
> And that fair form is thine.—

"HORSE" KETT

From a Portrait by Dighton

> How so? this riddle pray undo.—
> 'Tis no hard-laboured guess,
> For when I *lovely Charlotte* view,
> I then view *lovely Ness.*

He was a man of good family, hovering between London, Bath, and Oxford. A room in our house at Oxford was within my memory known as Mr. Dunbar's room. His walking-stick was handed down to me, a serpent-twined caduceus, with the names of the Nine Muses on the gold handle. *Styx novies interfusa* he called it.

Contemporary with Dunbar was "Horse" Kett, of Trinity. In his portrait by Dighton, here reproduced, the long face, dominated by the straight bony nose, explains and justifies the epithet. He was a man of considerable ability; Bampton lecturer, novelist; and just missed the Poetry Professorship. His Bampton Lectures of 1790, on the "Conduct and opinions of the Primitive Christians," show a historic insight surprising for that period. His critical powers were acknowledged by De Quincy, who referred to him the once burning, now forgotten, question of the plagiarism in White's Bampton Lectures. White had been assisted in their composition by Parr, by Parsons, Master of Balliol, by a Dr. Gabriel of Bath, and by a dissenting minister, Mr. Badcock. Kett, called in to arbitrate and reconcile, reprimanded the accomplices all round. But his repute was due to his strange equine face, inspiring from the seniors jokes in every learned language, and practical impertinences from the less erudite youngsters. When his back was turned in lecture, the men filled his snuff-box with oats. Dr.

Kidd used to relate how, attending him in his rooms for some ailment, he heard a strange rattle in the letter-box of the outer door: "Only a note (an oat)," said the good-natured victim. Walter Savage Landor tried on him his prentice hand—

> "The Centaur is not fabulous," says Young.[1]
> Had Young known Kett,
> He'd say, "Behold one, put together wrong;
> The head is horseish, but, what yet
> Was never seen in man or beast,
> The rest is human—or, at least,
> Is Kett."

He published a book which he called "Logic Made Easy," puffing himself on the title page as a public University Examiner. It was a dialogue between a father and his motherless daughter Emily; was a feeble production and filled with blunders. A pamphlet from Copleston's pen, entitled "The Examiner Examined," scourged it with merciless severity; and bore as its motto—

> Aliquis latet error; Equo ne credite, Teucri;

a stroke of personal impertinence better perhaps omitted. Dunbar, too, had ready his possibly premeditated impromptu. Some one asked him who were the Proctors in a certain year: they were Darnel, of Corpus, and Kett. Dunbar answered—

> Infelix *Lolium* et steriles dominantur *Avenæ*.

---

[1] A book notable in its day.—"Young (E.) 'The Centaur not Fabulous, in Six Letters to a Friend on "The Life in Vogue,"' 8vo, copperplate front., symbolic of the public's careless gaiety, calf, 3s. 6d., 1755." The parody on Byron in the "Rejected Addresses" contains the line "Centaurs (not fabulous) these rules efface."

ORIGINAL CHARACTERS

The mention of Copleston carries one to Oriel, peopled at that time with "characters" of a very exalted type. Copleston, substantial, majestic, "richly coloured," as T. Mozley calls him, was Provost; a man not without asperities of mind and manner—we recall his rudeness to J. H. Newman, dining in Hall as a newly-elected Fellow :—but, as a man of the world, in London society, regular contributor to the *Quarterly Review*, author of widely-read and accepted pamphlets on currency and finance, he held absolute ascendancy amongst the higher class of University men, and filled his College with Fellows strangely alien to the port and prejudice, the clubbable whist-playing somnolence, which Gibbon first, then Sydney Smith, found characteristic of Oxford society. I saw him only once, as Bishop of Llandaff; but his mien and presence were carefully preserved and copied by old Joseph Parker, the bookseller, who resembled him curiously in face and voice, and, in a suit of formal black, with frill at the breast and massive gold seals pendent from the fob, imitated his walk and manner. He carried on at Oriel the innovation of his predecessor, Provost Eveleigh, who had forced on a reluctant University the Public Examination for a B.A. degree;[1] and who gave his Fellowships not so much to technical attainment as to evidence of intellectual capacity; to Copleston himself, to Whately, Keble, Davison, Hawkins,

---

[1] The first Public Examination was held in 1802. Two men were placed in the First Class : Abel Hendy, who died in 1808; John Marriott, the friend of Walter Scott, who dedicated to him the Second Canto of " Marmion."

Hampden, Arnold; men who formed in Oxford what was known as the *Noetic* School, maintaining around them a continuing dialectical and mental ferment. Tommy Short used to say that Davison and Whately habitually crammed for after-dinner talk; and unfortunate outlanders, whose digestion of the dinner and enjoyment of the port wine was spoiled by it, complained that Oriel Common Room *stunk* of logic. A country clergyman once, after listening to Whately's talk throughout the evening, thanked him formally for the pains he had taken to instruct him. "Oh, no," said Whately, "not *instruct;* I did not mean to be didactic; but one sometimes likes having an anvil on which to beat out one's thoughts." Amongst them too was Blanco White—Hyperion they called him, as Copleston was Saturn—adopted not only into Oriel, but into English society and the English Church. He is believed to have not written, but inspired Hampden's famous Bampton Lectures: an old survivor of those days, Canon Hinds Howell, White's pupil at the time, told me how day after day for months before they were delivered Hampden was closeted with Blanco. Whately was a prominent Oxford figure, with blatant voice, great stride, rough dress. I remember my mother's terror when he came to call. She had met him in the house of newly-married Mrs. Baden-Powell, who had filled her drawing-room with the spider-legged chairs just then coming into fashion. On one of these sat Whately, swinging, plunging, and shifting on his seat while he talked. An ominous crack was heard; a leg of the chair had given way; he tossed it on to the sofa without comment,

and impounded another chair. The history of the
Noetic school has not been written; its interest was
obscured by the reactionary movement on which so
many pens have worked.

I cross, for the present only, from Oriel to
Christchurch, and encounter sailing out of Peckwater a very notable Canon of "the House," Dr.
Bull. Tall, portly, handsome, beautifully dressed
and groomed—he was known as Jemmy Jessamy
in his youth—I hail him as type of the *ornamental*
Don. For of Dons there were four kinds. There
was the *cosmopolitan* Don; with a home in Oxford,
but conversant with select humanity elsewhere;
like Addison and Prior in their younger days, Tom
Warton in the Johnsonian era, Philip Duncan in
my recollection; at home in coffee house, club,
theatre; sometimes in Parliament, like Charles
Neate; sometimes at Court, like William Bathurst
of All Souls, Clerk to the Privy Council. There
was the *learned* Don, amassing a library, editing
Latin authors and Greek plays, till his useful career
was extinguished under an ill-placed, ill-fitting
mitre. There was the *meer* Don, as Sir Thomas
Overbury calls him; Head of a House commonly
as the resultant of a squabble amongst the electing
Fellows, with a late-married wife as uncouth and
uneducated as himself, forming with a few affluent
sodales an exclusive, pompous, ignorant, lazy set,
"respecting no man in the University, and respected by no man out of it." Lastly, the *ornamental* Don; representative *proxenus* to distinguished
strangers, chosen as Proctor or Vice-Chancellor
against a probable Installation or Royal visit.

Bull played this part to perfection, as did Dr. Wellesley in the next generation. He had gained his double first and kindred decorations as a young man, but promotion early and plural lighted on his head, promotion, not to posts which tax and generate effort, but to cushioned ease of canonries; and he dropped into the manager of Chapter legislations and surveyor of College properties; a butterfly of the most gorgeous kind, a *Morpho*, such as dear old Westwood used to unveil before visitors to his museum, yet still only a butterfly. He was a man of pluck and determination; his overthrow of redoubtable Bishop Philpotts was immortalised by a delightful cartoon in an early *Punch*—a bishop tossed by a bull; he had the manner of a royal personage; you must follow his lead and accept his dicta; but he was a generous, kindly Dives, of a day when Lazarus had not come to the front with unemployed and democratic impeachments, to drop flies into the fragrant ointment, to insinuate scruples as to the purple and fine linen, to predict the evolutionary downfall of those who toil not neither spin. He would be impossible at the present day, and perhaps it is just as well. He was Canon of Christchurch, Canon of Exeter, Prebendary of York, and held the good College living of Staverton, *all at once*:—

> "On the box with Will Whip, ere the days of the Rail,
> To London I travelled ; and inside the mail
> Was a Canon of Exeter ; on the same perch
> Was a Canon of Oxford's Episcopal Church.
> Next came one who held—I will own the thing small—
> In the Minster of York a prebendary stall.

And there sate a Parson, all pursy and fair,
With a Vicarage fat and five hundred a year.
Now, good reader, perhaps you will deem the coach full?
No—there was but one traveller—DOCTOR JOHN BULL!"

An oddity *par excellence* was the "Senior Fellow": an oddity then, a palæozoic memory now. He vanished with the Forties; Railways, New Museums, University Commissions, were too much for him. He was no mere senior, *primus inter pares* only in respect of age; he was exceptional, solitary, immemorial; in the College but not of it; left stranded by a generation which had passed; a great gulf in habits, years, associations, lay between the existing Common Room and himself. He mostly lived alone; the other men treated him deferentially and called him Mister; he met them in Hall on Gaudy days and was sometimes seen in Chapel; but no one ever dropped in upon him, smoked with him, walked with him; he was thought to have a history; a suspicion of disappointment hung over him; he lived his own eccentric, friendless life, a victim to superannuation and celibacy.

Not a few of these venerable waifs come back to me from early years. There was old Tom Davies, Senior Fellow of Jesus, visible every day from 3 to 4 P.M., when he walked alone in all weathers twice round Christchurch meadow. He was the finest judge of wine in Oxford—"the nose of *haut-goût* and the tip of taste"—could, it was believed, tell a vintage accurately by the smell. Joyous was the Common Room steward who could call in his judgment to aid in the purchase of pipe or butt. He refused all the most valuable

College livings in turn, because the underground cellars of their parsonages were inadequate; lived and died in his rooms, consuming meditatively, like Mr. Tulkinghorn, a daily cob-webbed bottle of his own priceless port.

There was old Dr. Ellerton, Senior Fellow of Magdalen, who used to totter out of Chapel with the President on a Sunday. I have seen a laughable sketch of the pair, as Shuttleworth, Warden of New College, a dexterous caricaturist, spied them from his window shuffling along New College Lane to a convocation. Coævals they appeared, but Routh was really the senior by ten years. As time went on, Routh's intellect survived his friend's; he came to shake his wig at the mention of Ellerton's name; and say, "he is grown old and foolish, sir." He was a mild Hebrew scholar, and is embalmed as cofounder with Dr. Pusey of the small annual prize known as the Pusey and Ellerton Scholarship. His rooms were at the corner of the quadrangle, looking on to the deer park and the great plane tree. He was a picturesquely ugly man; the gargoyle above his window was a portrait, hardly an exaggeration, of his grotesque old face. Years before, when the building was restored and he was College tutor, the undergraduates had bribed the sculptor to fashion there in stone the visage of their old Damœtas; he detected the resemblance, and insisted angrily on alteration. Altered the face was: cheeks and temples hollowed, jaw-lines deepened, similitude for the time effaced. But gradually the unkind invisible chisel of old age worked upon his own octogenarian countenance; his own cheek was hollowed, his own jaw contracted, till the quaint projecting mask became again a likeness even more graphic than before.

I remember old Mr. Rudd, Senior Fellow of Oriel since 1819, who appeared always at the Gaudy in black shorts and silk stockings, travelling up from Northampton in a fly, and spending two days on the journey. Then I knew Edward Quicke, of New College, whose one lingering senile passion was for tandem-driving; the famous "Arter-Xerxes" story had its source in his groom and him. Twice a day he might be seen, sitting melancholy behind his handsome pair along the roads round Oxford. He died, I may say, in harness; for one dark night in the vacation he was run down near Woodstock by two scouts, and succumbed in a few days to his injuries. With him was old Eastwick, who after spending some years, poor fellow, in a lunatic asylum, reappeared to end his days in College. He had once, we supposed, been young; had lived and loved and gathered rosebuds; had certainly begun life as a briefless barrister. At a Gaudy dinner once sardonic Shuttleworth congratulated him "on an accession to his income." "I beg your pardon, Mr. Warden, I was not aware——" "Oh! I beg yours, but I was told that you had left o going circuit." He came back from durance vile a quiet, watery-eyed, lean old man, looking like a scarecrow in good circumstances, dining in Hall, where he was mostly silent, yet broke out curiously sometimes with reminiscences, forbodings, protests; spent the livelong day in eradicating dandelions from the large grass-plat in the front quadrangle, his coat-tails falling over his shoulders as he stooped, and leaving him, like the poor Indian of the parody, " bare behind." Once more there was old Maude, of Queen's, one of the *détenus* as they were called— the ten thousand English tourists seized brutally by Napoleon when war was suddenly declared in 1803, and kept in prison till his abdication. Maude came back to Oxford, eleven years of his life wiped out and his contemporaries passed away, to live alone in his old-fashioned, scantily furnished rooms, where I remember his giving me breakfast in my schooldays and quoting to me Dr. Johnson's "Vanity of Human Wishes."

These were curios of no great native force— spectacular oddities merely; two more remain, whose amusing outbreaks of indecorum and forcible gifts of speech deserve a longer notice: Dr. Frowd, of Corpus, and " Mo." Griffith, of Merton. Frowd was a very little man, an irrepressible, unwearied chatterbox, with a droll interrogative face, a bald shining head, and a fleshy under-lip, which he could push up nearly to his nose. He had been chaplain to Lord Exmouth, and was present at the bombardment of Algiers. As the action thickened he was seized with a comical religious frenzy, dashing round the decks, and diffusing spiritual exhortation amongst the half-stripped, busy sailors, till the first lieutenant ordered a hencoop to be clapped over him, whence his little head emerging continued its devout cackle, quite regardless of the balls which flew past him and killed eight hundred sailors in our small victorious fleet. Lord Exmouth rescued him from this incarceration, and to keep him out of mischief set him to unload and pack a large crate of port wine, presenting him with three dozen for himself. This gift was his pride through life; very rarely drunk, but boasted of to every guest in Common Room. At his death his will bequeathed to the Rev. George Hext, a brother Fellow, "all my wine in Corpus College cellars." It amounted only to seven surviving bottles of the famous port; the *deprome quadrimum* must have been repeated more frequently than was supposed. He was a preacher of much force and humour, if only one had the self-possession *risum tenere*. I heard him once in St. Clement's Church deliver a sermon on Jonah, which roused up his congregation quite as effectually as the shipmaster wakened the sleepy prophet. "There's a man in this church who never says his prayers: lies down at night, rises in the morning, without a word of gratitude or adoration for the God who made him and has preserved him. Now, I have a message to that man—what meanest thou, O thou sleeper? arise," &c., &c. "Hell," he began another time, with a knowing wag of his droll head, "Hell is a place which men believe to be reserved for those who are a great deal worse than themselves." Presently he became husky, drew out a lozenge and sat down in the pulpit to masticate it leisurely, while we looked at one another, wished that we had lozenges, and awaited the consumption of his lubricant. In reading chapters from the Old Testament, he used to pause at a marginal variation, read it to himself half audibly, and, like Dr. Blimber, smile on it auspiciously or knit his brow and shake his head in disapproval. I remember too his preaching in All

Saints Church, of which Thompson, afterwards rector of Lincoln, was incumbent. He climbed up the steep three-decker steps into the high-walled pulpit, and disappeared, till, his hands clinging to the desk and his comical face peering over it, he called down into the reading desk below, "Thompson, send up a hassock." A College living was offered to him : and a funeral being due, he went down to bury the dead and survey the place. Arrived at the nearest railway station, he found no conveyance except a carriage which had just deposited a wedding party. Into this he jumped— coachman, whip, horses, being all decked with favours—met the mournful procession, and finding the churchyard path muddy, climbed on the white-ribboned driver's back, and was borne to the church in front of the coffin amid the cheers and laughter of the amateur onlookers, who in the country assemble always at these instructive functions. He accepted the living after this escapade, but the College refused to present him, and were sustained on his appeal to the Visitor. To another prank they were unjustifiably lenient. A contested election of a member for the University was proceeding, the excitement high and the voting close. Frowd paired with four men against one of the candidates, then went up and voted. A London club would have expelled a man for such a feat ; but Frowd seems to have been looked upon as a chartered libertine, and the offence was passed over on receipt of an unintelligibly remorseful letter—"You have from me a *pœnitet* in duodecimo and a *habes confitentem reum* in quarto "—with a request, however, that he would absent himself from the College for a twelvemonth. His rooms were on the second floor looking out into the meadow; in the room below him lived Holme, a more advanced Bedlamite even than himself, a pleasant fellow as I remember him in his interlunar periods, but who died, I believe, in an asylum. Frowd used to take exercise on wet days by placing chairs at intervals round his room and jumping over them. Holme, a practical being, one day fired a pistol at his ceiling while these gymnastics were proceeding, and the bullet whizzed past Frowd, who, less unconcerned than at Algiers, ran downstairs, put his head into the room, and cried, "Would you, bloody-minded man, would you?" The feeling in the Common Room was said to be regret that the bullet had not been billeted; Frowd would have ceased to exasperate, Holme would have been incarcerated or hanged, the College rid of both.

Moses Griffith was son to a physician of the same name. In the hospital where the father practised a particular kind of poultice was long known as a "mogriff." The son, objecting to the nickname "Mo," obtained the royal licence to bear the name of Edwards, gradually dropping the Moses and the final letter s, and appearing in the later University Calendar as Edward Griffith; but though gods might call him Edward, mortals called him "Mo." Twice in the year he was compelled to sign his true name on receiving a dividend; and it was not well to go near him at those times. He was much more than an oddity—a real wit, racy in ironical talk, prompt in bitter or diverting repartee. In younger

28 REMINISCENCES OF OXFORD

days he was Whitehall Preacher, an appointment then made for life; but became so tedious as time passed that the Bishop of London, Howley, called on him to suggest his retirement. He was overpowered by Mo's formal politeness, and came away discomfited; and Griffith remained until Blomfield, succeeding to the bishopric, dismissed all the preachers, and replaced the best of them under fresh rules, mainly in order to get rid of Mo.[1] If you wished to rouse his anger, you had only to mention Bishop Blomfield, who had thus righteously deposed him from his Whitehall preachership. "Sir, he was born a blackguard; he's a Bury St. Edmund's blackguard, and he'll die a blackguard." Blomfield's father kept a school at Bury, and the future Bishop was there born, and was educated at the Grammar School. Mo. disliked the free use of oaths in conversation: one of the Senior Fellows, W——, retained this fault of his blood, as Queen Elizabeth called it, rather too faithfully; his every sixth or seventh word began with the letter D. Bishop Hobhouse, lately dead—*laus illi debetur et a me gratia maior*—remembered Griffith one day following W—— out of the Common Room, and calling through his door: "Mr. W——, Mr. W——, Walter Kerr says he won't dine in Hall if you continue to swear." Walter Kerr Hamilton was Denison's Curate at St. Peter's, and afterwards Bishop of Salisbury. But Mo. was not quite free from the habit himself; I was told by Archdeacon Bree that, returning one day from a powerful

[1] A history of the Whitehall preacherships is given in the Appendix S.

sermon at St. Mary's against profane swearing, he was overheard saying to himself, "I'm d——d if I ever swear again." W—— was a curious survival; a little, made-up old man, with the habits and the talk of long-ago West End clubs, attired always for evening dress in a satin scarf and a finely embroidered waistcoat. Going once to preach at Wolvercot, Mo. took with him William Karslake, a young Fellow of the College, who had found favour in his eyes. "How did you like my sermon, sir?" was the first question, as they walked through the fields homewards. "A very fine sermon, Mr. Griffith; perhaps a little above the audience." "Audience, my friend. I suppose these dear young turnip-tops would understand my sermon as readily as those rustics. Sir, that was a Whitehall sermon." He sometimes read the service at Holywell, a Merton living. The lesson happened to be the third chapter of St. Luke. Griffith read on till he came to the formidable pedigree at the end. "Which was the son of Heli," he began; then, glancing at the genealogical Banquo-line which follows—"the rest concerns neither you nor me, so here endeth the Second Lesson." He used to attend the St. Mary's afternoon service. A prolonged University sermon had retarded the parish service, and it was near five o'clock when Copeland, who sometimes preached for Newman, approached the pulpit. He was stopped in the aisle by Griffith, who said in one of his stentorian asides, "I am grieved to quit you, Mr. Copeland, but Merton College dines at five."

He spent the Oxford term-times usually at Bath

—"City of Balls and Beggars" he was wont to superscribe his letters thence—hating the sight of the Philistines, as he called the undergraduates. "Fetch a screen, Manciple," he said one day, when dining alone in Hall he beheld a belated solitary scholar who had not gone down; but he resided in the vacations, and always attended College meetings. The late Warden, I have heard, used to relate that when he was candidate for a Fellowship and Griffith came up to vote, his colleagues tried to impress upon him the duty of awarding the Fellowship according to the examiners' verdict. "Sir," said Mo., "I came here to vote for my old friend's son, and vote for him I shall, whatever the examiners may say." He would sometimes bring a guest to the College dinner, watching anxiously over his prowess with the knife and fork. Abstemiousness he could not abide: Dr. Wootten, an Oxford physician, dined with him one day, and did scant justice to the dishes: "My maxim, Mr. Griffith, is to eat and leave off hungry." Mo. threw up his hands as he was wont: "Eat and leave off hungry! Why not wash and leave off dirty?" So often as a haunch of venison was announced for the high table, he would invite my father, a renowned diner-out in former days, but made domestic by *tarda podagra*. I remember his exit once, fuming at my father's refusal. "My friend," laying hand upon his sleeve, "you will eat mutton till the wool grows out of your coat." Once, at a large party in our house, good-natured, loquacious Mrs. Routh, the President of Magdalen's wife, addressed him. "Mr. Griffith, do you ever take carriage exercise;

ORIGINAL CHARACTERS

drive in a fly, I mean?" "Madam, I thank God I am not quite such a blackguard." He used to ask me to his rooms when I was a boy, and regale me with strawberries. He would make me recite poetry to him—the "Elegy," "Sweet Auburn," "The Traveller," which I knew by heart—rewarding me with presents of books; on one occasion with a fine set of Pope's "Homer" in eleven volumes, bearing the bookplate of *Edward* Griffith. Much later, and shortly before his death, I met him at a Merton dinner. Edmund Hobhouse had brought Sir Benjamin Brodie. "Who is that gentleman?" asked Griffith in his sonorous whisper. He was told. A pause, during which Mo. glared at the great surgeon; then the word "Butcher!" was heard to hiss along the table. He comes before me in an unbrushed beaver hat, a black coat and waistcoat, nankeen trousers, and low shoes, with a vast interval of white stocking. *Requiescat in Pace!*

CHAPTER III

PRESCIENTIFIC SCIENCE

> " *We will be wise in time: what though our work*
> *Be fashioned in despite of their ill-service,*
> *Be crippled every way? 'Twere little praise*
> *Did full resources wait on our good will*
> *At every turn. Let all be as it is.*"
> —BROWNING.

Dr. Daubeny—His Physic Garden—His Monkeys and their Emancipation—A Pioneer of Science—Buckland and his Friends—His Wife—His Lectures—A Scotch Sceptic and how he was Silenced—The Buckland *Ménage*—The Buckland Collection in the Oxford Museum—Baden-Powell—Thomas, the Holywell Glazier—Chapman, the Discoverer of *Cetiosaurus*.

PRESCIENTIFIC unquestionably: in the Thirties the Oxford mind was inscient; its attitude first contemptuous, then hostile, towards the science that, *invita Minerva*, was hatching in its midst; a strange, new, many-headed, assertive thing, claiming absurdly to take rank with the monopolist Humanities of Donland, not altogether without concealed intent to challenge and molest the ancient, solitary reign of its theology. Yet science none the less there was, sustained by at least three famous names, making possible the Phillips, Brodie, Rolleston of a later date. Its first representative of note was Daubeny; Doctor, not Professor, Daubeny; Professor as a titular prefix came in much later; came, I am told, through

DR. DAUBENY
From a Photograph taken in 1860

the Scottish Universities, which had borrowed it from Germany. First Class and Fellow of Magdalen, he early forsook practice as a physician to devote himself to pure science; as a pupil of Jameson, Professor of Geology at Edinburgh, he studied, fifty years before his time, what is now known and valued as "Petrology"; became widely known by his works on the "Atomic Theory" and on "Volcanic Action"; and when Dr. Williams died in 1834, succeeded him as professor of chemistry, botany, rural economy, taking up his abode in the house built newly at the entrance to Magdalen bridge. He lectured, experimented, wrote; his books on Roman husbandry, and on the trees and shrubs of the ancients, are still invaluable to the Virgilian scholar; he carried out elaborately and with improved devices Pouchet's experiments on spontaneous generation, was the first to welcome and extend in England Schönbein's discovery of ozone. His chemistry lectures were a failure; he lacked physical force, sprightliness of manner, oral readiness, and his demonstrations invariably went wrong. But his lectures drew many noted University men; Pusey, Whately, Tait, Thomson, Charles Neate, Mark Pattison, Liddell, Acland, Ruskin, Frank Buckland, are all inscribed in his Pupil-book, which the College still preserves. He lavished care and money on his "Physic Garden," introducing De Candolle's system side by side with the old Linnæan beds, building new and spacious houses, in which flourished the Victoria lily, to be seen elsewhere for a long time only at Kew and Chatsworth, and where the aloe produced its one bloom of the century, its great raceme rising in seven days to the height of four-and-twenty feet. He cared little for outdoor plants, and could not condescend to rudimentary teaching; educational botany, prospering at Cambridge under Henslow, took no hold of Oxford. But it was pleasant to walk with him round the garden, and to hear his disquisitions on the Scammony and Christ's Thorn, the Weeping Willow from Pope's Twickenham Garden, the Pæstum Rose, the Birthwort from Godstow ruins, the Mandrake under the Conservatory wall, the Sibthorpia and Orontium in the little copper cisterns long swept away: and happily, the garden was for nearly eighty years in the care of the two Baxters, father and son, both of them amongst the best exponents in England of our native Flora. Their assiduity and knowledge resulted in a collection of hardy growths, exceptional in healthiness and size, arranged with little rigidity of system, but, with deference to each plant's idiosyncrasies, in spots which the experimental tenderness of near a century showed to be appropriate. They laboured for a posterity which hastened to undo their work. New brooms swept the unique old garden clean; young men arose who knew not Joseph; young men in a hurry to produce a little Kew upon the incongruous Cherwell banks,

> Parvam Trojam, simulataque magnis
> Pergama, et arentem Xanthi cognomine rivum.

So the time-honoured array was broken up, Baxter *fils* cashiered, the Linnæan borders razed, the

PRESCIENTIFIC SCIENCE 35

monumental plants uprooted. Thus I wrote in 1900; but better times have followed. The disaster has been repaired by the assiduity, zeal, knowledge, of the present professor, and his accomplished assistant Mr. W. G. Baker; and the garden is again amongst the most delightful spots in Oxford.

One of Daubeny's fads was a collection of monkeys, which he kept in a cage let into the Danby gateway. One night the doors were forced and the monkeys liberated, to be captured next day wandering dismal on the Iffley road, or perched *crepitantes dentibus*, on the railings in Rose Lane. The culprit was not known at the time; it was mad Harry Wilkins, of Merton, who had sculled up the river after dark and so gained access to the locked-up gardens. Daubeny was pained by the foolish insult, and the menagerie was dispersed. He was genial and chatty in society; in College Hall, or at evening parties, which he much frequented, we met the little, droll, spectacled, old-fashioned figure, in gilt-buttoned blue tail coat, velvet waistcoat, satin scarf, kid gloves too long in the fingers, a foot of bright bandanna handkerchief invariably hanging out behind. Or we encountered him on Sunday afternoons, in doctor's hood and surplice, tripping up the steps which led to the street, shuffling into Chapel, always late; cross old Mundy, the College porter, dispossessing some unfortunate stranger to make way for him in the stalls. But with all his retirement he did his work as a witness to the necessity of science; pleaded in pamphlets, letters, speeches, for its introduction into the University course, pressed on his own College successfully the establishment of science scholarships, helped on the time when, not in the Thirties, scarcely in the Forties, the hour and the man should come. He lived into old age, active to the last. Shortly before his death he visited me in Somersetshire, to meet his former schoolfellow, Lord Taunton. The two old men had not seen each other since they slept in the same room at Winchester fifty-five years before, along with one of the Barings, and Ford, author afterwards of the "Handbook to Spain." It was pleasant to hear the chirping reminiscences of the successful veterans, boys once again together. He died in 1867, and lies at rest beneath the stone pulpit in the Chapel court. A memorial tablet in the antechapel bears a Latin epitaph from the scholarly pen of his old friend John Rigaud. Ever I take off my hat when I pass his not forgotten grave, and pause, like Old Mortality, to clear encroaching moss from the letters which perpetuate his name.

The second *savant* of the time was Buckland, and there was certainly no overlooking him. Elected Fellow of Corpus in 1809, he gave his whole time for ten years to the fossil-hunting begun by him in the Winchester chalkpits as a boy, not then reduced into a science; till in 1819 the Prince Regent, at the instance of Sir Joseph Banks, created a professorship of geology, and nominated Buckland to the post. His lecture-room in the Ashmolean filled at once, not so much with undergraduates as with dons, attracted by his liveliness and the novelty of his subject. The Chancellor, Lord Grenville, visiting Oxford, sat beside and complimented him; Howley, afterwards Archbishop, Sir Philip Egerton, so famous later as a collector, were among his devotees; Whately, Philip Duncan, Shuttleworth, pelted their friend with playful squibs: "Some doubts," wrote Shuttleworth,

"Some doubts were once expressed about the Flood,
Buckland arose, and all was clear as—mud."

Alarms about the Deluge had not yet been generally awakened; in his early works, *Reliquiæ Diluvianæ* and *Vindiciæ Geologicæ*, he posed as orthodox and reconcilist; it was not till 1836 that his Bridgewater Treatise roused the heresy-hunters, that a hurricane of private and newspaper protests whistled round his disregarding head, that Dean Gaisford thanked God on his departure for Italy— "We shall hear no more of his geology"—that Pusey organised a protest against the conferring a degree on Owen, and Keble clenched a bitter argument by the conclusive dogma that "when God made the stones He made the fossils in them." Worse was still to come; the "Six Days" were to be impeached; the convenient formula "before the Flood" to be dispossessed; the old cosmogony which puzzled Mr. Ephraim Jenkinson to fade slowly from the popular mind, reposing as a curiosity, where it still occasionally survives, amid the mental furniture of the country clergy: and in the great awakening of knowledge which severed theology from science and recast Biblical criticism he was amongst the earliest and most energetic pioneers. The Clergy, the Dons, the Press, fell upon him all together; "Keep the St. James' Chronicles," wrote to him his wife, "every-one of which has a rap at you; but I beseech you not to lower your dignity by noticing newspaper statements." Wise words! which not every wife would unreservedly emit. Without her moral aid and intellectual support Buckland would not so lightly and so confidently have faced his difficulties and achieved his aims. An accomplished mineralogist before their marriage, she threw her whole nature into her husband's work. She deciphered and transcribed his horribly illegible papers, often adding polish to their style; and her skilful fingers illustrated many of his books. Night after night while his Bridgewater Treatise was in making, she sat up writing from his dictation till the morning sun shone through the shutters. From her came the first suggestion as to the true character of the lias coprolites. When, at two o'clock in the morning, the idea flashed upon him that the Cheirotherium footsteps were testudinal, he woke his wife from sleep; she hastened down to make pie crust upon the kitchen table, while he fetched in the tortoise from the garden; and the pair soon saw with joint delight that its impressions on the paste were almost identical with those upon the slabs. Genial as a hostess, sympathetic as a friend, she was not less exemplary as a mother. Her children, departed and surviving, called and call her blessed: "As good a man and wife," wrote Frank Buckland of his parents, "as

PRESCIENTIFIC SCIENCE 39

ever did their duty to God and their fellow-creatures." "Never," says her daughter, "was a word of evil speaking permitted. 'My dear, educated people always talk of things, not persons; it is only in the servants' hall that people gossip.'"[1] He was a wonderful lecturer, clear, fluent, apt, overflowing with witty illustrations, dashing down amongst us ever and anon to enforce an intricate point with Samsonic wielding of a cave-bear jaw or a hyæna thigh bone. Of questions from his hearers he was intolerant; they checked the rapids of his talk. "It would seem," queried a sceptical Caledonian during a lecture in North Britain, "that your animals always walked in one direction?" "Yes," was the reply, "Cheirotherium was a Scotchman, and he always travelled south."

Even more attractive than the lectures at the Clarendon were the field days; the ascent of Shotover, with pauses at each of its six deposits, the lumps of *Montlivalvia* hammered out from the coralline oolite, the selenite crystals higher up, the questionings over the ironsand on the summit, over the ochre and pipeclay on the rough moorland long since ploughed into uninteresting fertility. These are undergraduate memories; but I recall much earlier days, when I was wont to play with Frank Buckland and his brother in their home at the corner of Tom Quad: the entrance hall with its grinning monsters on the low stair-

---

[1] An unconscious echo of Plato: "ἀεὶ περὶ ἀνθρώπων τοὺς λόγους ποιουμένους, ἥκιστα φιλοσοφίᾳ πρέπον ποιοῦντας." "Ever chattering about persons, a proceeding quite inconsistent with philosophy."—*Republic*, vi. 12.

case, of whose latent capacity to arise and fall upon me I never quite overcame my doubts; the side-table in the dining-room covered with fossils, "Paws off" in large letters on a protecting card; the very sideboard candlesticks perched on saurian vertebræ; the queer dishes garnishing the dinner table—horseflesh I remember more than once, crocodile another day, mice baked in batter on a third—while the guinea-pig under the table inquiringly nibbled at your infantine toes, the bear walked round your chair and rasped your hand with file-like tongue, the jackal's fiendish yell close by came through the open window, the monkey's hairy arm extended itself suddenly over your shoulder to annex your fruit and walnuts. I think the Doctor rather scared us; we did not understand his sharp, quick voice and peremptory manner, and preferred the company of his kind, charming, highly cultured wife. Others found him alarming; dishonesty and quackery of all kinds fled from that keen, all-knowing vision. When Tom Tower was being repaired, he watched the workmen from his window with a telescope, and frightened a scamping mason whom he encountered descending from the scaffold by bidding him go back and bring down that faulty piece of work he had just put into a turret. At Palermo, on his wedding tour, he visited St. Rosalia's shrine,

> The grot where olives nod,
> Where, darling of each heart and eye,
> From all the youth of Sicily
> St. Rosalie retired to God.

It was opened by the priests, and the relics of the

DR. BUCKLAND

The Ansdell Portrait. From Mrs. Gordon's "Life of Buckland," reproduced by permission of the authoress and of the publisher, Mr. John Murray

saint were shown. He saw that they were not Rosalia's: "They are the bones of a goat," he cried out, "not of a woman;" and the sanctuary doors were abruptly closed.

Frank used to tell of their visit long afterwards to a foreign cathedral, where was exhibited a martyr's blood—dark spots on the pavement ever fresh and ineradicable. The professor dropped on the pavement and touched the stain with his tongue. "I can tell you what it is; it is bat's urine!"

I can see him now, passing rapidly through the quadrangle and down St. Aldate's—broad-brimmed hat, tail coat, umbrella, great blue bag. This last he always carried; it is shown in Ansdell's portrait, the best likeness of him by far. Sir H. Davy once expected him, and, disappointed, asked his servant if Dr. Buckland had not called. "No, sir, there has been no one but a man with a bag; he called three times, and I always told him you were out." His umbrella he was for ever losing; not through inadvertence, he declared, but through larceny: he set up a red umbrella: that too was pirated: engraved finally on the handle "Stolen from Dr. Buckland," that met the case; he became for the first time permanently umbrelliferous.

Suddenly, in the midst of unsurpassed energy and usefulness, came the blow which ended, not the life—better perhaps had it been so—but the vigour and beauty of the life. For eight years he lay torpid and apathetic; the only books he would open were the Bible and the *Leisure Hour!* His fine collection, with his own hammermarks and his wife's neat labels on every stone, he bequeathed to his successors in the Chair. It lies, or lay till lately, neglected, useless, unarranged, in the cellars of the Museum; yet, if not for the sake of education and learning, then for the sake of sentiment and reverence, one would think that the Conscript Fathers might accord, if they have not yet done so, a place conspicuous and honoured to the traditions and the autographs of the first great Oxford scientist.

A life-long friend and fellow pioneer of Daubeny and Buckland was Baden-Powell, who became Savilian Professor of Geometry in 1827. His earlier papers on Mathematics, Astronomy, Physics, had made him widely notable; and he distinguished himself from a very early time by discerning and urging the need of University reform. Of a nature eagerly participative, he did much by his popular addresses to create an appetite for science among the Oxford citizens, lecturing also to Polytechnics and Mechanics Institutes throughout the country. Alone amongst the Oxford teachers of his day he worked out with ability and boldness, with a single-minded aspiration after Truth, yet in a calm and temperate spirit, those attractive problems of the relation between Science and Religion, which his contemporaries for the most part handled only in support of personal and party preconceptions, or shirked through fear of the odium which they were certain to excite. As a member of the first University Commission, he did much to enforce the claims of Science to a prominent position in the University curriculum. He died, all too soon, in 1860.

I think the only Lectures besides Buckland's which drew students to a class-room were those on " ex-

PRESCIENTIFIC SCIENCE 43

perimental Philosophy," as it was called; delivered in the Clarendon by a cheery Mr. Walker, who constructed and exploded gases, laid bare the viscera of pumps and steam engines, forced mercury through wood blocks in a vacuum, manipulated galvanic batteries, magic-lanterns, air-guns. This last demonstration once, like decent David's dancing in "Don Juan," "excited some remark." A wicked wag loaded the air-gun before the professor entered, and when the trigger was pulled we saw some plaster fall from the ceiling, and a clatter was heard presently on the staircase. The bullet had gone up into the lecture-room above, and put to flight another professor with his pupils. Walker was a man of great ability; the first, I believe, to introduce into Oxford the analytical as distinct from the geometrical treatment of higher mathematics. He was also a notable preacher of the evangelical school; his sermons pure in style, and reflecting strong personal piety.

A humbler philosopher in the same line was Thomas, a Holywell glazier, who used to give gratuitous popular lectures in the music-room to working men, using implements and apparatus, magnets, galvanometers, induction coils, cleverly fashioned by himself. He was genuinely and widely scientific; made an interesting discovery as to the thinness at which decomposed glass yields complementary colours—I have some of his specimens in my cabinet—discovered that certain double salts, crystallised at particular temperatures, assume special forms and become beautiful microscopic objects—an electrician, a naturalist, an optician, a discoverer, a working man. A few years later came another self-taught genius, Chapman, a watchmaker with a shop opposite Balliol, whose large and well-stocked marine aquarium, a thing of beauty at that time rare, attracted wondering visitors. He it was who discovered and rescued the monster *Cetiosaurus* at Kirtlington Station. He had dismounted from the train with his son on a botanising expedition just as the first fragment was disclosed by the pick-axe; found the foreman, stopped the digging, telegraphed for Phillips, who superintended the removal of the enormous bones to the Oxford Museum. The credit accrued to Phillips, no one mentioned Chapman. "The page slew the boar, the peer had the gloire."

But the names of Phillips and the Museum are anticipatory: I must go back to clear the way for them. The man who made them and much else possible in Oxford has been dead only a few years, member of a family exceptional in longevity as in almost all besides. His advent in the early Forties, his regeneration of the Anatomy School at Christchurch, the Hope Bequest, the erection of the new Museum, the remarkable genius who was its architect, the impulse which it communicated at once to Science and Art, its welcome to the British Association, its handselling by the Great Darwin fight in its new Theatre from morn till dewy eve, when Huxley and S. Wilberforce were protagonists, and Henslow held the stakes,—I must keep for another chapter.

CHAPTER IV

SCIENTIFIC SCIENCE

"*Jam jam Efficaci do manus Scientiæ.*"
—HORACE.

Dr. Acland—His Influence—The New Museum—Its Erection—Pollen—Woodward—An Art Colony—William Morris and Rossetti—The British Association Meeting of 1860—The Darwinian Discussion—Wilberforce and the " Venerable Ape "—Huxley's Reply—The Statistician and the Symbolist—After the Battle—Darwinism a Decade Later—The Microscopical Society—J. O. Westwood.

IN 1844 Dr. Acland, settling in Oxford as a physician on Dr. Wootten's early and lamented death, was made Lee's Reader of Anatomy at Christchurch. The subject had not formed part of University studies; Sir Christopher Pegge had drawn small audiences to fluent desultory lectures; Dr. Kidd, who vacated the chair to Dr. Acland, had published an able monograph on the anatomy of the mole-cricket, whose novelty moved the mirth of his professional brethren. The small theatre contained a cast of Eclipse's skeleton with a few dreary preparations in wax; corpses were sent from the gallows for dissections, at which an intending medical student would now and then assist; there was a tradition that the body of a woman hanged for murder had once, when laid out on the table, shown signs of life, had been restored by the professor, and dismissed, let us hope to sin no more. In Oxford, or out of it, Invertebrate Zoology was a subject little studied, and Comparative Anatomy was unknown. Besides the regular students' course at St. George's Hospital, Acland had spent two valuable years in Edinburgh. Here he learned to handle the then unfamiliar microscope, and acquired under the famous Goodsir that insight into Comparative Anatomy and that conception of museum arrangement which were ere long to differentiate him from his medical brethren. The Readership of Anatomy fell vacant, and was offered to him by the Dean. With Goodsir's help he amassed preparations and slides; along with Edward Forbes visited the Shetlands for dredging and dissection; returned to Oxford with fourteen large packing cases, and set himself to create a little Hunterian museum on the banks of Isis. He employed for dissection the deft fingers of J. G. Wood, then an undergraduate: from the yet more skilful hands of Charles Robertson—who, under his tuition, became afterwards Aldrichian Demonstrator and tutor for the Science Schools, and whose "Zoological Series" gained a medal in the Exhibition of 1862—proceeded nearly all the beautiful biological preparations now on the Museum shelves. The lectures began in 1845; they were delivered in the downstairs theatre, whence we ascended to the room above, to sit at tables furnished with little railroads on which ran microscopes charged with illustrations of the lecture, alternately with trays of coffee. A few senior men came from time to time, but could not force their minds into the

SCIENTIFIC SCIENCE

new groove. Dr. Ogle, applying his eye to the microscope, screwed a quarter-inch right through the object; and Dr. Kidd, after examining some delicate morphological preparation, while his young colleague explained its meaning, made answer first, that he did not believe in it, and, secondly, that if it were true he did not think God meant us to know it. So we were mostly undergraduates; and greatly we enjoyed lectures, microscopes, and the discussions which Dr. Acland encouraged; though these last exercises were after a time suppressed, as endangering lapses into the *leve et ludicrum*. On one occasion, so fame reported, the men being invited to relate instances of surprising animal instinct, it was announced by an imaginative student, to the consteration of the professor, who did not appreciate jokes, that "he knew a man whose sister had a tame jellyfish which would sit up and beg."

We discerned his weaknesses, liked him, I think, all the better for them, as bringing him nearer to ourselves. His stiff sense of rectitude, oppressive sometimes both to his neighbours and himself, obstructed the easy relation, begotten usually by public school and College friction, which some teachers establish with their pupils. For neither at Harrow nor at Oxford was he on clubbable terms with his fellows. Lacking in a sense of humour, he often mistook fun for levity: denounced, I remember, as "unprofitable," Sydney Smith's hearteasing merriment; and his sensitiveness occasionally misinterpreted an impersonal frolic as an intentional offence against himself.

As he was by nature strongly emotional, the *hysterica passio* would "swell up," as poor Lear says, with disconcerting suddenness. Henry Furneaux, prince of *raconteurs* and mimics, used to relate how he once burst into tears at first sight of a pretty little window constructed by Woodward in his absence: he was ill in bed for a week after witnessing Tom Taylor's "Joan of Arc": and his broken-hearted self-tormentings over his own supposed religious deficiencies brought on him a manly rebuke from Liddell. His habit of assuming in argument a tone of moral superiority was wont to exasperate opponents. He would press his views upon his colleagues in conference with a sort of tremulous affectionateness—the *æterna mansuetudo* of the Thunny Squib (page 115)—breaking their heads, as Rolleston said, with precious balms; then, if disappointed, he would be peevish, lose temper, court defeat. Max Müller, asked how he had contrived to force through Convocation an extremely debatable measure, answered, "We got Acland to speak against it."

These were spots in the sun, to be recalled with lenient and good-humoured allowance, but essential to a complete understanding of the man.

Meanwhile his teaching bore fruit; and before the Forties had run half their course the question of a Museum arose. There were Buckland's treasures houseless, Dr. Acland's had outgrown their *sedem angustam*, and when Hope's noble entomological collection, accepted together with its curator, had to be stored away in drawers and boxes of a room in the Taylor building, it was felt that the old Ashmolean must be supplanted by a temple worthy of the University. The proposal was vehemently denounced; by economists on the ground of cost, by the old-fashioned classicists as intrusive, by theologians as subtly ministering to false doctrine, heresy, and schism. Sewell of Exeter strained the clerical prerogative of bigotry by protesting against it in a University sermon. Backed by Daubeny, Powell, Buckland, as later by Dean Liddell and Professor Phillips, Dr. Acland sedulously pressed it; till early in the Fifties the money was voted, the design adopted, the first stone laid by Lord Derby, and the work begun—due, as ought always to be remembered, to the initiative and persistence of Acland more than of any other man. Its erection popularised in Oxford Art no less than Science. The growth of artistic feeling had been for some time perceptible; the Eldon drawings were laid out in the Taylor; Mr. Combe's fine gallery of Pre-Raphaelites, the collections of choice engravings made by Griffiths of Wadham and by Manuel Johnson, were liberally and kindly shown; James Wyatt, the picture dealer, loved to fill his High Street shop with Prouts and Constables and Havills, and an occasional Turner water-colour; an exhibition of paintings at the Angel, promoted by Captain Strong, an accomplished amateur, brought out unknown talent and drew the artists together. Millais was often in Oxford as the guest of Mr. Drury at Shotover; Holman Hunt was working in Mr. Combe's house at "The Light of the World," brought with him from Chelsea; nor can any one who knew young Venables, curate of St. Paul's, an intimate with the Combes, doubt whence, consciously or unconsciously, Hunt drew the face of his Christ.

Another pioneer of Art was John Hungerford Pollen, Fellow of Merton. Calling on friends and finding the oak sported, he would leave his card in the form of pencil drawings on the staircase-wall without. Once at New College, when these walls were being newly coloured, we made intercession with the Bursar to leave untouched the *sacer paries* adjoining William Heathcote's rooms, which were inwrought with vigorous delineations of "Civitas Bethlehem, πόλις Nazareth, Urbs Jerusalem," from Pollen's pencil. He was a far-and-wide traveller, and with congenial friends would pour forth his experiences and show his sketches. Heathcote used to tell how one evening at the Skenes, when Miss Skene, a fine Handelian singer, was emulating the coyness of Sardus Tigellius, Pollen offered, if she would sing "Waft her Angels," to execute the Muezzin's call to prayer. This he did in perfection, sitting cross-legged on the floor with rocking body and resonant ascending drawling cry. He left his monument in the painted ceiling of Merton Chapel. I used to go in and watch him at work, recumbent all day long upon a scaffolding, his brush busy, and his black hair showing against the white blouse he wore. The cherubs filling the medallion were drawn from Magdalen Choristers: one was my brother, afterwards Rector of Stand-

WOODWARD, Architect of the Museum
From a Photograph

lake, another was Charles Corfe, son to the Christchurch organist; the Madonna was his mother, Mrs. Corfe; one of the angels was a Miss Smythe. Eight years after, when long cut off from College life, he came with Rossetti to decorate Woodward's Union Debating Room, his contribution being Arthur's investment with the brand Excalibur. We were all prepared for his secession in his Proctor's year, nor surprised to read in *The Times* one day that he had joined the Church of Rome. Two days later came a characteristic note from him to the premature journal: "As the statement is untrue, you will have the goodness to contradict it." Delane apologised, and gave up his informer, Oakley, who sent in his turn a furious remonstrance, which *The Times* snubbed. The report was untimely, that was all; he left us shortly afterwards.

Then into our midst came Woodward, architect of the Museum, a man of rare genius and deep artistic knowledge, beautiful in face and character, but with the shadow of an early death already stealing over him. He was a grave and curiously silent man: of his partners, men greatly his inferiors, the elder, Sir Thomas Deane, was a ceaseless chatterbox, the younger, son to Sir Thomas, stammered. Speaking in Congregation, Jeune hit off the trio after his manner: "One won't talk, one can't talk, one never stops talking." Woodward brought with him his Dublin pupils, drew round him eager Oxonians, amongst them Morris and Burne-Jones, not long come up to Exeter. The lovely Museum rose before us like an exhalation;

its every detail, down to panels and footboards, gas-burners and door handles, an object lesson in art, stamped with Woodward's picturesque inventiveness and refinement. Not before had ironwork been so plastically trained as by Skidmore in the chestnut boughs and foliage which sustained the transparent roof: the shafts of the interior arcades, representing in their sequence the succession of British rocks, sent us into the Radcliffe Library for the mastery of geological classification; every morning came the handsome red-bearded Irish brothers Shea, bearing plants from the Botanic Garden, to reappear under their chisels in the rough-hewn capitals of the pillars.

> "Nor herb nor flow'ret glistened there
> But was carved in the cloister arches as fair."

It seemed that Art was in the air: Mrs. Bartholomew Price, with Miss Cardwell's aid, painted her St. Giles' drawing-room in no Philistine taste; the graceful sunshade work outside Dr. Acland's windows found imitation in many another street; Ruskin, whose books in 1850 Sewell, the librarian of my College, refused to purchase for the library, was read as he had not been read before; while he himself hovered about to bless the Museum work, to offer cheques, and to suggest improvements which silent Woodward sometimes smiling put by. The Committee of the Union authorised Woodward to build a debating-room, to decorate which —alas! upon untempered mortar!—came down Rossetti and Val Prinsep, and Hughes and Stanhope, and Pollen, and Monro the sculptor. A

SCIENTIFIC SCIENCE 53

merry, rollicking set they were: I was working daily in the Library, which at that time opened into the gallery of the new room, and heard their laughter and songs and jokes and the volleys of their soda-water corks; for this innutrient fluid was furnished to them without stint at the Society's expense, and the bill from the Star Hotel close by amazed the treasurer. It was during this visit that Morris and Rossetti, with Rogers, a pupil of Woodward, hunting in the parish churches on Sunday evenings to find a Guinevere, met with the handsome girl who became afterwards the wife of William Morris and Rossetti's cherished friend. I well remember her sister and herself; she survives in sacred widowhood.

At last the Museum was so far finished as to receive the British Association of 1860. Sections fell conveniently into the lecture-rooms: the area, not yet filled with cases, held the evening gatherings; and the large Library, devoid of books and shelves, was dedicated to the Darwinian discussion, the great event of the week. The room filled early, and we waited long. Owen was to take the chair, but did not come; he was replaced by an unclerical-looking man in black, whom we in Oxford knew not, but whom all Cambridge honoured as Professor Henslow. The attack on Darwin's book was to be led by the Bishop of Oxford, who had written in the last *Quarterly* a denunciatory article inspired by Owen, and Huxley was to head the defence. The Bishop came late, trampling his way through the dense crowd to his place upon the platform, his face no longer refined and spiritual as in the early Richmond portrait; coarsened somewhat, even plebeianised, by advancing years, but resourceful, pugnacious, impregnable, not a little arrogant. On the chairman's other side sat Huxley; hair jet black and thick, slight whiskers, pale full fleshy face, the two strong lines of later years already marked, an ominous quiver in his mouth, and an arrow ready to come out of it. For a moment Daubeny beamed on us at the upper door, inviting all at three o'clock to his experimental garden on the Iffley Road. Professor Draper of New York, eminent, serious, nasal, read a paper on Evolution; then, during an expectant pause, out came the Derby dog in the person of old "Dicky" Greswell of Worcester, who, with great eyes, vast white neckcloth, luminous bald head and spectacles, rising and falling rhythmically on his toes, opined that all theories as to the ascent of man were vitiated by the fact, undoubted but irrelevant, that, in the words of Pope, Great Homer died three thousand years ago. Another pause, an appeal from the chairman to Huxley, his sarcastic response that he certainly held a brief for Science, but had not yet heard it assailed.

Then up got Wilberforce, argumentative, rhetorical, amusing; retraced the ground of his article, distinguished between a "working and a causal hypothesis," complimented "Professor Huxley who is about to demolish me," plagiarised from a mountebank sermon by Burgon, expressing the "disquietude" he should feel were a "venerable ape" to be shown to him as his ancestress in the Zoo: a piece of clever, diverting, unworthy clap-

PROFESSOR HUXLEY
From a Photograph taken at the Meeting of the British Association, 1860

trap. Huxley rose, white with anger. "I should be sorry to demolish so eminent a prelate, but for myself I would rather be descended from an ape than from a divine who employs authority to stifle truth." A gasp and shudder through the room, the scientists uneasy, the orthodox furious, the Bishop wearing that fat, provoking smile which once, as Osborne Gordon reminds us,[1] impelled Lord Derby in the House of Lords to an unparliamentary quotation from "Hamlet." "I am asked," Huxley went on, "if I accept Mr. Darwin's book as a complete causal hypothesis. Belated on a roadless common in a dark night, if a lantern were offered to me, should I refuse it because it shed imperfect light? I think not—I think not." He met Wilberforce's points, not always effectively, not entirely at his ease; the "venerable ape's" rude arms were choking him. The Bishop radiantly purged himself. He did not mean to hurt the Professor's feelings; it was our fault—we had laughed, and that made him pursue the joke. We laughed again, and Huxley was not appeased.

Another pause, broken by a voice from the crowd of a grey-haired, Roman-nosed, elderly gentleman. It was Admiral Fitzroy, and men listened; but when they found he had nothing more to say than that Darwin's book had given him acutest pain, the irreverent cry of "Question" silenced him. Another voice from the far end of the long room: a stout man waved and slapped a blue-book; told us that he was no naturalist but a statistician, and that if you could prove Darwin's theories you could prove

[1] Page 154, *note*.

anything. A roar of displeasure proclaimed the meeting's inaptitude at that moment for statistics, and the stout man made his exit with a defiant remonstrance. Now, we thought, for business; but no, there was another act of comedy. From the back of the platform emerged a clerical gentleman, asking for a blackboard. It was produced, and amid dead silence he chalked two crosses at its opposite corners, and stood pointing to them as if admiring his achievement. We gazed at him, and he at us, but nothing came of it, till suddenly the absurdity of the situation seemed to strike the whole assembly simultaneously, and there went up such an ἄσβεστος γέλως as those serious walls would, henceforth, never hear. Again and again the laughter pealed, as purposeless laughter is wont to do; under it the artist and his blackboard were gently persuaded to the rear, and we saw him no more. He was discovered to be a Cornish parson, scientifically minded; but what his hieratics meant or what he wished to say remains inscrutable, the thought he had in him, as Carlyle says of the long-flowing Turk who represented the human species at the heels of Anacharsis Clootz, conjectural to this day.

So at last the fight began, with words strong on either side, and arguments long since superannuate; so all day long the noise of battle rolled. The younger men were on the side of Darwin, the older men against him; Hooker led the devotees, Sir Benjamin Brodie the malcontents; till the sacred dinner-hour drew near. Henslow dismissed us with an impartial benediction, College Halls and hospitable homes received both combatants and audience; nor had Daubeny any visitors to his experimental garden. Next day I met Rolleston, and asked after Huxley's symptoms. "In my room," said he, "hang portraits of Huxley, and of S. Oxon. When I came down this morning I give you my word that Huxley's photograph had turned yellow." Ten years later I encountered him, anything but yellow, at the Exeter meeting of the Association. Again there was a bitter assault on Darwinism, this time by a Scottish doctor of divinity; with smiling serenity Huxley smote him hip and thigh, the audience, hostile or cold at Oxford, here ecstatically acquiescent. The decade had worked its changes: Darwin and Evolution, fighting in their courses against Inscience and Prejudice, had subdued the popular mind. Philistia herself was glad of them.

In Oxford for a time after this science was tolerated sceptically rather than cordially welcomed. "Brodie has done it at last, gentlemen," laughed Chaffers cheerfully to his Brasenose pupils, when during lecture was heard a tremendous explosion —issuing, as it turned out, from the new heating apparatus at St. Mary's, not from the Glastonbury laboratory. At this day, according to Professor Ray Lankester, it receives an indecently inadequate proportion either of recognition or emolument. Conservatism hated it as novel, Orthodoxy feared it as emancipating; even men like Jowett[1] proclaimed war against it on behalf of the "ancient studies," as encroaching on and menacing the "higher conception of knowledge and of the mind,"

[1] "Life and Letters of Jowett," vol. ii. p. 268.

as antagonistic to "morals and religion and philosophy and history and language"—curiously unaware that their own avowed ignorance of its nature, subjects, tendencies, precluded them from forming, much more from expressing, an opinion. Nevertheless, before the decade was far advanced science established itself in Oxford. The Museum buildings formed an object lesson which it was impossible to overlook; their contents, laid out and labelled, their minerals, fossils, insects, zoological specimens and preparations, appealed to the naturalist instinct which from many natures school and college had not quite extirpated; professors came amongst us, men already stamped with classical University distinction, Rolleston, Brodie, Balfour; or, like Mrs. Bayham Badger's second husband, "men of European reputation," such as dear old Phillips. The splendid show of microscopes at the British Association conversazione had excited interest and emulation; and when in 1861 an enthusiastic young New College naturalist projected a Microscopical Society the idea was warmly taken up. Dr. Acland was its first president, and delivered an inaugural address; it met and worked regularly, with papers and discussions, systematic investigation of the rich Oxford microscopic fauna, periodical exhibitions in the Museum, which drew large audiences and laid wide foundations.

Conspicuous at these gatherings was the famous entomologist and very lovable personage, J. O. Westwood, who had come to Oxford in the late Forties as controller of Mr. Hope's collection. As far as I know, he has never been memorialised in print, and I may appropriately end this science chapter with a brief tribute to his memory. His claim to eminence was not only biological; he was also a specialist in the archæology and palæography of art, the highest living authority on fictile ivories and inscribed stones. Born and brought up a Quaker, he was apprenticed to an engraver, acquiring the power of accurate delineation which enabled him so graphically to illustrate his various works. Articled for a time to a London solicitor and afterwards a partner in the firm, he was persuaded by Mr. Hope to remove to Oxford, first as curator of the Hope collection, then as earliest occupant of the Natural History Chair which Hope was founding; and at Oxford Westwood remained till his death. Sprung from the ranks, and a late-born son of the University, he received scant welcome from the Dons; the exclusiveness of that time being further aggravated by his Nonconformist origin and opinions, until rebuked by Richard Michell, the Public Orator, who reminded his friends that their new colleague was "not sectarian but *insectarian*." The good-humoured simplicity of his manner and his unfailing amiability to all who sought enlightenment in his department soon won men's hearts, and he became as popular as he deserved to be.

I knew him not till 1860. Attracted by a jar containing live specimens of the uncommon and beautiful *Cheirocephalus diaphanus*, which I had found in a rain-water pool near the Headington Asylum, and had sent to a natural history exhibition at the Town Hall, he begged me to call on him at the Museum; and finding that I was studying the *Coleoptera*, placed at my disposal books and specimens, sparing no pains to encourage and assist me. I happened to be dexterous in microscopical preparation, and he urged the Museum Delegates to employ me in mounting a series of insect anatomies after a conception of his own; but the plan fell through. His own technique was as remarkable as his knowledge; with no tools except scissors, forceps, lens, camel-hair brush, gum tragacanth, and colour box, he performed miracles of dissection and restoration. I remember his falling from a ladder in the Library, and crushing in his breast-pocket a pill-box containing a rare beetle. The ruin seemed hopeless, the insect a powder of fragments; but he set to work at once, and next day showed me the beetle restored to all its former beauty. His unerring instinct in diagnosing and locating a new species was made the subject of a practical joke. Some saucy young entomologists obtained a chocolate beetle, made and coloured under their directions, from a famous shop in Paris, and sent it to Westwood for identification fixed in a glass-topped box. He wrote that without handling it he could not be certain of the genus, but that it was a tetramerous beetle belonging to the family *Cerambycidæ*. The useful letter "h" he never succeeded in pronouncing. He once asked Mansel who was St. Bee. Remembering his peculiarity, Mansel answered that he was a near kinsman of St. 'Ives. At an electoral contest between Mr. Gladstone and Mr. Hardy, Westwood, coming in late, hurried and breathless, announced his vote for

"Glad——, no, no, I mean 'Ardy." Henry Smith claimed the vote for Gladstone. "Why," said the Vice-Chancellor, "he only pronounced the first syllable of Mr. Gladstone's name." "Yes, sir; but he did not pronounce the first letter of Mr. Hardy's."

He left more than one standard work : in science, the "Modern Classification of Insects," and a beautiful but costly monograph of "British Moths and Butterflies"; in art, the "Palæographia Sacra Pictoria," with "Miniatures and Ornaments of Anglo-Saxon and Irish MSS.," and the monumental "Lapidarium Walliæ." He was President of the Entomological Society, and received the Royal Society's gold medal. We felt when he passed away that a zoological professor as good, perhaps better, might be found; but that the minutely accomplished entomologist, holding in mind's eye and memory all the discovered and named insects in all the museums of the world, accessible from his fluent colloquial French and German to every Continental scientist, ready ever to display and expound his treasures, patiently to the unlearned, enthusiastically to the accomplished visitor, could probably never be replaced. Men said of him, as was said of Richelieu when he died, "Il laisse plus de vide qu'il n'a tenu de place." Entering the familiar room, I shall never cease to miss and to recall regretfully the short figure, shrewd kindly eye, welcoming voice, long wave of snow white hair and beard, which went to form the outward man of J. O. Westwood.

CHAPTER V

ÆSCULAPIUS IN THE THIRTIES

*"This is the Prince of Leeches: fever, plague,
Cold rheum, and hot podagra, do but look on him,
And quit their grasp upon the tortured sinews."*
—WALTER SCOTT.

An Oxford Medical Directory—Pegge—Wall—Bourn—Kidd—Ireland—West—Wood—Tuckwell—A Picturesque Survival—A Friend of Abernethy—His Wonderful Memory—His *jeux d'esprit*—The Last of the Old School.

"LONG and lasting," says Lockhart in his now forgotten "Reginald Dalton," while he recounts the blood-letting of an Oxford town and gown row—"long and lasting shall be the tokens of its wrath—long shall be the faces of Pegge, Wall, Kidd, and light shall be their hearts, as they walk their rounds to-morrow morning—long shall be the stately stride of Ireland, and long the clyster-pipe of West—long and deep shall be the probing of thy skilful lancet, O Tuckwell; and long shall be all your bills, and long, very long, shall it be ere some of them are paid." Lockhart wrote in the Twenties, but most of his doctors were walking their rounds ten years later; *walking*, for Oxford was a small place then, and our medicos performed their ambarvalia on foot. Sir Christopher Pegge was a showy, handsome man, a Fellow of Oriel in Oriel's prime of reputation; he had no great practice, but as

ÆSCULAPIUS IN THE THIRTIES 63

Regius Professor drew men to his spirited lectures. Though comparatively young, he wore the old-fashioned cocked hat and wig, with the massive gold-headed cane, which his successor, Dr. Kidd—a sensible, homely creature—was the first medical professor to abandon. Kidd, Wall, Bourn were the popular physicians of the decade. Kidd was a little man, trotting about the streets in a "spencer," a tailless greatcoat then becoming obsolete, and worn only by himself and Dr. Macbride. Bourn was an insinuating, smiling, soft-voiced man—"Have we any report from the bowels?" was his regular whispered question to lady patients suffering from what Epimenides the Cretan called γαστέρες ἀργαί. Wall I cannot recall, but I remember his widow and Bourn's, picturesque old ladies in black velvet and lace, whose card-parties, preceded by formal tea and closed by substantial suppers, attracted the clever genial men and women whom I have earlier mentioned. Dr. Ogle, father to a distinguished Fellow of Lincoln, who died all too early, lived on into the early Fifties; as did Kidd, with two droll little daughters something like himself. Eden, when Vicar of St. Mary's, once invited the pair to tea; stuffed them with cake and muffin;—for a tea was a square meal in those days—dismissed them with the farewell, which they received in the belief that it was a religious pastoral benediction:

Ite domum, *Saturæ*, venit Hesperus, ite, *Capellæ*.

Ireland represented the "matriculated apothecaries" of that date, men who, like the elder Pendennis in his lowly days, made up their own medicines, attended ladies at the most interesting period of their lives, sold Epsom salts, blisters, hair powder, across the counter of the shops which they called their surgeries. Some remained humble to the end; not so Ireland, who somehow obtained a Scotch degree, discarded the surgery, and set up a brass plate as Dr. Ireland on his house in Pennyfarthing Street. He was a grandiloquent, pompous man; Lockhart's "stately stride" exactly hits him off. I remember his swing along the street with cane held at attention; recall his stalking into my mother's drawing-room with his new honour fresh upon him, and bespeaking her congratulations on the fact that he would "enter the Kingdom of Heaven as a Doctor of Medicine." I saw him later in extreme old age; he said that he was ninety-nine years old—he was nothing like so old—but he added, with his hands aloft, "My memory is in ruins." He deserved credit, however, for discovering the mathematical talent of his servant lad Abram Robertson, who became afterwards Professor of Astronomy. West was his partner—tall, gentlemanlike, gold-spectacled, married to the daughter of a rich and notable Alderman Fletcher, whose hands continued to hold her cards long after they had ceased, through rheumatism, to be for other purposes prehensile. West's partner again and subsequent successor was Wood, father to the naturalist, who lived in the fine corner house opposite the King's Arms, built by Vanbrugh, and destroyed to make way for the Indian Institute.

But by far the most conspicuous and interesting of Lockhart's Hakims was Tuckwell, for thirty years

MR. TUCKWELL, SURGEON
From a Water-Colour Drawing by J. F. Wood, 1833

ÆSCULAPIUS IN THE THIRTIES

—from 1815 to 1845—the leading Oxford surgeon. In costume and demeanour he was a survival from the more picturesque and ceremonious past. He pervaded Oxford in a claret-coloured tail coat with velvet collar, canary waistcoat with gilt buttons, light brown trousers, two immense white cravats propping and partly covering the chin, a massive well-brushed beaver hat.[1] His manner and address were extraordinarily winning; a contemporary described him to me long ago, in a letter which I happened to preserve, as "the most fascinating man I ever met, a favourite with all who knew him; his cheery brightness invaluable in a sick room, supported as it was by his high repute and skill." Mr. Abernethy, discontinuing practice, entreated him to take his place; he was, said Sir Benjamin Brodie to me in 1853, "one of the cleverest surgeons of his day." He was not a member of the University, but had been educated at the then famous Aynho Grammar School, whose eccentric master, Mr. Leonard, was known for his scholarship and for his addiction to green tea, which he kept ever by his side to moisten his construes in Tacitus and Horace. So Tuckwell knew his Latin books minutely, and could quote them effectively. He was pupil to Abernethy, who became much attached to him; his dinner table after his marriage held a magnificent epergne, a wedding present from the famous surgeon. Amongst his comrades were the lads known

---

[1] *Beaver.*—There were no silk hats until late in the Thirties. The beaver cost two guineas; only gentlemen wore them. New College men of that day were known by their unbrushed hats.

afterwards as Dr. Skey and Sir George Burrows. He worked hard at his profession, and made himself a proficient besides in French, Spanish, and Italian. He went to Oxford, without introduction, friends, or money, about 1808, but rose rapidly into practice, establishing himself in the house opposite Magdalen elms, which a very few old Oxford men still associate with his name, and which was to bear in later years the door-plate of his son. His name is not only embalmed in Lockhart's novel, but points the moral of a bitter passage in the "Oxford Spy":—

> "If tutors punish what they seldom shun,
> Severe to all who do—as they have done—
> *Their* wild career at once pursue, condemn;
> Give fees to Tuckwell, and advice to them."

It was, as we have seen, the day of early dinners, late suppers, nightly cards. Ombre had gone out; though it was said that old Miss Horseman could still illustrate Belinda's game, and unfold the mysteries of Manille and Matador. Quadrille, piquet, whist, were the games in vogue; and at the last two Tuckwell was said to be one of the best players in England. David Gregorie, the Queen's Square magistrate, invited him to a three nights' contest at piquet. It took place at Oxford, in a select gathering of experts, and Gregorie returned to London three hundred pounds the poorer. He was no less skilful as a chess player, having learned from the famous Sarratt, the great chess teacher, whose fee was a guinea a lesson; and founding the club already mentioned in these papers. The marvellous memory which explains his prowess at cards was shown in his power of quoting poetry. Few men could beat him in capping verses; those present with him at a large party were challenged to write down the titles of Shakespeare's plays; all tried, but he alone succeeded. The story I am about to relate seems incredible, but I heard it long ago from not a few independent witnesses. A bet was laid, and heavy odds taken against it, that he would repeat ten consecutive lines from any one place at which he might be set on in Shakespeare, Milton, Dante, or Lope de Vega. The bet was won. What proverbs and riddles were to Solomon and his courtiers, that were impromptus and epigrams to the lively *convives* of that pleasant time. A lady sang one night a pretty Italian song by Metastasio, and the company appealed to him for a translation. He hastily pencilled it as follows:—

> "Gentle Zephyr, ah! if e'er
>   Thou meetst the Mistress of my heart,
> Tell her thou'rt a sigh sincere,
>   But never say whose sigh thou art.
> Limpid Rivulet, ah! if e'er
>   Thy murmuring waters near her glide,
> Say thou'rt swelled by many a tear,
>   But not whose eyes those tears supplied."

Catherine Fanshawe's poem on the letter H created much excitement when it appeared.[1] It was discussed one evening in his presence, and a Miss Harriett Lee, a very clever girl—afterwards Mrs.

[1] Appendix D.

Wingfield, of Tickencote Hall—disparaged it. "It's no great thing," she said; "Tuckwell would have done it just as well." Next morning he carried to her these lines on the letter W :—

"Its existence began with this World full of tears,
  And it first in the Work of Creation appears.
In the Whirlwind we feel and acknowledge its power,
  And its influence hail in each soft falling Shower.
Its presence the Woods and the Waters must own,
  And 'tis found in the Dwelling of monarch and clown.
It will never forsake us in Want or in Woe,
  And is heard in each Word that can comfort bestow.
It dwells with the Wealthy, the Witty, the Wise,
  Yet assistance to Wretchedness never denies.
'Twill be found in the Sweets of each opening flower,
  And hangs on each Dewdrop at twilight's soft hour.
In the mournful Farewell if you hear it with pain,
  In the sweet sound of Welcome 'twill meet you again.
'Tis the prop of our Laws, and the guide of our Will,
  Which without it would lead us to nothing but Ill.
It begins every Wish, every View it must bound,
  And still to our Welfare essential is found.
In the last dying Whisper of man it shall rise,
  And assist us with Wings to ascend to the skies ;
'Midst the Wonders of Nature its form we shall view,
  Until lost in the Wreck which shall Chaos renew."

His heart was as large as his brain was keen ; if he fascinated his equals, he no less won the love and gratitude of his humbler neighbours. During the thirty years of his celebrity his doors stood open for the first two hours of every over-busy day to the poor who chose to come, and who streamed in from the country round to be tended without a fee. He devoted to their care gratuitously the same minute and searching skill, the same unerring memory and rapid judgment, the same urbane and cordial presence, which had made him popular and fashionable among those who were glad to pay him highly for these gifts; and when the large heart ceased to beat and the keen brain to toil, while amongst a troop of friendly mourners I followed his remains along streets darkened by the signs of universal sorrow, I saw the crowd of poor —to be counted, it was said, by hundreds—gathered in from village and from slum for a final tribute to the friend who had dispensed among them health and healing through so many years. He was the last of the old Oxford school; the "Brilliant Man" —to quote from Henry Bulwer—amongst his University compeers, as was Canning among a wider and more high-placed set. He retained the "grand manner" of a fading age; the refined and pointed, not conventional and effusive, courtesy to women; the bounteous fund of ever-ready talk, alternating not monologist, seasoned not swamped with allusion, recitation, epigram. They played as well as worked, those fine old fellows—*luserunt satis atque biberunt*—lost and won their guineas gaily, chirruped their genial wit and anecdote, laid the ghosts of eating cares in floods of generous "Comet" port, which enriched and liberated, never dulled or overfraught, their brains. Some of us love them for it the more; let the "*sicci*" who start away from wine, the purists who spy sin in cards, remember that behind this radiant conviviality the higher virtues walked their round, moral excellence hand in hand with mental power; that often, as in Tuckwell's case, the day which culminated in joyous revelry began in self-devoted altruism, bidding us as our record closes turn from the catalogue of professional and social triumphs to

> " That best portion of a good man's life,
> His little, nameless, unremembered acts
> Of kindness and of love."

CHAPTER VI

CALLIOPE IN THE THIRTIES

*"The sound
Of instruments that made melodious chime
Was heard, of Harp and Organ; and who moved
Their chords and stops was seen; his volant touch
Fled and pursued transverse the resonant Fugue."*
—MILTON.

Early Amateurs—Blanco White—Newman—The Bewildered Butler—Musicians a Caste apart—A Notable Organist—Jonathan Sawell the Singer—A Letter from the Eighteenth Century—Jullien—The Amateur Society—Oxford becomes Musical—"Gregorian" Music—Jenny Lind's Visit—Sir Frederick Ouseley—Sir John Stainer.

WHEN Music, heavenly maid, was young in the last century, she had few votaries in academic Oxford. The traditions of the place were against her; to be musical was bad form. There was once, to be sure, a Dean of Christchurch who wrote charming glees and catches, and respectable church music; but the solecisms of Dean Aldrich were expiated by his successor, Cyril Jackson, who pronounced that a boy "with no more ear nor a stone nor no more voice nor an ass" would make an excellent chorister; and by Gaisford, who appointed as singing men worn-out scouts and bedmakers. In the Twenties and Thirties there were probably not half-a-dozen amateurs in Oxford. Blanco White was a violinist, so was Newman; and his noble passage on the Inspiration of Music, with its curious slip as to fourteen notes in the scale, has become a *locus classicus*;[1] but he records the bewilderment of the Provost's butler, when, sent to announce his election at Oriel, he found the new Fellow playing on the fiddle, and inquired anxiously if he had not mistaken the rooms or come to the wrong person. Donkin played both the violin and the piano; George Rowden of New College was one of the best double-bass performers in England : together with Donkin, Menzies, Driffield, Clifton, and Judge Bayliss, who in his 91st year still survives, he helped to form a Brasenose Harmonic Society, which practised and gave concerts. Now and then at the evening parties of the Heads a gifted lady would, with Handel, Haydn, or Mozart, compel, like Milton's nightingale, pleased silence; but from these gatherings music, as encroaching upon cards, was for the most part ostracised. Even so late as 1846 Max Müller, fresh from musical Leipzig, found that no young man, even if qualified, would stoop to the music-stool in public, and that to ask a Don to play "would have been considered an insult"; while Hallé, visiting England two years later, tells us that for a gentleman to be able to play upon the piano was looked upon as a sign of effeminacy, almost of vice. For by here-

[1] His sister challenged the passage in writing to him: "What do you mean by fourteen notes?" He answers: "I had already been amused and provoked to find my gross blunder about the 'fourteen.' Pray do not suppose I *doubled* the notes for semitones, though it looks very like it. The truth is, I had a most stupid idea in my head that there were fifteen semitones, and took off one for the octave. On reading it over when published I saw the absurdity."—"Letters and Correspondence," vol. ii. p. 411.

ditary prejudice the professional musician was looked upon as an inferior, to be paid for his services, to be kept socially at a distance. Prince Hal bore much from Falstaff, but broke his head for likening his father to a singing man at Windsor; Mrs. Thrale, we know, was deserted and denounced by all her friends, including ungrateful Fanny Burney, for marrying the blameless musicmaster, Piozzi. Stately Dr. Williams, when Headmaster of Winchester, took to hair-powder because a lady mistook him for a bass singer in the cathedral; I shall recall later on the consternation felt among the older men of Oxford, when Ouseley, baronet, gentleman commoner, Master of Arts, condescended to become Doctor of Music; and we all remember Mr. Osborne's contempt for the "Honourables" to whom his daughter introduced him — "Lords, indeed? Why, at one of her swarreys I saw one of 'em speak to a dam fiddler, a fellar I despise."

So music was relegated contemptuously to a quasi-professional set, the chaplains, singing men, Bible clerks, of the three choral Colleges; its Doctorate was a sham, the graduates not admitted to the sacred scarlet semicircle in the Theatre; its Professor, with a salary of £12 a year, appearing only at Commemoration to play the ramshackle old organ in the Theatre. The Professor at that time was Sir Henry Bishop, composer of deservedly popular part-songs, but inferior as a musician to his very eminent predecessor, Dr. Crotch. Of the three organists only one was notable, Dr. Stephen Elvey of New College, a good harmonist, an enthusiastic Handelian, though the loss of a leg prevented him from playing pedal fugues, but of rough manner and suspicious temper. On the death of his first wife he had married, with rather unusual promptitude, a pretty girl known as Perdita amongst the New College undergraduates, who used to crowd the "Slipe" gate on Sundays after service in order to see her pass from Holywell Church. He presided shortly afterwards at a concert, and the wag who arranged its programme had inserted a glee by his brother George, which appeared in the bill as "Ah! Why so soon—Elvey?"

I remember the performance of Sir George Elvey's Bachelor's exercise in the Music Room, I think in 1838, when Stephen Elvey conducted in the splendid robes which I then for the first time saw, the new Bachelor sitting at the piano. The choral services in the Chapels were not of a high order, though individual voices of special sweetness kept up their popularity. The finest adult singer of that time was Jonathan Sawell, chaplain of New College and Magdalen, who possessed the rare pure Mario-like tenor, almost touching alto in the higher range. He long survived his voice, singing with husky wooden notes into the Fifties; a cheery, popular fellow, and an admirable oar; he and Moon of Magdalen, son to Alderman or Lord Mayor Moon, placed on the river the first outrigger skiffs seen at Oxford. His window in Magdalen, opposite to the Physic Garden, was always beautifully floral; an adornment long since universal, peculiar then to him and to Dr. Peter Maurice of New College. As for the chorister boys, they ran wild. Their nominal master at Magdalen was an elderly Fellow, George Grantham, who came to a tragic end, falling out of his window at bedtime into the deer park, and found there next morning by his scout, dead with a broken neck, the deer crowding round him in an alarmed circle. His grave, with G. G. incised, is in the corner of the cloisters between the chapel door and the window opposite. There was a fire in the antechapel at that time, and the surpliced boys used as they passed it to deposit chestnuts and potatoes, which they recovered, *matura et cocta*, when they came out. The New College brats were not under better discipline. Many years ago, while lionising some strangers in the Chapel, I observed that the plaster wing of a sham oak angel had been broken off, and from the crevice behind protruded a piece of paper. I drew it out, yellow, stained, and creased. I suppose that interest accrues even to trivial personal records when ripened by the lapse of years. We take no note to-day of a child's naked footprint on the sand, but the impress of the baby foot on the Roman villa floor at Brading is a poem fertile in suggestion. So I copy the crumpled fragment as it lies before me : " When this you find, recall me to your mind. James Philip Hewlett, Subwarden's chorister, April 26, 1796." There follows the roll of boys ; then this edifying legend : " Yeates just gone out of chapel, making as if he was ill, to go to Botleigh with Miss Watson. Mr. Prickett reads prayers. Mr. Lardner is now reading the second lesson. Mr. Jenks read the first. Slatter shams a bad Eye because he did not know the English of the theme and could not do it.

A whole holiday yesterday being St. Mark. Only the Subwarden of the Seniors at Prayers." This last is significant. So we take our leave of naughty Master James Philip Hewlett—"*I, curre*, little gown boy," as dear Thackeray says.

The first pioneer of musical feeling in Oxford was Jullien, an affected, grimacing, overdressed Frenchman, but a clever *maestro*, whose brilliant band played the dance and march music which set elderly heads and bonnets wagging in imperfect time, and who brought out excellent soloists. He often came amongst us, and the men who heard Koenig and Richardson at his concerts themselves took up the cornet and the flute. Oppressive practising *à la* Dick Swiveller prevailed; but the taste for music spread. It was found that Thalberg and Madame Dulcken would fill the Star Assembly Room; that scientific and high-priced Chamber Quartetts, by Blagrove, Clementi, and the Reinagles, brought to Wyatt's room fit audience though few. In 1844 came Hullah; large classes working under him in Merton College Hall; mature and unmusical M.A.'s hammering away without much result at the "From his low and grassy bed," which formed the Pons Asinorum of the Hullah Manual. The practising soon died out; but the real musicians took the hint. An Amateur Society was formed, with W. E. Jelf of Christchurch for its president, Lord Seaham, afterwards Lord Londonderry, as secretary, a committee highly selected and unprofessional: and, with the help of Grimmet's band, concerts were given twice a term, at which men since famous made their *début*. Murray, of Queen's, was there, who sang subsequently with Louisa Pyne on the Opera stage at Boulogne; Thomson, afterwards Archbishop of York, sounded his magnificent baritone, publicly heard before only in the Boar's Head anthem upon Christmas Day; young Frederick Ouseley improvised at the piano; later on came the late Sir Herbert Oakeley, a slim boyish figure, with a passion for Handel. Musical talent was everywhere lying loose; it needed some one to combine it, and the someone was Dr. Corfe, who succeeded Marshall at the Christchurch organ. He formed classes of amateurs for practice of classical music, training them laboriously in his picturesque old house Beam Hall, in Merton Lane; until in 1847 they gave a public performance of "Acis and Galatea," Corfe rolling his *rs*, Staudigl-wise, in "O *r*uddier than the che*rr*y," Mrs. Corfe singing the exquisite Galatea solos. This was followed by "The Antigone," by "Alexander's Feast," and, more daring still, by Beethoven's Mass in C. At the opening of the new Magdalen School on May Day, 1851, an amateur choir, conducted by Blyth, who had followed old Vickery at Magdalen, performed, without instruments, a series of sacred pieces. We sang, I remember, the Ave Verum, lately brought to England by the Berlin choir; Croft's "We will rejoice"; "Teach me, O Lord," and many more. Our great feat was a Cantata of Bach's, which occupied twenty-one minutes, Blyth informing us with pride at its close that we had kept the pitch exactly. Amongst our performers was old G. V. Cox the Bedel, survival from a former age. He had been the first chorister whom

Dr. Routh appointed more than half a century before. Healthy development is apt to throw down morbid outgrowths, manifested here in a spurious but short-lived influx of the so-called "Gregorian" music, a reversion to the modes prevalent in Christian worship before the discovery of counterpoint. The freak was ecclesiological, not musical; part of the general putting back of clock hands which characterised the Church movement of the time. It was adopted by some amongst the clergy as a royal road to music, traversable without knowledge and without training; was rejected as an indefensible anachronism by musicians, who noted the unsuitableness of the "tones" to English words, their inexpressive baldness unless sung in unison by eighty or a hundred voices, the intolerable impropriety of appending to them harmonies for English Church performance. Meanwhile Ouseley brought his vast learning to pulverise the theory of their derivation from the Jewish Temple service, pointing out that the melodic intervals of Oriental music could have borne no resemblance to the Greek system of tones and semitones on which were founded the chants of the ancient Western Church. It is recorded that an old gentleman, whose time-honoured Sunday worship had been garnished by a new Rector with "Gregorians," ventured to expostulate, but was told that they were of consecrated antiquity, being in fact the very tones to which David set the Psalms. He deferred to the Rector's erudition, and thanked him for explaining a passage in the Old Testament which he had never understood before

—why it was, namely, that when David played the harp before King Saul, Saul threw a javelin at him.

Whether, without its incipient musical awakening, Oxford would have gone crazy over Jenny Lind in December, 1848, I cannot say. She came as Stanley's guest, having stayed with his father at the Palace when she sang at Norwich. The Bishop, a little black figure, hopping about the Cathedral aisles like Vincent Bourne's "Cornicula," was known locally as the Crow; a nickname previously borne by his brother, Lord Stanley of Alderley, the husband of Maria Josepha Holroyd; and Jenny's visit produced the epigram :—

> "Ornithologists ancient and modern attest
> That the Cuckoo-bird visits the Nightingale's nest,
> But not Stanley's own Alderley Bird-book can show[1]
> That the Nightingale roosts in the nest of the Crow."

She sang in the Theatre, which was crowded from area to roof; here, as elsewhere, winning every heart. That the sight of the interior with its thousand black gowns should have impressed her to tears is perhaps a tradition difficult of acceptance; there were tears in the hearts if not in the eyes of many amongst her hearers. Great was the demand for her autograph; most good-naturedly she acceded to it. One undergraduate, who rushed into poetry and sent her his effusion, still retains her answer—the verse from Brady and Tate :

> "Happy are they and only they,
> Who from Thy judgments never stray,
> Who know what's right, nor only so,
> But also practise what they know,"

---

[1] "A Familiar History of Birds," by the Rev. Edward Stanley, Rector of Alderley, Cheshire (afterwards Bishop of Norwich).

with "In remembrance of Jenny Lind," and the date. On the day after the concert she came, veiled and *incognita*, to New College Chapel: but the Subwarden, Stacpoole, near whose stall she sat, detected her. It happened that the Hall was lighted and its piano open for the Thursday glee club practice; Stacpoole, after showing her the Chapel, cunningly brought her on to see the Hall, by this time filled with men, and unceremoniously asked if she would sing. She looked surprised, but unaffectedly consented; bade the lady with her accompany, and sang to us a cavatina from *Der Freyschütz*. I remember her, poising herself like a fisherman about to throw a casting-net, before she flung out her wonderful trills. Many years afterwards I heard her again in Max Müller's drawing-room; the old execution was there; the nightingale warble, the *timbre-argentin*, was gone. She told us that A. P. Stanley, who had no ear and hated music, or at least was bored by it, usually left the room when she warbled. But hearing her one day sing "I know that my Redeemer liveth," he told her she had given him an idea of what people mean by music. Only once before, he said, the same feeling had come over him, when in front of the Palace at Vienna he had heard a tattoo performed by four hundred drummers! So, Eothen Kinglake, we are told, also tone-deaf, astray by some mischance at a *matinée musicale*, and asked by the hostess what kind of music he preferred, answered—"I certainly have a preference; it is for the drum." One thinks too of M. Jourdain's passion for *la trompette marine*.

CALLIOPE IN THE THIRTIES

Not till 1855 was music validly recognised by the University; that achievement was reserved for Sir Frederick Ouseley. Sir Henry Bishop died; the appointment rested with the Proctors, and through one of them, Holland of New College, a good musician, it was conferred on Ouseley. The necessary reforms were two: that the degree should become a reality, and that the Professor should not only profess, but teach. Hitherto any one seeking the Mus.Doc. had merely to inscribe his name as a nominal member of some College, send in an orchestral thesis, which was invariably accepted, pay a band for its performance, and take rank as an Oxford Doctor. Ouseley instituted a public examination by three competent examiners in historical and critical knowledge of music, and in elementary classics and mathematics, demanding also from each candidate a lengthy written composition to be submitted to himself. The stringency of the test was shown by the fact that in its early application fifty per cent. of the candidates failed, not a few of the plucks being a judgment on "cribbed exercises," which his immense knowledge enabled him to expose. I remember how the Professor, kindest-hearted of men, suffered in inflicting rejections. He was beset by piteous, even tearful, appeals, or by fierce expostulations; had sometimes to escape into a friend's house from imploring remonstrants who chivied him in the streets; but he kept conscientiously to the line he had drawn, with the result that in a few years' time the Oxford Doctorate came to be estimated as it had never been before. His lectures, somewhat obscure and cramped in style, owed popularity to the practical illustration of them on the organ or piano by his friend Mr. Parratt, and to the volunteer assistance of a well-coached vocal and instrumental band. So at last Queen Calliope came down from heaven and made a home in Oxford. I am told she abides there still; that Ouseley's white and crimson mantle fell upon a worthy Elisha, whose advent to St. Paul's had been hailed by the innocent quatrain:—

> "St. Paul's had a loss
> In Dr. T. Goss;
> I'm sure it's a gainer
> In Dr. J. Stainer;"

that by his promotion to the vacant Chair Oxford was a gainer in her turn; that if Sir Frederick Ouseley made music respectable in the University, Sir John Stainer made it beloved. But this is more recent history; and the Neleian sovereign old, though his confidences to Patroclus were sometimes garrulous in their old-world reminiscence, never bored that Homeric Man Friday by recapitulation of contemporary events.

> "Plague on't, quoth Time to Thomas Hearne,
> *Whatever I forget*, you learn."

NOTE.—A lady reading this chapter recognised her great-grandfather in the recording chorister, Master James Philip Hewlett. She tells me that he grew up to be Chaplain of New College and Curate of St. Ebbe's, dying young. His brother was the author of "Peter Priggins," mentioned on page 85.

CHAPTER VII

UNDERGRADUATES IN THE THIRTIES

*"The seedsman, Memory,
Sowed my deep-furrowed thought with many a Name,
Whose glory will not die."*
—TENNYSON.

An old Diary—Oxford in the Thirties as depicted in Fiction—Its more Essential Aspects—Some Great Undergraduates—And a Great Tutor—"Tom" Acland—His Achievements at Oxford—His Torrential Eloquence—The "Uniomachia"—Tom Brancker—Solomon Cæsar Malan—His Seventy Languages—Stanley—Matthew Arnold—Clough—Thorold Rogers—A Kindly Action—An Interchange of Amenities.

MANY years ago, with a collector's instinct, I exhumed for sixpence a ragged manuscript from the rubbish heap of a Barbican bookstall. It was the diary of an old Rugbeian, covering his residence at Oxford through 1830 and 1831. His name was Trevor Wheler, cadet of a Warwickshire family living in their ancient manor-house at a village called Leamington Hastings, and he came to Oxford by the Regulator coach, going on to London when the term was over on the box of the Royal Defiance. The Trevor Whelers of to-day have tried to identify the diarist. They think he was Henry Trevor Wheler, who went to India, returned and took Orders. His name, I think, spelled Wheeler, occurs near the bottom of the M.A. list in my 1836 Oxford Calendar. I lent the manuscript to old

Bloxam, the Rugby antiquary, who died without returning it. This Wheler seems to have been a quiet, orderly fellow: he kept morning chapel strictly, went always to St. Mary's, where on one occasion he heard Keble preach; and usually read a sermon in his own rooms on Sunday night. He corresponds with several female Christian names, and has written Byron's stanzas on "Woman, lovely woman" in the first page of his journal, with the date June 14th attached, evidently Commemoration Week. He gives frequent wine parties, among the guests being Roundell and William Palmer and Piers Claughton, and always carefully records the number of corks he drew. He breakfasts with Tommy Short of Trinity, of whom I shall speak anon. He goes to New College Chapel, and to the Tyrolese singers at the Music Room. He frequents the Union, where seven men are blackballed in one evening, where Acland senior (the late Sir Thomas), is elected treasurer and Gladstone secretary, and where debates are held on Jewish disabilities, and on the superiority of Byron to Shelley, Sunderland coming express from Cambridge, with Arthur Hallam and Monckton Milnes, to speak upon the latter theme. Sunderland, we may remember, was the contemporary of Tennyson, who described him as "a very plausible, Parliament-like, self-satisfied speaker at the Union," and sketched him mercilessly in the poem called "A Character." His sad story is told in Sir Wemyss Reid's "Life of Lord Houghton" (vol. i., p. 76). Wheler "sits" in the Little-Go school, and hears a man construe *spicea virga* a "spicy virgin." He buys the new edition of the Waverley Novels, and, attending Wise's sale-room, has a lot of seventy books knocked down to him for £1, 2s. The composition is neither incisive, eventful, nor picturesque; but it is interesting, not only as all diaries are interesting by lifting the curtain of a fellow-mortal's mental privacy, but as raising from the shades with contemporary vividness the Undergraduate Oxford of seventy-seven years ago.

We may read of this Oxford in forgotten novels: its vulgar side in Hewlett's "Peter Priggins"; its rollicking side in Dickinson's "Vincent Eden," published in *Bentley's Miscellany*, and abruptly ceasing through pressure on the editor, it was believed, from apprehensive University authorities. In "Loss and Gain" we have its obscurantist side, due to the author's teaching; the picked men of ability in its pages—Sheffield, Reding, Carlton—ranging over not high themes of philosophy, science, culture, but the nightmares of Tractarian theology and the characteristics of a true Church. Mere foils were men like those, setting off the nobler Oxford of their time; and never in the history of the University has a decade opened and progressed amid a group so brilliant. In 1830 we have Gladstone, Liddell, Charles Wordsworth, Hope, T. Acland, Manning, Church, Halford Vaughan, William Adams, Walter Hamilton, Lords Dalhousie, Elgin, Lincoln, Canning, to take names almost at random. Nor was this dawn of golden times confined to Oxford; at Cambridge in the very same year gathered a not less rare group of *conjurati fratres:* Spedding, Thomson, Brookfield, Trench, Tennyson, Monckton Milnes, Charles Buller, Merivale, Arthur Hallam, Kinglake, Sterling. There is deep pathos in these sparkling catalogues. We see the band of friends, cheerful, united, sanguine, starting together on life's path. Pass sixty years, we check the list, to find a scattered remnant of survivors, telling sadly of havoc wrought in their train by the storms of life, themselves too often alienated at its close. But the record of their deeds survives. Outworn, disappointed, hostile, not one of them lived in vain. The severances of party and of creed are incidents of independent warfare; but the soul that is fervent and heroic not only fights its own way to perfection, but makes ignoble sloth more odious, brings high aim within the readier grasp of the generation and the men who follow it.

> "And O, blithe breeze ! and O, great seas,
>   Though ne'er, that earliest parting past,
> On your wide plain they join again,
>   Together lead them home at last.
> One port, methought, alike they sought,
>   One purpose hold where'er they fare—
> O, bounding breeze ! O, rushing seas !
>   At last, at last, unite them there !"

First among the Oxford comrades of that time, *juvenum publica cura*, universal undergraduate theme, ranked Charles Wordsworth; tutor to Gladstone and Manning, to Sir Francis Doyle and Walter Hamilton, Acland, Hope, Lords Lincoln and Canning; the best scholar, cricketer, oar, skater, racquet player, dancer, pugilist, of his day.

CHARLES WORDSWORTH
From the Richmond Portrait

His proficiency in this last branch of antique athletics was attested by a fight at Harrow between himself and Trench, which sent the future Archbishop to a London dentist, in order to have his teeth set to rights. "That man," whispered Lord Malmesbury to Lord Derby, when Wordsworth had shaken hands with the Chancellor on receiving his honorary degree, "that man might have been anything he pleased." His attainments and capacities were set off by an unusually tall and handsome figure,

Gratior et pulchro veniens in corpore virtus.

His aunt, the Poet's wife, told me that of all the young men she had ever known he was the most charming in manner, mind, and person. He was beyond all his contemporaries an adept in Greek and Latin versification; whatever of noble thought, of touching sentiment, of transient humour, gained access to his mind, came draped in one or other of the classic tongues. His grief at his wife's death found expression in a perfect Latin couplet, untranslated, untranslatable.[1] A junior boy whom he once found eating cake in "Meads" at Winchester, artlessly offered him a piece, which he accepted, sending to the boy next day a pile of cakes and cream from the confectioner, with the note,

δέξαι, πλακοῦντος ἀντιδωρεὰν, τόδε.
(Requiting guerdon, cake for cake, receive);

and his very inscriptions in hotel books when on a tour were Greek Iambics.[2] His career as Master

[1] Appendix E.   [2] Ibid.

in College at Winchester justified the promise of his youth: he raised the scholarship as well as the morality of the boys. His Greek Grammar was accepted by every school in England except Eton, which, preferring to go wrong with Plato, clung to its old inferior manual; and he imparted to Winchester a tone of unaffected, thoughtful piety which long outlived his rule. At Gladstone's entreaty—High Churchmen saw in the reviving Episcopal Church of Scotland a happy hunting ground for English Tractarianism—he undertook the Headship of Glenalmond College, becoming soon afterwards Bishop of St. Andrews. It was a sacrifice; had he remained in England he was to have been Dean of Rochester. Through no fault of his own he failed as Warden; as Bishop he did all that man could do, but the post was not worthy of his powers; and the illustrious Oxford paragon ended, like his Swedish namesake, amid the trivial surroundings of a petty fortress and a barren strand. Having been his pupil in early years, I reviewed his Autobiography in a London Weekly. He was pleased by my notice of him, sought my name, and we exchanged many letters lively with memories of the past. The last I received from him was a New Year Greeting, with closing invocation of *multos felices annos, ultimum felicissimum.* It was his own *annus ultimus;* he died before the day came round again.

One more confederate in this ἱερα νεοτής, this sacred band of youthful brothers, let me commemorate. Double First Class, when Double

Firsts meant much, Fellow of All Souls, heir to beautiful Killerton with its mighty trap rocks, forest scenery, wild ponies, and red deer, Mr. or "Tom" Acland, as every one called him, was heralded into public life by unusual expectations. He was in Parliament for a time, made no great mark, married, early lost his wife, threw himself heartbroken into agriculture, under the tuition of his friend and relative Philip Pusey. He came late to his inheritance, for the Aclands are a longæval race, and old Sir Thomas lived to a great age. The contrast between them was amusing; the father with manners regal in their measured graciousness and polish, the son jerky and discursive in talk, movement, ideas. "Tom thinks so fast," said a near relation, "that none of us can keep up with him." During the Fifties it was my lot to see a good deal of him in Oxford: he used to walk with me in the streets, recalling his early life, the Newmania and its influence on his mental growth, his association with the "Young England" movement, whose last surviving representative was the late Duke of Rutland. Stopping opposite to St. Mary Magdalen Church one day, he told me how he and Jacobson had taken there F. D. Maurice, when an undergraduate, to be baptised. He was full at that time of the "Middle Class Examinations," which, with Canon Brereton, he had initiated in Devonshire, and which developed ultimately into the Oxford Local Examinations. To him especially, to his experience of West Buckland School, his patience, wisdom, and enthusiasm, that great educational experiment was due. I remember, too, that we went together to Max Müller's opening lecture on Comparative Mythology; he was disturbed, fidgeted, bit his nails. "It frightens one," he said. I was reading the "Odyssey" with a pupil one day; he came in, and I handed him a book; he listened for ten minutes, then gave me back the volume, saying: "How quickly one forgets! but for the Latin translation at the foot I could not have followed"; going on to tell me how with Bunsen and Philip Pusey he used to read Homer daily through a winter in Rome, and imitating Bunsen's Continental pronunciation of the sonorous lines.

In 1865 I gave evidence on School Teaching of Science before the Schools Inquiry Commission, of which he was a member. He questioned me at great length as to examination methods, as to the machinery needful for extending the local examination to the public schools, as to the desirableness of a Government Board of Higher Education, with a special Minister at its head. He became somewhat iterative; and the chairman, Lord Taunton, cut him short; he rose with an impatient gesture and went to the fire, but said to me afterwards, "I kept my temper." We travelled down to Oxford together; he was in high spirits, having just re-entered Parliament after twenty years of exile, and poured forth optimistic talk. My sceptical interjections grated on him once or twice; he was uneasy, too, lest my science teaching should overshadow the imaginative and reverential side of the boy-mind. "Don't be too materialistic," he shouted into my cab from the pavement, as I dropped him at his brother's house in Broad Street. Yet again I was to know him, in his home at Killerton. I had left Taunton School: and finding that I was uncertain as to my next move, he made me his Chaplain, and put his house at Sprydoncote at my disposal for a time; an act of kindness for which I shall ever think of him with gratitude. He was now Sir Thomas—a far abler man than his father in all the higher requirements of a great country gentleman's position, yet, somehow, never filling his father's place in local sentiment; less outwardly imposing, less captivating, suasive, patriarchal. I saw him constantly; he used to drop in and talk on the winter afternoons. He was not a man of reminiscences, nor did his speech linger on scholarship and books; present problems, social chiefly and theological, seemed to fill his mind. He would question me repeatedly as to my own mental development, wishing to trace the process by which High Church rigidity in the green salad-days changed into independent rationalism later on. He was devoted to agriculture, of which I had some experience; to allotments, to cottage building in its sanitary, profitable, moral aspects. My microscope, which stood constantly in employ, used to puzzle him—he always went to see what new marvel I had got, with an ever-renewed protest against the cult of the infinitely little.

He was not amœbæan in his talk; it sped forth torrential, and you had to listen; it fascinated for the first half-hour, then to the hearer followed loss of sequence, logical perplexity, swamped surrender, boredom, headache, desperation. I once compared notes with a kindred patient, who had the day before dined with him *tête-à-tête*. He described the eloquence, so genial in its opening, endurable during dinner by manducative and bibulous supports, by degrees assuming nightmare proportions, tempered only with faith in inevitable bedtime. That arrived, the good-nights were spoken, the staircase reached ; and then, stimulated by a fresh *œstrus*, the host began again, and the evening closed with a long supplementary harangue in the hall by the light of the bedroom candlesticks. This habit made him in society the terror of *raconteurs*, demanding as they do attentive auditors with interlocution just enough to start successive topics and give fresh chances to their wit. I recall meeting at his table Mr. Massey, M.P. for Tiverton, one of the brilliant London talkers of the day, a member, with Kinglake, Count Stzrelecki, American Ticknor, and others, of the famous Athenæum "corner." He led off at the opening of dinner with a delicious anecdote of the well-known Mrs. Thistlethwayte ; but his incidental mention of a certain other lady inspired Sir Thomas to interrupt with a genealogical disquisition : the aroma of the story exhaled, and the narrator looked depressed. He recovered himself, and another good story was begun ; but when a second time Sir Thomas cut in *mal à propos*, Mr. Massey collapsed, and we heard no more of him. And so in this and other ways it came to pass that with all his great attainments he was not a man with whom you ever felt at ease. That he would be polite and kind you knew ; knew, too, that until submerged by vocables, as Carlyle said of Coleridge, you would gain abiding knowledge from his boundless stores; yet everywhere in his talk and temperament lurked sharp points on which you feared to tread—the conversational smoothness was *suppositus cineri doloso*. It used to be said that God made men, women, and Aclands, (it was said, I think, originally of the Herveys), and he lent full flavour to the epigram. He gave one always the idea of a superlatively good thing unkindly impaired by Fate. To his birth thronged the fairy god-mother with gifts of intellect, fluency, loftiness of standard, philanthropy of aim, generosity of nature; then came the malignant Uninvited, with the marring supplement of position, fortune, ease, to annul the bracing, shaping discipline which moulds the self-made man. Covered with University distinctions, Fellow of All Souls, rich in Parliamentary promise, protagonist in a great social and religious movement—all older men looked on at him expectantly with a *Ce garçon ira loin*. But inherited wealth absolved him from compulsory struggle, rank and repute secured him unearned deference—he was admirable, useful, honoured, loved; but he disproved the augury of greatness, he failed to realise the promise heralded by his splendid youth.

Faster than Homer's leaves the Undergraduate generations pass. Three years, or four at most, push them from their stools, and a fresh succession enters on the stage. In 1833 the "Uniomachia," Battle of the Union, embalms another scarcely less remarkable relay.

I well knew Tom Brancker, who was believed to be *dux facti*, originator of the social war. Coming from Shrewsbury in jacket and turn-down collars, he had, while still a schoolboy, though matriculated, beaten Gladstone and Scott for the Ireland. Butler had sent him up by Scott's advice, for the sake of practice merely, but he came out scholar, surpassing his two great competitors, as Vowler Short told them, in the points of taste and terseness. He failed afterwards to get his First, but became Fellow of Wadham, and dropped finally into the lotos-eating of a College incumbency. He was hated and dreaded as a bully in the Schools, but I always found him kind and friendly. It was usual, as matter of course and compliment, to re-elect each year the committee of the Union; but just then was the time of the Reform Bill, the outgoing committee was Tory; and Brancker, with Bob Lowe, Massie, and other zealous Whigs, successfully opposed them, and were elected in their place. The exiles formed an opposition club called the Rambler, so popular and successful that the new committee proposed to expel its members from the Union. In hope of lulling the storm, two St. Mary Hall men, Jackson and Sinclair, produced the "Uniomachia," a mock Homeric poem with a dog-Latin Interpretatio and notes, and, in a second edition, with an additional "Notularum Spicilegium" by Robert Scott, afterwards Master of Balliol. There followed an English translation from the pen of Archdeacon Giles, and an "Emollient and Sedative Draught" by Lenient Lullaby, F.R.S., whom I have never been able to identify. The characters, besides the three innovators, were Cardwell, W. G. Ward, Roundell Palmer, Mayow, Tait, Pattison, and Charles Marriott. The fun fell upon the combatants like Virgil's *pulveris exigui jactus* on the bees, and the hatchet was buried in a reconciliation dinner at the Star. Of Marriott I shall speak later on, as also of Mark Pattison, who in these years, not yet disappointed, melancholy, and vindictive, was struggling with undigested reading, half-awakened intelligence, morbid self-consciousness, progressing towards that love of learning for learning's sake which, agnostic, cynic, pessimist as he was, gave unity to his sad, remonstrant life.

Contemporary with these was a genius perhaps more remarkable, certainly more unusual, than any of them. In 1833 Solomon Cæsar Malan matriculated at St. Edmund's Hall, a young man with a young wife, son to a Swiss Pastor, speaking as yet broken English, but fluent Latin, Romaic, French, Spanish, Italian, German; and a proficient at twenty-two years old in Hebrew, Arabic, Sanskrit. He won the Boden and the Kennicott Scholarships, took a Second Class, missing his First through the imperfection of his English, was ordained, became Professor in Calcutta, gathered up Chinese, Japanese, the various Indian, Malay, Persian tongues, came home to the valuable living of Broadwinsor, where he lived, when not travelling, through forty years, amassing a library in more than seventy languages, the majority of which he spoke with freedom, read familiarly, wrote with a clearness and beauty rivalling the best native caligraphy. In his frequent Eastern rambles he was able, say his fellow-travellers, to chat in market and bazaar with every one whom he met. On a visit to the Bishop of Innereth he preached a Georgian sermon in the Cathedral. He published twenty - six translations of English theological works, in Chinese and Japanese, Arabic and Syriac, Armenian, Russian, Ethiopic, Coptic. Five-fold outnumbering the fecundity of his royal namesake, he left behind him a collection of 16,000 Proverbs, taken from original Oriental texts, each written in its native character and translated. So unique was the variety of his Pentecostal attainments that experts could not be found even to catalogue the four thousand books which he presented, *multa gemens*, with pathetic lamentation over their surrender, to the Indian Institute at Oxford.

I encountered him at three periods of his life. First as a young man at the evening parties of John Hill, Vice-Principal of St. Edmund's Hall, where prevailed tea and coffee, pietistic Low Church talk, prayer and hymnody of portentous length, yet palliated by the chance of sharing Bible or hymn-book with one of the host's four charming daughters. Twenty years later I recall him as a guest in Oxford Common Rooms, laying down the law on questions of Scriptural interpretation, his abysmal fund of learning and his dogmatic insistency floated by the rollicking fun of his illustrations and their delightful touches of travelled personal experience. Finally, in his old age I spent a long summer day with him in the Broadwinsor home,

IN THE THIRTIES 97

enjoying his library, aviary, workshop, drawings; his hospitality stimulated by the discovery that in some of his favourite pursuits I was, *longo intervallo*, an enthusiast like himself. He was a benevolently autocratic vicar, controlling his parish with patriarchally imperious rule, original, racy, trenchant, in Sunday School and sermons. It was his wont to take into the pulpit his college cap: into it he had pasted words of Scripture which he always read to himself before preaching. They were taken from the story of Balaam : "And the Lord opened the mouth of the ass, and she said——" He died at eighty-two, to have been admitted, let us hope, in the unknown land to comradeship of no ordinary brotherhood by spirits of every nation, kindred, tongue; to have found there, ranged upon celestial shelves, the Platonic archetypes of the priceless books which it tore his mortal heart to leave.

Skip two or three more years, and we come to a scarcely less interesting student stratum, to the period of Stanley, Matthew Arnold, Clough. Think of them walking among the Cumnor cowslips and the fritillaries of the Eynsham river side, bathing in the abandoned lasher, noting from Hinksey Hill on winter afternoons the far-off light of the windows in Christchurch Hall, mounting to the Glanvil elm, which yet stands out clear against the flaming sunset sky. Imagine the talk, now glad, now pensive, of their still illusioned youth; its poetry, speculation, criticism, Wordsworthian insight into nature, valiant optimism, rare communion of highest and most sacred thoughts;—as one reads "Thyrsis" and "The Scholar Gypsy," airs from Paradise seem to breathe around one, airs which only Oxford could have inspired, only high natures such as theirs could have exhaled. I heard Stanley recite his "Gypsies" in the Theatre in 1837; the scene comes back to me as of yesterday—the crowded area, the ladies in their enormous bonnets; handsome, stately Dr. Gilbert in the Vice-Chancellor's chair; the pale, slight, weak-voiced, boyish figure in the rostrum; the roar of cheers which greeted him. Clough, too, I knew; read with him for half a year in his tiny Holywell lodging immediately after his election to Oriel, working the first hour in the morning, while he ate his frugal breakfast of dry bread and chocolate. It was his happy time, before his piping took a troubled sound; his six golden Oxford graduate years of plain living and high thinking, of hopeful fight for freedom, of the rapturous Long Vacations in Wales, the Highlands, the English Lakes, summed up immortally in his "Bothie." The original edition in its blue cloth lies before me as I write, a present from his son. I have noted in it the undergraduates represented, so far as they are now recoverable.[1] Side by side with these men were Donkin, Lord Hobhouse, Brodie, Henry Acland, young gentleman-commoner Ruskin; little, white-haired, cherub-faced Jowett; James Riddell, whose $\phi\theta\iota\nu\omega$, $\phi\theta\iota\nu\omega$, $\phi\iota\lambda\iota\sigma\tau\eta$, Moberly used to quote as the unsurpassable gem of all the Anthologies; and, perhaps a year or two earlier, "Jem" Lonsdale, great in estimation rather that in

[1] Appendix F.

production as a scholar, the tales of his wit and genius ephemeral and for the most part lost. Let me give one specimen. Asked to preach at Eton by his old tutor, Bishop Chapman, he sent this answer :—

> "Cur imparem me cingis honoribus,
> Me, triste lignum, me vetulum, pigro
> Sermone, fundentemque tardo
> Ore soporiferum papaver?"

Henry Furneaux, who was his colleague in the Moderation Schools, used to speak of him as the most winning of men from his extreme simplicity and absence of all self-consciousness; his scholarship not so much an acquirement as an intuition, inherited probably from his father. It was amongst the answers to a Paper set by him that occurred the delicious explanation of the Lupercalia, "Lupercalia is the name of a she-wolf that suckled Romeo and Juliet." Riddell's quiet manner concealed a turn for comedy. I once saw him in a charade act with much humour the Parliamentary Candidate in the gentlemanly interest, opposing Henry Wall, who was the demagogue. And one day at Zermatt, the party being bored by a cockney who was destitute of Miss Catherine Fanshawe's letter, and was afraid of losing his 'at on the mountain, Riddell wrote in the hotel book :—

> "A gent who was late at Zermatt,
> Dropped an H on the Hoch Taligat;
> If he'll fetch it away
> He'll find it some day
> Of use in the front of his 'at."

He was thus embalmed by a contemporary poet.

"The other, of an ancient name, erst dear
　　To Border hills, though thence too long exiled;
　In lore of Hellas scholar without peer,
　　Reared in grey halls on banks of Severn piled.
　Reserved he was, of few words and slow speech;
　　Yet dwelt strange power that beyond words could reach
　In that sweet face by no rude thought defiled."

The Forties were years of strife; of Ward's expulsion, Newman's perversion, Hampden's challenged bishopric; a time none the less of great youthful names. Thorold Rogers I knew slightly as an undergraduate. He was then a loud, dominating, rapid talker, deluging his company with a shower-bath of Greek choruses, not more regardful of the skins into which he poured the wine of his erudition than was Tom Jones when in company with Ensigns Northerton and Adderley. He so frightened men, in fact, that he could find no College to take him as a Fellow. Altered and saddened by his young wife's death, he plunged into politics as a relief, obtained the Act of Parliament which enabled him to resign his Orders, and sat in the House of Commons till not long before his death, valued there as a walking dictionary, and always the centre of a laughing group in the smoking-room or on the Terrace. From this time I knew him closely; we stood together on many political platforms, and I pleased him by an appreciative review in *The Spectator* of his book on Holland, which had been coarsely attacked, as I thought, in *The Pall Mall*. He was an unequalled story-teller; some men affect nonchalance in repeating a good thing, but Rogers's face used to flash and his eyes start out with contagious joy in a clever saying. That football is the accomplishment of a hippopotamus, that the Athanasian Creed was an election squib—a saying Rogeresque but justified, as readers of Foulkes's investigation are aware—and his happy comparison of a serious, hairy-faced Birmingham M.P. to a costive terrier, are amongst his countless epigrams which occur to me. His was the pun which disqualified Mundella of the big nose, ὁ μεγαλόρρινος, as Chairman of Committees, because "when Mr. Mundella was in the Chair the Noes would always have it." Some prolix creature had told one day in the House the ancient story of a miser swallowing a guinea, from whose niggard interior an emetic persuaded him to refund only ten and sixpence. Rogers seized a pencil, scribbled and handed round the following:—

χθὲς νομικὸς δέκ' ἀποκρύψων κατεβρόχθισε δραχμάς,
καὶ βυσθεὶς θάνατον Πρόκλος ἔδεισε μόρον.
νῦν δὲ μόγις τέχνῃ Παρακέλσου δῆθεν ἰατροῦ
ἡττηθεὶς ὀβολοὺς εἴκοσιν ἐξέμεσεν.
τῶν δὲ τριῶν μερίδων γλισχρῶς ἀπενόσφισε διπλῆν
ἀνθρώπου γαστὴρ, τὴν δὲ κάτεσχ' ἰδίαν.

Translated in the manner of Swift :—

"Attorney Proclus, so they say,
   Swallowed ten drachmas 'tother day.
He choked, he gasped ; to ease his ill
   Came Paracelse with purge and pill.
Seven coins the emetic spew obeyed—
   Cries Proclus, 'Curse your plundering trade!
Of my loved store three-fourths are gone ;
   So help you Plutus, leave me one!'"

When news came down to the Lobby of Lord Derby's death, he wrote :—

"Reckless in speech, and truculent in face,
  Geoffrey, the fourteenth Earl of Derby, died :
Only in this superior to his race,
  He left the winning for the losing side."

He used to quote, as the cleverest retort ever made, the answer of a notorious admiral to the Duke of Clarence : "I hear, sir, that you are the biggest blackguard in Portsmouth !" "I hope your Royal Highness has not come down to take away my character!" I met him one day laughing along Beaumont Street; he had just overheard a scout talking to a waiter at the door of the Randolph : "So he says to me, his lordship says, 'You don't seem to think much of them bishops.' 'No, my lord, I don't,' says I ; 'I remember them all coming up here with pockmantles not worth five shillings, and now they're as fat as Moses's kine.'" Beneath his coarseness and profanity lay not only political morality and ardent patriotism but active kindness of heart. A clever girl at Somerville had exhausted her funds after two years' residence and was about to leave. Rogers heard of it, told the circumstances about the House in his forcible way till he had collected £80, which he sent to the young lady, who is now a successful and distinguished professor. Of his *bons mots* the majority, perhaps, will not bear repetition ; there was truth as well as pungency in the saying which explained his writing a book on Holland by the fact that it is "a low country full of dams." When Freeman came up to examine in the newly-founded History school, he and Rogers, an equally ursine pair, were maliciously brought together at a dinner party. In compliment to Rogers the host led the talk to political economy. "Political economy," said Freeman, "seems to me to be so much garbage." "Garbage is it?" said Rogers; "the very thing then for a hog like you." Readers of Walter Scott's note in Boswell (vol. v. p. 114) will recall the meeting between Adam Smith and Dr. Johnson.

CHAPTER VIII

MORE ABOUT UNDERGRADUATES

"*Præteritos extollens, Recentiorum incuriosus.*"
—CICERO.

Goldwin Smith—John Conington—Hayman and Rugby and Moredecay—Frank Buckland—J. G. Wood—His Many-sidedness—The "Common Object"—Blaydes of Oxford and Calverley of Cambridge—R. E. Bartlett—The Schoolboy and the Queen—Walter Wren—The Great Henley Race of 1843: "Septem contra Camum"—George Cox—"Black Gowns and Red Coats"—The Early Fifties—Harry Wilkins—Herbert Coleridge—His Mother, Sara Coleridge—Dress at Oxford Fifty Years Ago and Now—Unathletic Oxford—The Supremacy of the Spirit.

GOLDWIN SMITH—"vastiest Goldwin," Rolleston always called him—towered above his fellows as undergraduate and bachelor. We all saw in him the coming man; but he married, settled in America, and never came. Close to him was John Conington, whose extraordinary visage, with its green-cheese hue, gleaming spectacles, quivering protrusive lips, might be encountered every day at 2 o'clock on his way to a constitutional, which he would have liked, he said, to conduct between two high walls, shutting out all irrelevant topics such as surroundings and scenery might suggest. He ranked in Oxford as a scholar of the very highest character and industry, attested by his fine translations of Horace and of Virgil. He was a lonely, melancholy man, out of harmony with the young athletes who were his pupils; prevented from voluntary advances to them by his own insuperable shyness; but eagerly making friends with any who would seek his confidence, and sparing no pains with promising students. He was passionately fond of the best English poets, by whom he illustrated his classical teaching. His pupils learned from him what University teaching should have been, learned too how its realisation was made impossible by the imperfection of previous public school training. From an *esprit* and a Liberal he suddenly became Conservative and Puseyite; died early, leaving a profuse diary of his Oxford life, which his executors unfortunately thought it their duty to destroy. In the same class list with Goldwin Smith and Freeman, a Second where they were Firsts, stood the name of Hayman, the unfortunate *ad interim* Headmaster of Rugby. I first met him in our younger days on the top of a Devonshire coach. I was quoting Pope's "Character of Narcissa," and hesitated for a word, which a voice behind me supplied, and its owner joined in our talk with spirit. He was a pleasant fellow and a good scholar, though what the waiter in the "Newcomes" would call a "harbitrary gent"; but his election to Rugby was unfortunate for everybody. Only a Hercules could have succeeded an Atlas such as Temple; and Hayman's inferiority in generalship, teaching, preaching, capacity for work, at once armed against him boys and masters. His forlorn position won him public sympathy, but the numbers fell; it became clear even to the Philistines who had appointed him that he must go :—

> "When Rugby, spite of priest or layman,
> Began to fall away,
> The Governors suspended Hayman
> For fear of More-decay."

The next year brings us to Frank Buckland. Few men can now recall those unique breakfasts at Frank's rooms in the corner of Fell's Buildings; the host, in blue pea-jacket and German student's cap, blowing blasts out of a tremendous wooden horn; the various pets who made it difficult to speak or move; the marmots, and the dove, and the monkey, and the chameleon, and the snakes, and the guinea-pigs; the after-breakfast visits to the eagle, or the jackal, or the pariah dog, or Tiglath-pileser the bear, in the little yard outside. "Why Tiglath-pileser?" several inquiring correspondents asked me; "why give unexplained these cryptic names and jokes of long ago?" Thus it was. On a certain morning in May the bear escaped from Buckland's yard, and found his way into the chapel, at the moment when a student was reading the first Lesson, 2 Kings xvi., and had reached the point at which King Ahaz was on his way to meet Tiglath-pileser, King of Assyria, at Damascus. So far as that congregation was concerned, the meeting never came off; the bear made straight for the Lectern, its occupant fled to his place, and the half-uttered name on his lips was transferred to the intruder. Gaisford sent for Frank: "You or that animal, Mr. Buckland, must quit the College." The undergraduate was father of the man. His house in Albany Street became one of the sights of London; but to enter it presupposed iron nerves and *dura ilia*. Introduced to some five-and-twenty poor relations, free from shyness, deeply interested in your dress and person, you felt as if another flood were toward, and the animals parading for admission to the Ark. You remained to dine: but, as in his father's house so in his own, the genius of experiment, supreme in all departments, was nowhere so active as at the dinner table. Panther chops, rhinoceros pie, bison steaks, kangaroo ham, horse's tongue, elephant's trunk, are recorded among his manifestations of hospitality; his brother-in-law quotes from the diary of a departing guest—"Tripe for dinner; don't like crocodile for breakfast."

Of the same standing—acquaintances I think they were not—was J. G. Wood, the well-known lecturing naturalist. He was a Bible clerk of Merton, of the class typified in Tom Brown's "Hardy," one of two pariahs compelled by chill penury to accept the coarse munificence of the College, who pricked Chapel attendance and said grace, knowing no one, living alone, dining in Hall alone on the remnants sent from the high table. I used to go with him down the river in the Long Vacation, with gun, fishing rod, collecting net. He was a redoubtable athlete, champion of the St. Clement's gymnasium; for Maclaren's rooms were not then built, though he had come lately to Oxford, succeeding little Angelo, who taught fencing to the previous generation. Wood was skilled and imperturbable at singlestick, and a first-rate boxer. I saw him once put on the gloves with Maclaren at Parson's Pleasure when both were stripped for a bathe, hitting Mac in the face during the first round, and receiving the good-natured professional's warm congratulations. Large-boned and muscular, he had a small, facile, lady-like hand; was a dexterous anatomist; many of his dissections being still in the Museum; mounted skilfully for the microscope, manufactured for himself electrical and optical apparatus, took calotypes, as photographs were called before the collodion process was invented, drew spirited caricatures. He was not then, if ever, a scientific naturalist; he picked up knowledge as he went on, and cleverly made the most of it; and his authorship was due to accident. He was intimate with Buckley, a Christchurch chaplain, who did cribs for Routledge; the publisher asked him to recommend a man who could produce for moderate payment a popular work on Natural History, and Buckley named Wood. He accepted, and came to me for suggestions, which I gave rather inventively. The bull terrier "Crab" who figures in his first book was mine; some of that quadruped's recorded feats, with other surprising incidents, one in particular of a pointer standing at a pig, were, I fear, not founded on fact. But the little book had a great sale, was followed by "Common Objects of the Country," and led to a long series of more pretentious works. Wood was ordained to the curacy of St. Thomas, then, under "Tom" Chamberlain, of Christchurch, the most ritualistic of Oxford temples; in doubt to the last moment whether he was to serve under Chamberlain or under a Low Church friend of Ben Symons, he bid the tailor leave his clerical waistcoat uncompleted, that it might be open or M.B. according to his rector's tenets. He made no mark as a clergyman, his vocation lay in writing and in lecturing. Plain in features and rough in dress—men called him the "Common Object"—and with a somewhat indistinct voice, he was yet on the platform extraordinarily popular, fascinating, by his anecdotic itch, as Peter Pindar calls it, and his skill in blackboard drawing, not certainly scientific or highly cultivated hearers, but the half-educated intelligence of a middle-class or schoolboy audience. He died suddenly while at work, struck down on a lecturing tour.

I pass to a very different man, who came up to Oxford as Blaydes in 1847, and left it in 1849 to be better known as Calverley at Cambridge: his encounters with the little "Master," the stone thrown up at his library window, the "Well, yellow-belly, how's Jinks?" the surmise at Collections that it might perhaps be some time since the Master had read Longinus, were long current in Balliol. When one of his escapades made it probable that the authorities would invite him to adorn with his liveliness the groves of some other Academe, R. E. Bartlett, afterwards Fellow of Trinity, wrote:—

> "Oh, freshman, redolent of weed,
> Oh, scholar, running fast to seed,
> This maxim in thy meerschaum put—
> The sharpest Blades will soonest cut."

He answered:—

> "Your verse is tolerable; but
> My case you understand ill;
> For though the Dons want Blades to cut,
> They cannot find a handle."

Bartlett's, too, were the lines on Weatherby, a fast scholar of Balliol, who was sent down for being drunk in Quad, and prostrating the porter who tried to get him to bed:—

> "Why was his term, at first so short,
> Cut prematurely shorter?
> The reason was, he floored the Port,
> And then—he floored the Porter."

The catastrophe occurred in the "short" three-week summer term, which gives point to the opening line. Conversing with an old Harrovian the other day, I asked what sort of reputation Blaydes left behind him at the school. Not, it appeared, for wit and verse-writing, but as the only boy who ever jumped from the top to the bottom of the old school steps. So Matthew Arnold's leap over the Wadham railings used to be familiar to many who had never read his books; so a clever boy named Selwyn earned immortality at Winchester by jumping for a bet over "Nevy's hedge" into the road far below. He broke his leg, had been thought sure of the Queen's gold medal for that year, locked from ink and paper lost his chance. The young Queen heard the story through his cousin, a maid of honour, and sent him a gold watch, with an inscription more precious than Wyon's shop full of medals.

By the way, what becomes of old school and

college medals? One rarely meets with them in after life. A greatly beloved London preacher sold all his the other day that he might subsidise a deserving institution; and Macaulay did the same through want of money for himself in early struggling days. My own, gold and silver, repose under a glass case, and perhaps those who survive me may value them.

Calverley retained his saltatory power at Cambridge. Professor Allbutt kindly writes to me that one evening, in the presence of himself, Walter Besant, and Wormald, then stroke of the Christ's boat, he suddenly sprang like a skipjack off the floor of the Christ's gatehouse porch, over the bar which crossed (and still crosses) from the wall to fasten one valve of the gate, alighting safely in the triangular space within. The marvel was not so much the height ($37\frac{1}{2}$ inches) as the rise without a run and clean descent into the narrow triangular enclosure, free from collision with door or wall: he must have jumped straight upwards, clearing his feet easily, and then dropping vertically downwards. He possessed enormous thighs and large gluteal muscles, enabling him to spring like a grass-hopper. The Professor adds that Calverley was the most indolent man of parts he ever knew; his reading casual and intermittent, but his memory prodigious, with power of absorbing from a book as though by some ethereal process the matter demanded and assimilable by his genius. His Cambridge life has lately lost an honest chronicler in his great friend Walter Wren, who boasted that he had answered all the questions in the Calverley Pickwick Paper except the "red-faced Nixon."

More than once I have sat with Wren into the small hours, listening to his reminiscences of his friend's lampoons, epigrams, miracles of scholarship and wit. Wren had often pressed him for a scholarly *tour de force;* caught him one wet morning in his room, and seized his chance. The "Excursion" lay on a table; Calverley handed it to his friend—"Read me any five-and-twenty lines." Wren did so. "Again, more slowly." Then for ten or fifteen minutes Calverley sat with his head in his hands. "Now write"; and he dictated the translation in fluent Virgilian hexameters. The remaining story I cite with special pleasure as revealing a very noble aspect of his many-faceted character. He heard from a profligate acquaintance of a country girl, turned out of home by her parents for disobedience in some love affair, come to seek service at Cambridge, not yet ruined, but in a house where ruin was inevitable and imminent. He was reading for the Craven, which he won; to be seen by tutor or proctor in questionable company or at a house of ill-repute would mean rustication or expulsion; but he went to the place at once, extricated the girl, took her with him to the station, paid her fare, and sent her home with an earnestly written letter to her father which brought about a reconciliation, and saved her. Clever as Blaydes in epigram and pun, though not in sustained satire, was Arthur Ridding, of New College, elder brother to the late Bishop of Southwell. When every one was celebrating in Latin verse the Duke of Wellington's funeral he was asked how to render "lying in state." "Splendide mendax," was the answer. At Winchester once during a cricket match we passed on the "Tunbridge" towpath a miserable horse, who with drooping head, glassy eyes, protruding bones, was dragging a heavy barge. "Τὸ-πάθ-ος" (*Tow-path-'oss*) was Ridding's comment.

I must not leave the Forties without a reminiscence of the Henley race, the "Septem contra Camum," in 1843. It was the event which really popularised boating at Oxford; the College races were before that year a mere pleasant incident in a summer term; there were no College barges on the river; even the Oxford and Cambridge race, except in 1829, the first race rowed, excited languid interest. I stopped on Battersea bridge one day in 1841 to watch the Oxford boat practising against a Thames crew; there was hardly any one on the bank, where to-day thousands would be running. It was, I think, in 1842 that a new oar, Fletcher Menzies, of University, arose, under whose training the Oxford style was changed and pace improved, with prospect of beating Cambridge, which had for several years been victor; and the '43 race at Henley between the two picked crews of Oxford University and the Cambridge Subscription Rooms was anxiously expected as a test. A few hours before the race Menzies, the stroke, fell ill, and the "Rooms" refused to allow a substitute. The contest seemed at an end, when some one—Royds, of Brasenose, it was said—

proposed that the Oxford seven should pull against the Cambridge eight. The audacious gallantry of the idea took hold; George Hughes, of Oriel, brother to Tom Hughes, was moved from seven to stroke, and his place taken by the bow, Lowndes, of Christchurch.[1] So, with the bow-oar unmanned, the race began, the crew hopeless of more than a creditable defeat; but as their boat held its own, drew up, passed ahead, the excitement became tremendous; and when the Oxford flag fluttered up, the men on the bank, as the guard said of his leaders in "Nicholas Nickleby," went mad with glory; carried the rowers to the Red Lion, wildly raced the street, like horses on the Corso in a Roman carnival, tore up a heavy toll-bar gate, and flung it over the bridge into the river. The boat was moored as a trophy in Christchurch meadow at the point where Pactolus poured its foul stream into the Isis, and was shown for twenty-four years to admiring freshmen; until in 1867, rotten and decayed, it was bought by jolly Tom Randall, mercer, alderman, scholar, its sound parts fashioned into a chair, and presented as the President's throne to the University barge. One of the seven, John Cox, of Trinity, who pulled six, died quite recently.

His elder brother, George Cox, of New College, an extraordinarily promising man, died young. Besides one or two coarse, clever, very popular songs,

[1] I give the names of the seven in Appendix C. I believe that two of them, Royds and Bourne, are still alive. R. B. Mansfield, author of the "Log of the Water-lily," a brother Wykehamist, wrote to me that he was appointed *locum tenens* for Royds, who was unable to come up till just before the race.

such as the "Oxford Freshman," and "A Drop of Good Beer," he left behind him a satire of unusual power, called "Black Gowns and Red Coats," published in 1834. It is now very scarce, its author so forgotten that Mr. Hirst in the Cassell "Life of Gladstone," quotes him as George Fox. He draws a lurid picture; proclaims the teaching barren, the teachers sunk in crapulence and sloth, the taught licentious, extravagant, idle. Of the Dons only three are excepted from his lash, the two Duncans and Macbride; of recent undergraduates only one:—

> "Yet on one form, whose ear can ne'er refuse
> The Muse's tribute, for he loved the Muse,
> Full many a fond expectant eye is bent,
> Where Newark's towers are mirrored in the Trent.
> Perchance ere long to shine in senates first,
> His manhood echoing what his youth rehearsed,
> Soon Gladstone's brows will bloom with greener bays,
> Than twine the chaplet of a minstrel's lays,
> Nor heed, while poring o'er each graver line,
> The far faint music of a lute like mine."

There are passages of terrible force, as in the portrait of the profligate freshman; memorable photographs of contemporary follies, as in the fast exquisite's career; echoes of conservative alarm at the muttering thunder of reform; momentary lapses into prize poem jingle, redeemed by abundant resonant epigram; one special episode, "A Simple Tale of Seduction," rising very nearly to the highest strain of poetry. Was it a faithful portrait? No more than was the "Oxford Spy," whose author, Shergold Boone, lived to express his deep regret for having written it in a curious penitential University sermon. It generalised from a single and a limited side of Oxford life, as it was said of Simeon Stylites that he discerned the hog in Nature and mistook Nature for the hog. Amongst the Heads whom Cox indiscriminately chastises were Routh, Gaisford, Cramer, Jenkyns, Ingram, Hawkins, Hampden; his "untutored Tutors" with their bloated pedantry and screechowl throats numbered in their ranks such men as Hussey, Newman, the two Fabers, Robert Wilberforce, Vowler Short, and Hurrell Froude; his one blameless junior was but a notable comrade in the splendid youthful band sampled, and sampled merely, in my last chapter. We must bemoan the untimely loss of genius so prodigal in its shortened promise; but, remembering his own admission that the fingers were not always clean which held the pen, we discount the Censor's satire with the banished Duke's reply to sneering Jaques :—

> "For thou thyself hast been a libertine;
> All the embossed sores and headed evils
> That thou with license of free foot hast caught,
> Wouldst thou disgorge into the general world."

My undergraduate reminiscences must stop short with the early Fifties, at the line of cleavage between the Old and New Oxford Comedy. They include mad Harry Wilkins of Merton, manumitter of Daubeny's apes, who once, an M.A. and Fellow of his College, in broad daylight and full term, led a mob of rowdy Christchurch undergraduates in a duck hunt at the Long Bridges. He came up from Harrow in 1840 with a Gregory Exhibition and high scholarly repute, but with incipient deafness, which increased as years went on. I remember his examination in the Schools, his inability to hear questions, his cataclysmal answers when they reached him. Probably his deafness was calculated; Liddell, one of the examiners, remarked that the way to make Mr. Wilkins hear was to question him on subjects which he knew; but there was no doubt about his First Class. He was an eloquent talker, used to sit kicking his legs on a table, pouring out to a crowd of listeners classically poised sentences like extracts from a review. His life's occupation was writing school-books, by which he made large sums; his unrealised ambition was to become a nobleman's chaplain, as the next best thing to being a nobleman: "My dear fellow, think what it would be to be a Marquis—a *Marquis!* my dear fellow." He was a *bon vivant*, declined into a fat Phæacian, abrogated his Orders, and latterly did nothing.

A very different man was Herbert Coleridge, whose Double First in 1852 marked the close of the old system, as Sir Robert Peel's in 1808 shed lustre on its commencement. The most successful Etonian of his day, Newcastle Scholar, and winning the Balliol while still in the Sixth Form, he was unappreciated in a school where athletic eminence was the sole title to distinction; at Oxford he found and enjoyed a higher, more congenial level. His richly endowed and beautiful mother, Sara Coleridge, "last of the three, though eldest born" in Wordsworth's *Triad*, theologian, scholar, poetess, her father's spiritual child in philosophy, learning, genius, yet feminine in grace and sweetness, in domestic tenderness and self-sacrifice, died just before his Class was known. She had read with him, his Greek books especially, throughout his school and college career. He used to acknowledge, it was said, that, while he beat her latterly in trained scholarship, she was always his superior in vigour of phrasing and in delicate verbal felicities. He was fond of talking about "my famous grandfather," insomuch that he gained the nickname of οὐκ ἄπαππος. He never took his degree : by an absurd rule then prevalent —now, I am told, extinct—men taking the B.A. with £300 a year of their own, ranked as "Grand Compounders," and, bedizened in scarlet gowns— Cox's tulips they were called—paid £100 in fees to old Valentine Cox, the Esquire Bedel; and this Coleridge would not do. He turned his attention to Philology, inducing the Philological Society to announce a new English dictionary on a vast scale, to be compiled with aid from volunteers throughout the country, and edited by himself. I was one of his humble coadjutors, and preserve many letters which he wrote to me as the work went on. With his death the enterprise fluttered broken-winged and fell, to be revived in our own time by Dr. Murray. He died in 1861, only thirty years old. Throughout a prolonged and distressing illness he laboured steadily and cheerfully; beside him at his death lay an unfinished review of Dasent's "Burnt Njal," which had employed him almost to the last; like another heroic student, J. R. Green, "he died learning." Eighteen months before the end it was announced to him that recovery was hopeless. "Then," said he, "I must begin Sanskrit to-morrow."

To close this chapter of retrospect, let me set down the main differences which to an old man surveying modern Oxford point the contrast between then and now. The first lies in the category of dress, whose strict unwritten rules were in the Thirties penally enforced and universally observed. Men *wore*, not carried, their academicals in the streets; the Commoner's gown, now shrunk to an ugly tippet, floated long and seemly, a sweet robe of durance. Even to cricket and to the boats black coats and beaver hats were worn, with change and re-change upon the spot; a blazer in the High Street would have drawn a mob. A frock or tail coat was correct in Hall; in some Colleges even a cut-away, as it was called, provoking a sconce or fine. A clever group of undergraduates in the Forties who presumed to dress carelessly—Irving, son to the famous preacher; Henry Kingsley, who ranked as one of the three ugliest men in Oxford[1]—and some three or four besides, incurred universal obloquy, and were known as the intellectual bargees. Nowadays the garments of a gentleman are reserved, as high school girls tell me that they keep their Longfellow, for Sundays; while men pulling ladies on the river go near to earn the epithet suggested by Jonathan Oldbuck for his nephew Hector's Fenians, through the frank emergence from amputated trousers (Calverley's *crurum non enarrabile tegmen*) of

---

[1] I shall not give the names of the other two Calibans. One having curly teeth, was known as *Curius Dentatus*; the extraordinary visage of the other was hit off by the inspired nickname, "The Exasperated Oyster."

what Clough's Bothie calls their lily-white thighs. Even a more potent factor in University change is the development of athleticism. At that time there was no football and no "sports"; only one cricket field, the "Magdalen ground," at the Oxford end of Cowley marsh. Comparatively few men boated; outriggers, dinghies, canoes, apolaustic punts were unknown. Rich men hunted, followed the drag, jumped horses over hurdles on Bullingdon Green, drove tandem. This last was more common than to-day: from West's, Tollitt's, Figg's, Seckham's stables the leader was trotted out a mile or so to await an innocent-looking gig, taken off again on the return so as to outwit the Proctor. When Osborne Gordon was Proproctor, he took his chief in a fly one night to the edge of Bagley Wood, told the driver to unfasten the horse and push the fly into a ditch. The expected tandem came—pulled up—"Can we help you?" said the Jehu dismounting, when out stepped the velvet sleeves with "Your name and College." The plant was complete; but Gordon had made the Proctor promise amnesty, and the men were unmolested.

These were amusements of the wealthy; the great mass of men, whose incomes yielded no margin for equestrianism, took their exercise in daily *walks*—the words "constitutional" and "grind" not yet invented. At two o'clock, in pairs or threes, the whole University poured forth for an eight or ten miles' toe and heel on the Iffley, Headington, Abingdon, Woodstock roads, returning to five o'clock dinner. The restriction told undoubtedly in favour of intellectual life. The thought devoted now to matches and events and high jumps and "bikes" moved then on loftier planes; in our walks, no less than in our rooms, then, not as now,

> "We glanced from theme to theme,
>   Discussed the books to love and hate,
>   Or touched the changes of the State,
> Or threaded some Socratic dream.
>
> There once we held debate, a band
>   Of youthful friends, on mind, and art,
>   And labour, and the changing mart,
> And all the framework of the land."

Only I fear in unathletic days was possible the affluent talk of a Tennyson and Hallam on the Cam, on the Isis of a Whately and a Copleston, a Newman and a Froude, a Congreve and Mark Pattison, Stanley and Jowett, Clough and Matthew Arnold—brain as against muscle, spirit as against flesh, the man as against the animal, the higher as against the lower life.

CHAPTER IX

SUMMA PAPAVERUM CAPITA— CHRISTCHURCH

*" See unfading in honours, immortal in years,
The great Mother of Churchmen and Tories appears."*
—NEW OXFORD SAUSAGE.

" Presence-of-Mind " Smith—" Planting Peckwater "—Gaisford— His Achievements as a Scholar—His *brusquerie*—Helen Douglas —" Brigadier" Barnes—Dr. Jelf—Pusey—A Veiled Prophet— His Mother, Lady Lucy Pusey—Pusey's Personal Characteristics —His Brother the Agriculturist—Roots, Esculent and Hebrew— A Religious Vivisector—How Pusey got his Hebrew Professorship —My Relations with him—The Sacrificial Lamb—Attitude towards Biblical Criticism and Free Thought—His Sermons— *Dicta*—The Year 1855—Other Chronicles of Christchurch— Liddell—His Greatness—Max Müller—Ouseley—The Jelf Row— The Thunny—Lewis Carroll—His Girl Play-fellows—Why his Friendships with them Ended—A Personality Apart.

OF men, no less than plants, the upgrowth and stature are unequal. The tallest ears in Thrasybulus' cornfield, the proudest poppies in Tarquin's garden, were, to use the metaphor of Prospero, "trashed for overtopping"; and so, *inter silvas Academi,* some men stand out conspicuous to the backward glance of memory above the haze which shrouds the lower levels of the generations past, claiming to be "taken off" in milder sense than by the enigmatic cruelty of the Grecian or Etruscan tyrant. Let me embalm in fragmentary guise some relics of the wit and wisdom of those once laurelled now half-forgotten heroes.

In the august procession of Colleges Christchurch leads the way. Its Dean at the opening of the Thirties—καὶ γὰρ ἔτι δὴν ἦν—was "Presence-of-Mind" Smith. The tradition which explains the name, and which has diverted many University generations, may perhaps now be consigned to oblivion. Smith's daughter Cecilia was engaged (and afterwards married) to Richard Harington of Brasenose. Harington was Proctor, and with the young lady and her party attended a concert at the Star. Behind them sat some Christchurch men, who amused themselves by removing with a sharp knife the "penwiper," of no utility and of uncertain origin, worn by noblemen and proctors. What was to be done with the trophy? They hurried home, pinned the penwiper to the Dean's door, and retired into the obscurity of the adjacent archway. Tom Gate opened, the carriage drove to the steps, the party ascended to the door. A hand, stretched to ring the bell, was arrested by the novel ornament; it was taken down and handed round. "Why, it is Dick's penwiper," said Miss Cecilia's voice, as she fingered the back-piece of her lover's toga; and a chorus of Samsonic laughter was heard retiring up to Peckwater.

Peckwater enriched the Oxford vocabulary with a proverb in the reign of Smith's successor, Gaisford. During one of his periodical quarrels with the men, some of them scaled his garden wall in the night, dug up a quantity of shrubs, and planted them in Peckwater, which was found next morning verdant with unwonted boskage; and for many years "planting Peckwater" was synonymous with a Christchurch row. Gaisford became Dean unexpectedly; the men came up in October, 1831, to find his grim person in Smith's vacated stall. Smith appears to have been uneasy at Oxford, while Gaisford longed to return to it from Durham. So in some occult fashion Bishop Van Mildert, whose niece was Gaisford's wife, effected an exchange; Gaisford came to the deanery, Smith subsided into one of the Silver Canonries of Durham; his portrait hangs in the Castle. Gaisford was no divine; he preached annually in the cathedral on Christmas Day, and a sentence from one of his sermons reverberated into term-time.

"Nor can I do better, in conclusion, than impress upon you the study of Greek literature, which not only elevates above the vulgar herd, but leads not infrequently to positions of considerable emolument."

The muse had taught him, as she taught Horace, *malignum spernere vulgas.*

He was a rough and surly man; had owed his rise originally to Cyril Jackson, who discovered the genius of the obscure freshman, gave him a Christchurch studentship, and watched over him. "You will never be a gentleman," said the "Great Dean" to his *protégé* with lordly candour, "but you may succeed with certainty as a scholar. Take some little known Greek author, and throw your knowledge into editing it: that will found your reputation." Gaisford selected the great work on Greek metres of the Alexandrian grammarian Hephæstion, annotated it with marvellous erudition, and became at once a classical authority. In 1811 Lord Liverpool, with a highly complimentary letter, offered him the Professorship of Greek: he replied: "My Lord, I have received your letter, and accede to its contents. Yours, etc." The *gaucherie* came to Cyril Jackson's ears; he sent for Gaisford, dictated a proper acknowledgment, and made him send it to the Prime Minister with a handsomely bound copy of his Hephæstion. He never lectured; but the higher Oxford scholarship gained world-wide lustre from his productions. His Suidas and Etymologicon Magnum are glorified in Scott's Homerics on the strife between Wellington's and Peel's supporters for the Chancellorship.

> Ἀλλ' ὅσοι εἰς Καθέδρην περὶ Βόσπορον ἠγερέθοντο
> Γαισόφορος κόσμησε, δύω δολιχόσκια πάλλων
> λέξικα, δυσβάσταχθ', οἷς δάμνησι στίχας ἀνδρῶν
> ἡρώων, κριτικῶν· ἅπερ οὐ δύο γ' ἄγδρε ἰδέσθαι
> τλαῖεν ἀταρμύκτοισι προσώπασι, σήματα λυγρά,
> οἷοι νῦν βροτοί εἰσ'· ὁ δέ μιν ῥέα πάλλε καὶ οἷος.

In a facetious record of the Hebdomadal Board Meeting in 1851 to protest against University Reform, he is quoted as professing that he found no relaxation so pleasant on a warm afternoon as to lie on a sofa with a Suidas in one's arms. These *Lexica*, with his Herodotus, won cordial respect from German scholars, who had formed their estimate of Oxford from third-rate performances like Dr. Shaw's "Apollonius Rhodius." His son used to relate how, going with his father to call on Dindorf at Leipsic, the door was opened by a shabby man whom they took to be the famulus, but who on the announcement of Gaisford's name rushed into his arms and kissed him. Poor Shaw's merits, on the other hand, they appraised with contumely. The "Apollonius" was re-edited, I think, by Böckh, whose volume was eagerly scanned by Shaw in hopes of some complimentary recognition. At last he found cited one of his criticisms with the appended comment "*Putidissime Shavius*"! Gaisford was an unamiable Head, less than cordial to the Tutors, and speaking roughly to his little boys. He nominated my old schoolfellow, "Sam" Gardiner the historian, to a studentship. Sam became an Irvingite, and thought it right to inform the Dean, who at once sent for the College books and erased Gardiner's name. He had a liking for old Hancock, the porter at Canterbury Gate, with whom he often paused to joke, and whom he called the Archbishop of Canterbury. Hancock once presumed so far as to invite the Decanal party under that name to tea: I do not think they condescended to immure themselves in those unwholesome subterranean rooms of his. The story of the Dean of Oriel's compliments to the Dean of Christchurch is true in part. The Dean Minor was Chase; the Dean's remark, not written but spoken to his neighbour, was, "Oh! yes—Alexander the Coppersmith to Alexander the Great." Equally confused is the tradition of his daughter's suitor. It runs that W. E. Jelf proposed to Miss Gaisford, who refused him; that Gaisford urged his deserts, as of a scholar knowing more about γε than any man in

Oxford:—that the young lady answered "it might be so, but she herself knew too much about μὲν to accept him." Those who remember Gaisford will doubt if his respect for Greek would overbear his indignation that a mere Tutor should cast eyes upon his daughter; those who knew Osborne Gordon will give a tolerable guess at the origin of the story. A story indeed there was; of love strong as death, of brave and patient constancy, of bright too brief fruition, not to be profaned by mention here. *Est et fideli tuta silentio merces.* I am growing tragic, and, as Wordsworth sings, the moving accident is not my trade. Let me end off old Gaisford's cenotaph with lines composed, it was believed, by Henry Cotton, afterwards Archdeacon of Cashel, who assumed certainly in conceiving them the sock rather than the buskin, when Gaisford, unloverlike, slovenly, black-a-vised, wooed and won his first wife, the beautiful Helen Douglas:—

"Here's to the maid who so graceful advances;
　'Tis fair Helen Douglas, if right I divine.
Cupid, thou classical god of soft glances,
　Teach me to ogle and make the nymph mine.
　　　Look on a Tutor true,
　　　Helen, for love of you,
Just metamorphosed from blacksmith to beau—
　　　Hair combed and breeches new,
　　　Love has changed Roderick Dhu,
While every gownsman cries, wondering, 'Oho!'

In Greek, I believe, I must utter my passion,
　For Greek's more familiar than English to me;
And Byron of late has brought Greek into fashion,
　There's some in his 'Fair Maid of Athens'—let's see.

But this vile modern Greek
Never will do to speak;
Let me try—Ζώη μὸν σᾶς ἀγαπῶ—?
　　Pshaw! I don't like the tone;
　　Let me now try my own—
κλῦθι μεῦ Ἑλένη, σοῦ γὰρ ἐρῶ.

But here comes a handsome young spark whom I plucked once.
　Perhaps he'll make love to her out of mere spite;
Aye, touch thy cap and be proud of thy luck, dunce,
　But Greek will go farther than grins, if I'm right.
　　　By Dis the infernal god,
　　　See, see—they smile—they nod—
ʼΩ μοι δύστηνος—ὦ τάλας ἐγώ.
　　　Oh! should my faithless flame
　　　Love this young Malcolm Græme,
Ὀτοτοῖ τοτοτοῖ φεῦ πόποι ὦ.

Thank heaven! there's one I don't see much about her,
　'Tis her townsman, the Tutor of Oriel, Fitz-James;
For though of the two I am somewhat the stouter,
　His legs are far neater, and older his claims.
　　　Yet every Christchurch blade
　　　Says I have won the maid;
　Every one, Dean and Don, swears it is so.
　　　Honest Lloyd, blunt and bluff,
　　　Levett and Goodenough,
　All clap my back and cry 'Roderick's her beau.'

Come then, your influence propitious be shedding,
　Ye Gnomes of Greek metres, since crowned are my hopes;
Waltz in Trochaic time, waltz at my wedding,
　Nymphs who preside over accent and tropes.
　　　Scourge of false quantities,
　　　Ghost of Hephæstion, rise!
　Haply to this my success I may owe;
　　　Come sound the Doric string,
　　　Let us in concert sing,
　Joy to Hephæstion—Black Roderick, and Co."

Gaisford's senior Canon was "Brigadier" Barnes, a name persistent to the end of his long life because he had borne it in the Oxford Volunteer Corps of 1803. To him was always attributed what is I suppose the archetype of leading questions, launched at a floundering youth in a Homer examination—"Who dragged whom how many times round the walls of what?" All the Canons, except Pusey, were more or less nepotist in their nomination to Studentships; but none of them came up to Barnes. "I don't know what we're coming to! I've given studentships to my sons, and to my nephews, and to my nephews' children, and there are no more of my family left. I shall have to give them by merit one of these days!" I knew him as a large, red-faced, kindly, very deaf old gentleman, with three pleasant daughters, who gave evening parties. To one of these came upon a time Mrs. and the Miss Lloyds, widow and daughters of Bagot's predecessor in the Oxford See. The youngest girl had engaged herself to Sanctuary, an undergraduate of Exeter. The mother frowned on the attachment; the sisters favoured it. Sanctuary's rooms in Exeter commanded the Lloyd's dwelling, which was next door to Kettel Hall; and so it came to pass that when mamma went out, a canary was hung outside the drawing-room window, and the young gentleman walked across.[1] Old Barnes had imbibed from his daughters some hazy notion of the *liaison*, and greeted the pretty rebel, of whom he was very

---

[1] "Je l'ai vu," wrote old Canon Tristram on reading this.

I

fond, with a loud " How do you do, dear Miss ——, and how *is* Mr. Tabernacle ?"

Another Canon meriting record was Dr. Jelf. He was also Principal of King's College, London, and therein instrumental in expelling F. D. Maurice from his Professorship, as a tribute to the majesty of everlasting fire. He had been tutor of the blind King of Hanover, whose full-length portrait in oils adorned the drawing-room, and he had married a Hanoverian, a highly accomplished Countess Schlippenbach. Her presence, and that of two young musical daughters, made his house exceedingly attractive during his canonical residence. I remember taking the tenor part with the young ladies in Mendelssohn's Quartetts, while Thomson, afterwards Archbishop, sang the bass. I recall too a dinner party one day when I championed Johnson's "Rambler" against general disparagement, until from the head of the table Jelf interposed, thanked me for what I had said, and told us that at a critical period in his own life he had owed very much to certain Papers in the "Rambler."

Of Buckland and of Bull I have spoken; there remains Pusey. In those days he was a Veiled Prophet, always a recluse, and after his wife's death, in 1839, invisible except when preaching. He increased as Newman decreased; the name "Puseyite" took the place of "Newmanite." As mystagogue, as persecuted, as prophet, he appealed to the romantic, the generous, the receptive natures; no sermons attracted undergraduates as did his. I can see him passing to the pulpit through the crowds which overflowed the shabby, inconvenient, unrestored cathedral, the pale, ascetic, furrowed face, clouded and dusky always as with suggestions of a blunt or half-used razor, the bowed grizzled head, the drop into the pulpit out of sight until the hymn was over, then the harsh, unmodulated voice, the high-pitched devotional patristicism, the dogmas, obvious or novel, not so much ambassadorial as from a man inhabiting his message; now and then the search-light thrown with startling vividness on the secrets hidden in many a hearer's heart. Some came once from mere curiosity and not again, some felt repulsion, some went away alarmed, impressed, transformed. It was in the beginning of the Fifties that I first came to know him well, sometimes in his brother's house at Pusey, sometimes in his own. His mother, too, I knew, Lady Lucy Pusey, a dame of more than ninety years, preserving the picturesque dress and sweet though formal manners of Richardson's Cedar Parlour. She remembered driving under Temple Bar with her mother as a little girl, and being told to look up and see the last "traitor's" head still mouldering on its spike. She would tell me stories of her school, where the girls sat daily in a horrible machine constructed to Procrusteanise a long and graceful neck by drawing up the head and chin; of her wedding introduction to Queen Charlotte's drawing-room, borne in her sedan chair by brown-coated "Johnnies" and attended by running footmen with silk coats and wax flambeaux; of the "reverend gentleman" from Oxford who rode over to Pusey each Sunday morning in boots and cords, read prayers in the little church, *dined in the servants' hall*, and carried his ministrations and his boots to two other parishes for the afternoon. She used old-fashioned pronunciations, such as t'other, 'ooman, 'em for them. "Green tea poisonous? look at me. I'm an old 'ooman of ninety-two, and I've drunk strong green tea all my life!" She loved to talk of Ed'ard, as she called her famous son, relating how, when he gained his First Class and his father begged him to claim some valuable commemorative present, he asked for a complete set of the Fathers; and how in the Long Vacation he used to carry his folios to a shady corner in the garden which she pointed out, and sit there reading with a tub of cold water close at hand, into which he plunged his curly head whenever study made it ache. She died, I think, in 1858; her sedan chair, in which she regularly went to church on Sunday from her house in Grosvenor Square, and which attracted always a little crowd of onlookers, was one of the last used in England.

Two things impressed me when I first saw Dr. Pusey close: his exceeding slovenliness of person; buttonless boots, necktie limp, *intonsum mentum*, unbrushed coat collar, grey hair "all-to-ruffled"; and the almost artificial sweetness of his smile, contrasting as it did with the sombre gloom of his face when in repose. He lived the life of a godly eremite: reading no newspapers, he was unacquainted with the commonest names and occurrences; and was looked upon with alarm in the Berkshire neighbourhood, where an old lady, much respected as "a deadly one for prophecy,"

PUSEY
From a pen-and-ink drawing of the Thirties
Photographed from the Print by Mrs. Frieda Girdlestone

had identified him with one of the three frogs which were to come out of the dragon's mouth. His brother, the renowned agriculturist, would introduce him to visitors with the aphorism that one of them dealt in esculent, the other in Hebrew roots; but, like his friend and follower Charles Marriott, he had no small talk, and would sit absolutely silent in strange company. Into external society he never went; was once persuaded by his old friend and neighbour Sir Robert Throgmorton to meet at dinner the Roman Catholic antiquary and theologian Dr. Rock; but he came back bewailing that Dr. Rock had opened controversy so soon as they sat down, had kept it up after the ladies had left the table, had walked homewards with him in order to pursue it, flinging a last word after his opponent as they parted at Mr. Pusey's lodge-gate. In contrast to his disinclination for general talk was his morbid love of groping in the spiritual interiors of those with whom he found himself alone. He would ask of strangers questions which but for his sweet and courteous manner they must have deemed impertinent. I had not been in his company a week before he had extracted my past history, habit of mind, future aims. Persons who evaded his questionings fell in his opinion; he denounced as reprobate a sullen groom who drove him in and out of Oxford, and who had repelled his attempts at inquisition: the habit of acting towards others as a confessor seemed to have generated a scientific pleasure in religious vivisection. He had countless clients of this kind; women chiefly, but young men, too, as readers of Mark Pattison's

"Memoirs" will recollect. Flys came to the door, from which descended ladies, Una-like in wimple and black stole, "as one that inly mourned," obtained their interview, and went away. He paid frequent visits for the same purpose to Miss Sellon's institution—Chretien's wicked witticism will recur to some who read [1]—and on our occasional visits to Wantage, where Butler reigned as vicar, with Liddon and Mackonochie as his curates, we were detained till late at night while he gave audience to ladies of the place. Sisterhoods were his especial delight and admiration; he had begun to work for their establishment in 1840, somewhat against Newman's judgment; his eager support of them being rooted less in the benefit they might confer on the community than as a means of securing their votaries in the virginity which he had come to look upon as the highest state of life. He made an idol of celibacy, exerting all his influence on one occasion and setting many springs in motion to enlist in the Clewer Home a young orphan lady whose friends deemed her not old enough for such a life, and treating his ultimate discomfiture as a victory of Evil over Good. His obscurantist dread of worldly influences begot the feeling that no young woman was safe except in a nunnery, no young man except in Orders. He would urge men to be ordained at the earliest possible period: controversial knowledge, systematic reading, theological erudition, might come afterwards; if only

[1] There was a foolish report of his contemplated marriage to Miss Sellon : Chretien of Oriel remarked that the offspring of the alliance would be known as the "Pusey *Miscellany*."

the youth were pious, earnest, docile, the great thing was to fix, to secure, to *capture* him.

In learning Pusey stood probably supreme amongst English divines of his century: the other leaders of the movement—even Keble, much more Newman—were by comparison half-educated men. They knew no German—he was an adept; they were not Orientalists—he had toiled over five years for sixteen hours a day at Hebrew, Arabic, Chaldee, under the Semitic scholar Freytag. His vast patristic knowledge is shown in his exhaustive catenæ, and in the "Library of the Fathers" which he conceived and conducted. He was familiar with the entire range of Protestant Reformation literature, with the English Deists of the seventeenth century, with the German Rationalists of the nineteenth. His appreciation of language as the vital genius of cultured human thought was not so much an acquirement as spontaneous; corresponding felicities of diction in one or another tongue seemed to present themselves to him instinctively and without effort: Keble, his examiner in the Schools, used to say that Pusey's construe of Pindar revealed to him for the first time a perfect English equivalent of the magnificent dithyrambic roll which he had believed to be untransferable.

Pusey's religious development was gradual. Brought up in lax traditional English Churchmanship, he was early attracted by, and always loved, the Evangelicals, sharing their deep reverence for the written Word, and their dislike of what he called "Orthodoxism," the "godless orthodoxy" of Mark Pattison's essay—an exaltation, that is, of form and phrase above the realities they were constructed to convey. He was initiated into controversy through a brilliant schoolfellow and friend, Julian Hibbert, who, a sceptic even while at Eton, became later a pugnacious atheist. Pusey determined to face and fight out the difficulties which Hibbert's arguments had raised, and, after taking his degree at Oxford, betook himself to the German Universities, where, more vigorously than elsewhere in Europe, Rationalism at that time flourished. He often spoke in after years of the kindness shown to him by the professors at Göttingen and Berlin; they listened to his arguments, maintained or sometimes modified their own. Their influence on his mind appeared in his first published work, a defence of German teaching against a powerful attack made upon it by Hugh James Rose. Later he came to think that he had judged his friends too leniently, felt alarm at the tendency of their destructive criticism, and withdrew his book from circulation.

In one of our walks he told me of his appointment to the Hebrew Professorship. He had been a favourite with Lloyd, who held besides his Oxford bishopric the post of Divinity Professor, and who when at Cuddesdon or in London gave up his Christchurch house and library to his young friend's use. Pusey owned a Hebrew Bible with large folio interleavings, and these were filled with the notes of ten years' study. Once the Bishop came suddenly to his house, and Pusey, vacating it in a hurry, left his folio behind. It caught Lloyd's eye : he examined it, and gave it back without remark; but when soon afterwards Dr. Nicol died and Sir Robert Peel consulted Lloyd as to the appointment, he strongly recommended Pusey, who became Regius Professor at the age of twenty-nine. Lloyd cautioned him—"Remember, you must be circumspect, you will be φθονερῶν φθονερώτατος." Lord Radnor, the head of the family, was just then in vehement Opposition, and the Duke of Wellington's colleagues attacked him for patronising a Bouverie. "How could I help it," said the Duke, "when they told me he was the best man?" He was a laborious Professor, but a dull lecturer. His lectures, given in his library, were conversational, not continuous or methodised; his manner hesitating, iterative, involved; you had to look out for and painfully disentangle the valuable learning they contained. Rarely his subject would inspire him. Once at the close of a wearisome disquisition on Isaiah xxi. he suddenly woke up at the words, "Watchman, what of the night?" gave a swift, brilliant, exhaustive paraphrase of those two oracular verses, sent us away electrified and wondering. Two other incidents from the lecture room rise up before me. He was laying down the probable site of ancient Tyre, when an eccentric student broke in to quote from memory Grote's dictum on the subject, differing altogether from the Doctor's. He looked scared for a moment at the interruption, then smilingly reserved the point, and told us next time that he had read Grote's note and acceded to his view. Another day I noticed that he was unwontedly *distrait*, casting glances towards the same student, who, always nervous and restless, was crumpling in his fingers a scrap of written paper. When the room cleared and I remained to chat, as I sometimes did, he joyously pounced upon the paper, which had fallen under a chair, and showed it to me crammed with manuscript in his own minute handwriting, representing as he told me two days' labour, which would have been lost to him had young Fidgety destroyed it.

He early gave me a proof of his regard, vouchsafed I was told only to a few, in setting me to work for him : successive pages from Greek and Latin which I translated look me now in the face when I open his " Catena on the Eucharist." But he would let no one else overwork me, for I had much on my hands at the time ; and when he heard poor Edward Herbert, then an Eton boy, murdered afterwards by Greek brigands, petition me to read Virgil with him in the evenings, interposed an eager negative— " Mr. Tuckwell's evening is the poor man's one ewe lamb, and I will not have it sacrificed." Twice he spoke to me of his wife, whom he had loved at eighteen, married at twenty-eight, lost at thirty-nine. A common friend was sacrificing an important sphere of work in order to seek with his delicate wife a warmer climate, and I asked him—no doubt a priggish query—if the abandonment were justifiable on the highest grounds. " Justifiable ? " he said, " I would have given up anything and gone anywhere, but——" ; his voice shook, the aposiopesis remained unfilled. Once afterwards I was with him in his drawing-room at Oxford. It had been newly papered when the family from

CHRISTCHURCH

Pusey came to live with him. He told me that the former paper had been chosen by his wife, and that to cover it up had pained him, but pointed with a sad smile to a corner where the fresh paper had been rubbed away (by his own fingers I suspected) and an inch or two of the old pattern disclosed. He was greatly amused by a report, which I repeated to him as current in Oxford, that he punished his children for their misdeeds by holding their fingers in the candle as an antepast of hell-fire. He said he had never punished his children in his life, and his son Philip, to whom the tradition was repeated, added that the nearest approach to punishment he could recollect was when his father, looking over his shoulder as he read a novel on a Sunday, pulled his ear and said, "Oh, Phil, you heathen!" The well-known anecdote of the lamb he corrected for me. He was in the three-horse omnibus which used to run from Oxford to the railway at Steventon, and a garrulous lady talked to him of the Newmanites and of Dr. Pusey, adding that the latter, she was credibly informed, sacrificed a lamb every Friday. "I thought I ought to tell her," he said; "so I answered, 'My dear madam, I am Dr. Pusey, and I do not know how to kill a lamb.'"

In argument he was always modest and candid. Mr. Algernon Herbert, the eccentric, the omniscient, the adorable, was referring Christ's miracles to personal magnetism and *medica fides*; to no innate thaumaturgic power that is, but to a passionate belief on the part of the recipients which acted on their bodily frames. Pusey frankly accepted the theory as regarded the healing of *functional* maladies, citing modern instances in support of it, but pointing out that the explanation failed to cover the removal of *organic* disease; that when, for instance, a man born blind was reported to have gained eyesight, you must accept the miracle or deny the fact. He owned that a six days' Creation could not be literally maintained, for he had attended Buckland's lectures; and he renounced on Rolleston's remonstrance his belief in a simultaneous universal deluge. When Darwin's book came out, he asked Rolleston whether the species existing upon the globe five thousand years ago might not have been so few as to be contained in an Ark of the dimensions given in Genesis. "I would not answer him," said Rolleston in his blunt way; "I knew he would quote me as an authority." I pressed him once to say whether, in his opinion, morality without faith or faith without morality were the more hopeful state. He did not like my way of putting it, and fenced with the question for a time, giving the preference at last to faith without morality, but owning his verdict to be paradoxical, and laughing heartily when I reminded him of the sound Churchman in Boswell's "Johnson,"[1] who never entered church, but never passed the door without pulling off his hat. I quoted a recent Charge by Bishop Blomfield containing strong

---

[1] "Boswell," vol. ii. p. 195; ed. 1835. "Campbell is a good man, a pious man; I am afraid he has not been in the inside of a church for many years, but he never passes a church without pulling off his hat. This shows that he has good principles."

doctrinal statements. He said that he had not read and should not read it: "He has been a Bishop twenty years, has given, they say, eight hours a day to the merely mechanical work of his diocese; what time has he had to read, or what is his opinion worth on questions of theology or doctrine?" The ritualistic practices just beginning to appear he regarded with distaste, as presumptuous and mistaken; his strong disapprobation of their later developments is recorded in a recent "Life of Goulburn." We called upon an adjacent rector, who showed us proudly as a *virtutis opus* his newly made reredos surmounted by a large cross, admitting that in consequence of its erection several parishioners had ceased to attend the service. Pusey said to me as we drove away, "I would *never* put up a cross in any church, feeling certain that it would offend some one." Alluding once to his own alleged heterodoxy, he challenged us to find any rule of the Church which he had ever broken. Rubric in hand, we catechised him, but he stood the test, owning indeed that he always stayed away from the Gunpowder Plot Service, but refusing to recognise a Royal Warrant as canonical.

He had no familiar acquaintance with our older English classics; a quotation from Cowley, Dryden, Pope, seemed to touch in him a latent string, but awoke no literary association; for Dr. Johnson indeed he professed loyal admiration—less, I fancy, for the author of "Rasselas," the "Rambler," and the "Lives," than for the scrupulous High Churchman who drank his tea without milk and ate his buns without currants upon Good Friday. Of modern publications not theological he read absolutely nothing; one of his nieces pressed on him for a railway journey Miss Yonge's "Heartsease," just then in vogue, but he could not get through the opening chapter; his sympathies, all wide as they were, failed to vibrate to the poor child-bride's sorrows. He was a staunch defender of absent friends; when a visitor spoke disparagingly once of Dr. J. M. Neale, another time of Dean Lake, he flared up on their behalf with an energy for which he afterwards apologised. For freethinkers he had the deepest repugnance; his outbreak when I quoted admiringly Froude's fine paper on the Study of History in the "Oxford Essays" reverberated through the family. He seemed to feel something like alarm in the presence of neologian writers, English or German, as of antagonists whose arrows threatened weak points in his armour. He recounted to me the curiosity first, the later uneasiness, with which, while in Germany, he listened to the Professors' lectures. I told him how Shuttleworth, when at Holland House as tutor and engaged in controversy with Allen, "Lady Holland's infidel," demolished his attacks on prophecy by citation of Isaiah liii. "The Germans," he said with a groan, "would have shown Allen how to meet it." The close of his life was darkened by this cloud. Newman found that Rome, failing him on many points, could at least shelter him from Rationalism. To Pusey it was a Brocken spectre, dilating in proportion as he approached it. Sir Henry Acland has told for us the dismay with which he looked upon its advance; has recorded, too, the adapted line from Horace,

"Nil desperandum, Christo duce et auspice Christo,"

which, amid all his anxieties, summarised his abiding solace.

He preached every Sunday at Pusey in the little church, a tonic change from the ordinary occupant of the pulpit, whose homilies Mr. Pusey pronounced to be Blair infused with Epictetus. His sermons there gave the same overwhelming impression of personal saintliness as breathed from them in the Christchurch pulpit; but the language was laboriously simple, arresting the crass Berkshire rustics by pithy epigrams which fastened on their minds, and which some of them used afterwards to repeat to me: "Find out your strong point and make the most of it"; "Seek heaven because it is God's throne, not because it is an escape from hell"; "Holiness consists not in doing uncommon things, but in doing common things in an uncommon way." Of his *obiter dicta* I recall the following: "In the study of theology books are better than topics." "The best ecclesiastical history is Fleury's." "It is a good thing to know a large number of minds." "A carefully written sermon or essay cannot be recast or expanded; its integrity is marred by reconstruction." "Discontinue fasting as dangerous if you feel exhausted on the following day." (His own regular Friday meal was a poached egg on spinach, with one glass of port.) "Bennett, of St. Paul's, Knightsbridge, is the only man I know who went abroad with wavering Anglican allegiance and returned an English Churchman." "Hooker's chapter on the Eucharist is disappointing; he shirks the logical sequence of his grand argument on the Incarnation and passes off into mere pious rhapsody." "Luther had an irreverent mind; he says that if God had pleased to make a bit of stick the Sacrament He might have done so." I failed to see the irreverence, but he spoke the words whisperingly and with a shudder, and I could not question him further.

The year 1855, with which these experiences end, marked a transitional period in his life-history. In the autumn of the previous year, greatly to his surprise, he was elected at the head of the Professoriate a member of the enlarged Hebdomadal Council under the new Act, was fascinated at their first encounter, as he told me, by the dashing talk and practical energy of his colleague, Jeune, became, I think, for a time a weapon in that clever tactician's hands, at any rate came out of his Achilles tent and flung himself with a keen sense of freedom and enjoyment into active legislation for the liberated University. Mark Pattison used to say that no man of superior intellect and character could be yoked unequally to the machine of public "business" without moral and mental deterioration; and certainly the Pusey of later years, as useful for aught I know, was not so *great* as the imposing hierophant of the Forties. He is handled saucily in the clever fragment which sprang from young Balliol about 1856 :—

CHRISTCHURCH

" Now, stilled the various labours of the day,
Student and Don the drowsy charm obey.
E'en Pusey owns the soft approach of sleep,
Long as his sermons, as his learning deep ;
Peaceful he rests from Hebraistic lore,
And finds that calm he gave so oft before."[1]

The lines are quite good-humoured, but no longer reverential; they could not have been written ten years earlier. I had known him as a devout Casaubon, unconscious of contemporary trivialities, aloof in patristic reverie and in spiritual pathology. That at any rate he ceased to be; these earlier reminiscences, nowhere hitherto recorded, indicate the close of a chapter in his inner as in his outer life.

But the chronicles of Christchurch are not all in canon type. In my bookcase is a finely bound Delphin Virgil, a school prize with the legend *Honoris Causa* on its cover, which belonged to Charles Atterbury, Senior Student, and Vicar of St. Mary Magdalen. A well-bred gentleman, a finished scholar, a devoutly efficient pastor, he was also an enthusiastic whip, never so happy as when handling Costar's thoroughbreds. He was destined, like Pope's Cobham, to feel his ruling passion strong in death : while driving the Birmingham coach he was upset and killed. The text of his sermon on the Sunday before had been " Set thine house in order ; for thou shalt die, and not live."

In the Thirties Liddell strode the quadrangles, already magnificent in presence, less superbly

[1] Appendix I.

Olympian than he afterwards became; I think Westminster saw the meridian of his personal beauty. Sweeping into the Abbey with his boys on a Sunday afternoon, he belittled and uglified all the surpliced dignitaries around him; venerable to the last, he yet made one rejoice that the gods do not grow old. "None knew," wrote to me at his death one of his most distinguished colleagues—

"None knew how great Liddell was. I rather hope they will not have his Life written. Only those who worked with him could tell what a depth of tenderness and generosity there was in him. He was strangled by the Don, and spent his great powers on the Dictionary. Do the greatest of men achieve more than one-tenth of their powers?"

The Life has been written, and we may be grateful for it. It has set him right with a half-appreciating world; has taught those who needed to be informed that beneath the stern, reserved, austere outside lay a man humble, reverent, tender-hearted; his severity straight-forwardness, his *hauteur* shyness, his reticence born of the strong self-restraint which guarded all utterances by exactest truth, his Stoicism like that of the Roman Aurelius, like that of the Hebrew Preacher—"death so dark, and all dies; love it before it dies; love it because it dies; fear God, love one another, this is the whole of man." The cathedral which he beautified, the University which he helped to reform, the College whose intellectual and moral strain he raised, will not behold a nobler man.

Of Christchurch, too, his friend of many years, Max Müller, was an adopted son. I recall the black-haired slight young foreigner in 1847, or thereabouts, known first as a pianist in Oxford drawing-rooms, whose inmates ceased their chatter at his brilliant touch. I remember the contest for the Sanskrit Professorship, wherein I voted, and as far as I could worked for him; an inferior candidate being preferred before him, first because Max was a "Germaniser," secondly because a friend of Bunsen must of necessity be heretical, thirdly because it was unpatriotic to confer an English Chair on any but an Englishman. The horror of everything German was of very ancient date. Old Tatham of Lincoln, in his famous two-and-a-half-hour sermon on the Three Heavenly Witnesses, wished "all the Jarman critics at the bottom of the Jarman Ocean." The sermon ended thus: "The further elucidation of this subject I leave to those learned Doctors and dignitaries whom I see before me; who, receiving large emoluments for doing little, are content with doing less. And *now*, &c." I attended his stimulating philological lectures; learning from his lips the then novel doctrine of the Aryan migrations and the *rationale* of Greek myths: the charm of his delivery heightened by a few Germanisms of pronunciation and terminology; *moost* for "must," *dixonary* for "vocabulary." He consulted me later about two matters in which, strange to say, I was better informed than he, the art of budding roses and the conduct of marine aquaria. He watched me one day in my garden putting in some buds, and tried his hand; but gave it up presently, saying: "While you are budding a dozen standards I can earn £5 by writing an article." I was his guest sometimes in his pretty home opposite the Magdalen elms, where played Deichmann—

"Whose bowing seemed made
For a hand with a jewel,"

where Jenny Lind warbled, Charles Kingsley stammered in impassioned *tête-à-tête*. I read with delight some years ago his "Auld Lang Syne," pasting into it an 1860 portrait of his then clear-cut face, as a corrective to the more commonplace outlines of the elderly presentment, which, hardly suiting the title, decorates the frontispiece of his book.

As I think of him in his earlier musical Oxford days, there comes before me a more wonderful pianist, who had taken his degree, but was still resident at Christchurch, when Max Müller first appeared. Few now remember Sir Frederick Ouseley's playing at the amateur concerts in the earlier Forties; the slight form and dark foreign face, the prolonged rubbing and twisting of the mobile hands before they were placed upon the instrument; the large, prominent, opal eyes, in fine frenzy rolling over the audience as the piece went on, the executant brilliancy of the marvellous performance, with constructive development and contrapuntal skill which the highest English adepts professed themselves unable to emulate. Like Handel, Mendelssohn, Mozart, he was born a musical prodigy; but he lacked serious training; the early golden years were wasted by his relatives in petting, not instructing, him; Greek and Latin, which he hated, were forced upon him; a clerical career and

SIR FREDERICK OUSELEY
From a Photograph taken about 1856

ritualistic excitements distracted him. Even so, he was nothing short of a very great musician. He was probably—there is wealth of competent consensus in the verdict—one of the greatest extempore players who ever lived. Often, in days of yore, have I stood amongst a group round his piano challenging him to improvise. He always asked for a subject. Some man would supply a theme, perhaps intentionally intricate. In a few moments he would begin, and the piece would grow under his hand with a wealth of resource, a command of technical device, a fertility of imagination, and a skilful elaboration of complicated texture,

> "Untwisting all the chains that tie
> The hidden soul of harmony—"

which raised it to the rank of a great classical masterpiece. His knowledge of the history of music was unique; his library, finely equipped in other departments of literature, inherited from his father, contained not only endless autograph and unpublished scores, but several hundred works on music in many languages, all of which, an accomplished linguist, he had read and mastered. His musical degree and his acceptance of the Professorship were looked upon by the Dons as ignominious condescensions; though old Gaisford loyally attended the performance in the Theatre of his Mus.Doc. exercise, the oratorio of "Polycarp," in which his friend Madame Dolby sang the sweet contralto solos. As Professor he raised to a very high pitch the standard of graduate qualification, and delivered erudite lectures, of which only meagre reports remain. From his many compositions a couple of anthems and two or three hymns alone seem likely to survive; his ultimate repute will, I fear, be altogether incommensurate with his vast powers.

Apart from exceptional men like these, intellectually as historically, Christchurch held its own. The Common Room in the Thirties contained seniors such as Foster Lloyd, F.R.S., and Political Economy Professor; Robert Hussey, a monument of erudition, not yet grimly saturnine as he became in later years; Jacob Ley, the greatly beloved, who probably, like Dominie Sampson, "evinced, even from his cradle an uncommon seriousness of disposition." Of the juniors were Bode, Hertford Scholar, author of the hymn "O Jesus, I have promised"; W. E. Jelf; Osborne Gordon, Ireland Scholar and Double First; Linwood, Hertford, Ireland, Craven Scholar, and, a little later, Kitchin, Double First, now Dean of Durham. Linwood was nephew to the once celebrated Miss Linwood, whose needlework imitation of great paintings drew crowds to her Exhibition Rooms in Leicester Square. He is known to the present generation as compiler of the "Anthologia Oxoniensis." He was a rough, shabby fellow when I remember him, living in London, and coming up to examine in the Schools, where he used to scandalise his colleagues by proposing that for the adjudication of Classes they should "throw into the fire all that other rubbish, and go by the Greek Prose." It was said of him that somewhat late in life, reading St. Paul's Epistles for the first time, and asked by Gaisford what he thought of them, he answered "that they contained a good deal of curious matter, but the Greek was execrable."

By Jelf hangs a tale. He was younger brother to the Canon, an accomplished scholar, author of a Greek Grammar which furnished to English students what Matthiæ had achieved for Germans. But his reputation rests upon the historic "Jelf row" of 1843. Proctor in that year, he was the most unpopular official of the century, beating "Lincoln Green" and Merton Peters, who ranked next to him in odium. He seems to have found enjoyment in what Proctors usually hate, the punitive side of his duty. Dexterous in capturing, offensive in reprimanding, venomous in chastising his victims, he had accumulated against himself a fund of hatred which abode its time, until it might find relief in the Saturnalia of Commemoration. It happened that the uproar which ensued gave voice to a *duplex querela;* hostilities were rampant in the area as well as in the gallery of the Theatre. The young lions of the Newmania, sore from Pusey's suspension and Isaac Williams' defeat, and led by Lewis of Jesus and Jack Morris of Exeter, chose to be furious at the presentation of a Unitarian, the American Minister Everett, for an honorary D.C.L. Early in the morning they called on the Vice-Chancellor, Wynter, President of St. John's, to protest. Wynter, serene, indifferent, handsome—"St. John's Head on a charger" men called him as he went out for his daily ride—urged that Mr. Everett conformed in England; that honorary degrees had no reference to theological opinion; would not, in short, withdraw the distinguished heretic. So finding remonstrance vain, the angry malcontents attended in formidable numbers to *non placet* the degree. On the other hand, the smarting undergraduates had sworn a solemn oath, like John Barleycorn's royal foes, to stop all proceedings until Jelf was driven out of the Theatre. From his first appearance in the procession the yells and groans went on without a moment's slackening. In dumb show the Vice-Chancellor opened the Convocation, Garbett declaimed inaudible his Creweian Oration, Bliss presented Everett, who, red-gowned, unconscious, smiling, took his seat among the Doctors. An opposing Latin speech by Marriott and a volley of *non placets* from his friends were imagined but unheard amid the din, and ignored by Wynter, who at the expiration of an hour dissolved the Convocation, to the fury of the Puseyites, the triumph of the gallery, and, so all believed, to his own concealed but genuine relief from a very difficult position. After-protests poured in upon him, to be met by bland assurances, which no one credited, but no one could disprove, that in the ceaseless uproar he had not heard the *non placets;* that, in short, *factum valuit*, the thing was done. His well-known hostility to the High Churchmen added poignancy to their defeat: when soon afterwards he was succeeded as Vice-Chancellor by Ben Symons, one of them said "Solvitur acris *Hyems Grata Vice."* Three or four men were expelled; amongst them Parnell, a Double First of Wynter's own College, who had not yet put on his gown, and

CHRISTCHURCH

who, according to the testimony of those who sat near him, was inconspicuous if not innocent in the turmoil; while the posthumous indignation of the M.A.'s fizzled out in the appointment of a committee. "So," says the Introduction to a recent edition of "Eothen," "while Everett was obnoxious to the Puseyites, Jelf was obnoxious to the undergraduates; the cannonade of the angry youngsters drowned the odium of the theological malcontents;

> "Another lion gave another roar,
> And the first lion thought the last a bore."

The Tractarian element in the tumult is described in a richly humorous letter to Lord Blachford[1] from Dean Church, himself prominent in the following year as interposing with Guillemard of Trinity to crush by their proctorial *non placet* the decree against "Tract 90": a dramatic incident which had not occurred during the entire century, except when in 1836 the measure to suspend Hampden was veto'd by Bayley of Pembroke and Reynolds of Jesus. I possess the address of thanks presented to Church and Guillemard, signed by about six hundred notable graduates, not by any means confined to the High Church party.

The memory of Osborne Gordon is, I fear, already fading. The authors of the "Life of Stanley" think that "some few readers may have met with his Greek lines on Chantrey's children." I should hope every scholar can repeat them— *non obtusa adeo gestamus pectora!*[2] Less known,

---

[1] "Life of Dean Church," p. 40.   [2] Appendix J.

154 REMINISCENCES OF OXFORD

and very scarce, are his "Sapphics on the Installation of Lord Derby as Chancellor," a parody on Horace's "Quem Virum."[1] With solemn irony he glorifies his hero; lauds him, in fiction such as Phœbus loves, a consistent Proteus, skilled to veil base thoughts in noble words; recalls in a felicitous stanza his savage assault on smiling Bishop Wilberforce in the House of Lords; sneers at the tail of followers brought with him to be decorated—"sorry wreck of a defeated crew, to be refitted in the harbour of quiet Isis." Young men and maidens in the Theatre cheer him and them; with malign smile the country looks and listens. I know not what fly had stung him— what motive winged and pointed a shaft so keen; it must have pierced the Chancellor's embroidered panoply, vulnerable to elegant academic taunts, though impervious to vernacular Parliamentary vituperation.

One more skit let me be permitted to recall, emanating from the same College, partly from the same pen. In 1857 Dr. Acland went with Dean Liddell, then in delicate health, to Madeira. On his return voyage a large thunny was caught by the sailors, rescued when the ship was wrecked on the Dorsetshire coast, taken to Oxford by the Professor, articulated by Charles Robertson, and mounted in the Anatomy School. Brought thence to the new Museum in 1860, it was placed in the area, with a somewhat inflated Latin inscription on *Thunnus quem vides* affixed to its handsome case. Soon appeared a sham Congregation notice,

[1] Appendix K.

CHRISTCHURCH

announcing a statute for the abrogation of the label and substituting another, *Thunnus quem rides*, a line-upon-line travesty of the first, as derisively satirical as its model was affectedly complacent.[1] It was believed to have been rough-hewn by Lewis Carroll, handed round the Common Room, retouched by Gordon, Bode, and Chaffers, who happened to be dining as Gordon's guest: a delightful change at the close, ἐσκελετένθη, *skeletonised*, to ἐΣκιδμωρεύθη, *Skidmoreised*, Skidmore having constructed the supporting iron foliage of the area, was ascribed to Mr. Prout, who is still in green old age an admired ornament of "The House." Would that we had more of Osborne Gordon! Marshall of Christchurch edited a volume of his sermons with an inadequate Memoir. Those who can still remember that queer, mocking face with its half-closed, inscrutable eyes (he was known as "the debauched crow"), and who knew the humour, wisdom, benignity, which lay behind it, are fewer every day—

> "Slowly we disarray; our leaves grow few,
> Few on the tree, and many on the sod."

He is a memory only, and will some day cease to be that.

A recent diarist in a book of "Memoirs" calls his old tutor a vulgarian and a tuft-hunter. Probably Gordon snubbed him, deservedly no doubt, but forgetting Shallow's advice to Davy, and this is his revenge; the valet-de-chambre was no hero.

[1] Appendix L.

He was accused of obsequiousness to "Tufts." Polite to them he was, and they were fond of him. When one of them was sent down in disgrace, he passed Gordon as he left by Canterbury Gate. "Sorry to leave *you*, Mr. Gordon," he said; "I always enjoyed attending your lectures." "Did you really?" was the answer, " I must say that you showed a great deal of self-denial." A conceited undergraduate said to him one day : "I am afraid, sir, that I have rather a contempt for Plato." "And *I* am afraid, Mr. ——, that your contempt has not been bred by familiarity."

I have mentioned Lewis Carroll. He was junior to these other men, and has been fully biographised since his death. Of course, he was one of the sights of Oxford: strangers, lady strangers especially, begged their lionising friends to point out Mr. Dodgson, and were disappointed when they saw the homely figure and the grave, repellent face. Except to little girls, he was not an alluring personage. Austere, shy, precise, absorbed in mathematical reverie, watchfully tenacious of his dignity, stiffly conservative in political, theological, social theory, his life mapped out in squares like Alice's landscape, he struck discords in the frank harmonious College *camaraderie*. Away from Oxford, and especially in home life, I am told that he was cheery and would unbend himself. The irreconcilable dualism of his exceptional nature, incongruous blend of extravagant frolic with self-conscious puritan repression, is interesting as a psychological study now that he is gone, but cut him off while living from all except the "little misses" who were his chosen associates. His passion for them was universal and undiscriminating; like Miss Snevellici's papa, he loved them every one. Yet even here he was symmetrical and rigid; reaching the point where brook and river meet, the petted loving child friend was dropped, abruptly, remorselessly, finally. Perhaps it was just as well: probably the severance was mutual; the little maids put away childish things, he did not: to their maturer interests and grown-up day-dreams he could have made no response: better to cherish the recollection unimpaired than to blur it by later consciousness of unsuitability; to think of him as they think of nursery books; a pleasant memory, laid by upon their shelves affectionately, although no longer read. And to the few who loved him this faithlessness, as some have called it, seems to reveal the secret of his character. He was what German Novalis has called a "grown-up child." A man in intellectual range, severe self-knowledge, venturesome imagination, he remained a child in frankness, innocence, simplicity; his pedantry cloaking a responsiveness which shrank from coarser, more conventional, adult contact, yet vibrated to the spiritual kinship of little ones, still radiant with the visionary light which most of us lose all too soon, but which shone on him through life.

CHAPTER X

MAGDALEN AND NEW COLLEGE

"Lordly is Christchurch, with its walks and quadrangles; lovely is Merton, as it were the sister of Christchurch, and gracefully dependent; New College is majestic; All Souls worthy of princes; but Magdalen alone is all that is the charm of others, compendious in itself; yielding only a little to each rival in particular, but in the whole excelling them all."—CLEVELAND COXE.

The Most Beautiful of Colleges—Dr. Routh—His Old Young Wife—His Mania for Books—His Friends—Some Famous Men of Magdalen—New College—Shuttleworth—Whately and Manning—The Abingdon Ball and the Brigands of Bagley Wood—Public Orator Crowe—Christopher Erle—His Sharp Tongue—Lancelot Lee—One of the *Détenus* of 1803—Dr. Nares—His Drollery written for Miss Horseman—Warden Sewell.

THE "College of the Lily" pairs naturally with its *Mater Pulchra*, New College. I knew Magdalen in the Thirties; the rambling Greyhound Inn, with large glass-warehouse adjoining, on the site of the present schoolroom; the trees, tall and umbrageous then as they are not to-day; the choristers' playground, in front of which used to pace up and down the Usher, Lancaster of Queen's, who once enlivened a University sermon by speaking of Hampden as "that atrocious Professor." I recall the noble Inigo Jones gateway, removed early in the Forties in deference to the Puginesque craze which had just then set in; Pugin's erection in its turn, *prope funeratus arboris ictu*, damaged by the

DR. ROUTH, PRESIDENT OF MAGDALEN

From the Pickersgill Portrait, 1851 (?)

fall of a vast elm branch, and looked upon as somewhat paltry by a succeeding generation, giving way after several experiments to the present unsatisfying entrance.

Architecturally, Magdalen is to other Colleges what Oxford is to other towns and cities. Even at New College we miss the indescribable charm of its Hall and Chapel; in its walks and grove we have, as nowhere else, the "hallowed haunt" of Milton and the "classic ground" of Addison. No other College pretends to match the felicitous grouping of its clustered buildings; and its campanile dominating the whole is supreme among the third-pointed towers of all England. Nowhere else does the *Numen inest* so inspire and enthral. But its prime of rarity in those days was its President, Dr. Routh, "of olden worth the lonely leaf and last"; who, born in 1754, was in the later Thirties past fourscore, and was to live into his hundredth year. It was as a *spectacle* that he excited popular interest; to see him shuffle into Chapel from his lodgings a Sunday crowd assembled. The wig, with trencher cap insecurely poised above it, the long cassock, ample gown, shorts and buckled shoes; the bent form, pale venerable face, enormous pendent eyebrows, generic to antique portraits in Bodleian gallery or College Halls, were here to be seen alive—

"Some statue you would swear
Stepped from its pedestal to take the air."

After 1836 he was rarely visible in the streets, but presided at College Examinations, and dined in

Hall on Gaudy days, occupying the large State Chair, never profaned by meaner loins, constructed from the immemorial Magdalen elm, which, much older than the College, fell with a terrific crash in 1789. In front of his lodgings stood a scarcely less venerable acacia tree, split from the root originally, and divagating in three mighty stems, of late years carefully propped. Once while he was at Tylehurst, his country home, word was sent to him that a heavy gale had blown his acacia tree down: he returned a peremptory message that it should be put up again. Put up it was; the Magdalen Dryads owned their chief; it lived, and long survived him. I stood for a Demyship early in the Forties; nominated, according to the custom then prevalent, by Frank Faber. He was confined to his rooms by illness, and had failed to comply with some essential preliminary, of which he ought to have been informed. But—so it was said—the Vice-President, with the Fellow next in order, to whom Faber's nomination, if forfeited, would lapse, conspired to keep it from the invalid; and when he was carried into Hall to vote for me, they sprang the objection they had husbanded, and disqualified him. I went in for *vivâ voce* immediately afterwards, and I remember how old Routh, shaken by the contest, wept while I construed to him the lines from the Third Book of the "Iliad," in which Helen, from the walls of Troy, names the Grecian chiefs below. My supplanter was a Winchester boy named Wickham, who died shortly afterwards.

Mrs. Routh was as noticeable as her husband. She was born in the year of his election to the

Presidency, 1791; so that between "her dear man," as she called him, and herself—"that crathy old woman," as *he* occasionally called *her*—were nearly forty years. We are told that she three times asked him to marry her before he consented; and some of his love verses are preserved, resembling, George Eliot would say, the cawings of an amorous rook. But she had become rapidly and prematurely old: with strongly marked features, a large moustache, and a profusion of grey hair, she paraded the streets, a spectral figure, in a little chaise drawn by a donkey and attended by a hunchbacked lad named Cox. "Woman," her husband used to proclaim, when from the luncheon table he saw Cox leading the donkey carriage round, "Woman, the ass is at the door." Meeting me as a boy, she sometimes used to take me in to lunch, where the old President, who was intimate with my father, talked to me good-naturedly, questioned me about my school work; showed me one day the scar on his table which had been left by Dr. Parr's tobacco; and enjoyed my admiration of the books which lined hall, rooms, staircase. He was proud of possessing many not on the Bodleian shelves. To himself and to Dr. Bandinel the London catalogues were regularly sent: Bandinel would mark off the treasures which he coveted and write by return of post, but was constantly informed that the books had gone to Dr. Routh. One day, calling at Tegg's shop, he saw the boy bring in a pile of catalogues wet from the press. Now is my time, he thought; noted some sets of rare books, and said, "I will take these books away with me." The shopman went to consult his chief. "I am very sorry, sir, but they are all bespoken by Dr. Routh." "How can that be? Are not the catalogues freshly printed?" "Yes, sir, but proofs of all our catalogues are sent to Dr. Routh." Dr. Jacobson was another disappointed rival; he obtained the proofs, but was still too late: remonstrating with the bookseller, he was told that while he *wrote* for the books he wanted, the President sent a man up by the early coach to secure and bring them back. The story gives delightful point to the generous caution which he is said to have impressed on Jacobson: "Beware, sir, of acquiring the habit of reading catalogues; you will never get any good from it, and it will consume much of your time."

Old Marshall Hacker, going through the papers of his uncle, W. A. Jenner, found a bundle of slips on which Jenner, a Fellow of Magdalen, had for years, after leaving Common Room in the evening, written down stories told, noteworthy observations and jokes, many of them from Routh's lips. Some were coarse; and Marshall Hacker, without making any selection, burned the whole. Herostratus still walks amongst us.

His especial friend was Dr. Bliss; I have a letter to him from Routh, sealed with his favourite ΙΧΘΥΣ seal, deploring my father's death. Bliss once asked him to say, supposing our language to become dead to-morrow, who would take the classic rank in English which Cicero had held in Latin. "I think, sir, our friend Tom Warton," he replied; an answer bespeaking no great knowledge of older English Prose. In later years

Burgon, fussy, obsequious, adulating, hovered about him. Henry Coxe, an accomplished mimic, used to render dialogues between the two, bringing out, as in the "always verify quotations," and the recipe for theological study, the absurdity of which Burgon's narrative is all unconscious. He much admired J. H. Newman, who dedicated to him his " Lectures on Romanism in 1837 "; speaking of him always as "that clever young gentleman of Oriel." Having come to Oxford from his Suffolk home in 1770, he was a mine of anecdote as to the remote past; had seen two undergraduates hanged for highway robbery on the gallows which ornamented the corner of Long Wall near Holywell Church—the "church by the gallows" it is called in a skit from Anthony Wood's collection—remembered stopping in High Street to gaze on Dr. Johnson as he rolled up the steps into University College. One of his aunts, he used to say, had known a lady who saw Charles I. in Oxford. He died, so John Rigaud averred, and so Blagrave, his brother-in-law and man of business admitted, through chagrin at the fall of Russian Securities, in which most of his hoards were invested, at the time of the Crimean War—a very respectable way of breaking one's heart, according to Mr. Dombey, but which would have formed an anticlimax to Burgon's rhapsodies. Rigaud imitated his voice and manner with startling accuracy; his stories of the old man owed their force to this, and would be pointless written down. Rigaud preserved too his queer shoes and gown, and one of his wigs; another was secured by Daubeny, who sent it to be petrified in the Knaresborough Spring. It would have been indestructible without this calcifying process: when in 1860 a grave was sunk in New College antechapel to receive the remains of Warden Williams, an ancient skeleton was found extended, the bones partly dissolved, the wig fresh as from the maker's hands. The old man's spectacles passed from Bloxam to Rigaud, and are now preserved by Dr. Macray of the Bodleian.

Of the Magdalen Fellows in the Thirties I have mentioned Daubeny; I recall also Chambers, riding from Swerford into Oxford in a broad-brimmed hat, followed by a pack of little dogs; and Sibthorp, whose oscillation to and fro between the English and the Roman Church were viewed as comic rather than serious at a time when "'verts" had not begun to come upon the stage. I recall Frank Faber, a kindly careless valetudinarian, lecturing in dressing-gown and slippers, his head sheltered by an umbrella from every gleam of sunshine. An old Fellow of the College used to relate that, riding once out of Oxford, and resting at Shillingford Inn, he was told that Mr. Faber was in the house. He went to his room, and found him sitting up in bed with an umbrella over his head. James Mozley's shy, cold outside hid a genial nature and a mind of rarest power. "Dick" Sewell was a frank Bohemian; his vigorous Newdigate on the "Temple of Vesta" was said to have been written in a single night. A barrister on the Western circuit, he used to get me leave out at Winchester, sending me to dine alone at his lodgings, where I found a roast fowl, a pint of champagne, a novel, and a tip. Henderson's First Class in 1839 was long memorable in the history of the Schools; he became Headmaster successively of Hatfield Hall, Durham; of Victoria College, Jersey; and of Leeds Grammar School. He died, as Dean of Carlisle, in 1905. Charles Reade, just beginning to write novels, would beguile acquaintances into his ill-furnished rooms, and read to them *ad nauseam* from his latest MS. Bloxam, Newman's curate at Littlemore, incarnation of all that was ideal in the College, its mediævalism, sentiment, piety, was the first man to appear in Oxford wearing the long collarless coat, white stock, high waistcoat, which form nowadays the inartistic clerical uniform. Like his better known brother Matthew, he was a laborious antiquary, and compiled a Register of the Members of his College from its foundation. He established the delightful Christmas Eve entertainment in the College Hall which has been annual now for fifty-eight years. Held first in his own rooms as a treat to the choristers, then in the Summer Common Room, it came in 1849 to fill the Hall with a hundred guests or more. Hymns, carols, parts of the "Messiah," were sung through the evening; the boys were feasted at the high table, the visitors waiting upon them, and eating Christmas frumenty. Then, when midnight drew near, a hush fell on the assembly, the choir gathered round the piano; twelve o'clock pealed from the tower, and as the last stroke ceased to vibrate, Pergolesi's "Gloria" rose like a stream of rich distilled perfumes, and sent us home in tune for the worship as well as for the festivity of the Christmas Day. I am told that the gracious custom still abides, to keep fresh and green the memory of dear old Bloxam. Of the remaining Fellows I will say no more than that they were, for the most part, *fruges consumere nati*, born to eat their founder's venison and drink his wine; and justified their birthright zealously. Two among them, Whorwood and T. H. Newman, claim a kindly though certainly not a reverential notice. Whorwood was the last and landless descendant of an ancient line, which had owned for centuries the wide manors of Shotover and Headington. His mother, "Madame Whorwood," a stately old lady in antique dress, lived with him in the house overhanging the Cherwell on the north side of Magdalen Bridge; the top of her high cap usually visible to passers-by. They moved afterwards to a house in the High Street, over which her ancestral hatchment was suspended when she died. He was a fresh-coloured, smooth-faced, vivacious, whist-playing, amiable lounger. Later in life he took the College living of Willoughby, leading there a lonely, melancholy life, cheated and ruled by five domestics, whose service was perfect freedom. Dining once in his old College, he was boasting of their docility and devotion; Rigaud scribbled and handed round his own rendering of the facts—

"Sunt mihi quinque domi servi, sunt quinque magistri;
Quod jubeo faciunt, quodque volunt jubeo;"

Englished promptly by Octavius Ogle into—

"Five servants I have whom I handsomely pay,
Five masters I have whom I always obey.
To do what I bid them they never refuse,
For I bid them do nothing but just what they choose."

Alas! The human butterfly in its later stages is a sight more cautionary than pleasing; I met poor Whorwood not long before his death, pallid, weary, corpulent; and he cried as we talked over old times. Newman was a practical joker; his rooms overlooked the river, and he sometimes fished out of his window. The men coming in from Cowley Marsh cricket and constitutionals were arrested one afternoon to see him struggling with a fish, which Sawell announced through a speaking trumpet from another window to be an enormous pike. Great was the concourse, passionate the excitement, profuse the advice; till at last the monster was hauled up, gaffed, and drawn in at the window. It was on view in his rooms ever after, ingeniously constructed of cardboard overlaid with tinfoil. He was not related to the future Cardinal; but his initials, T. H. N., caused him often to be confounded with, and to receive letters intended for, his Oriel namesake, J. H. N.; and their handwriting was curiously alike. An accomplished artist and connoisseur, he once, by borrowing the Cardinal's signature, gained access to Claude's *Liber Veritatis* at Chatsworth—of course in the absence of the Duke, who would have detected him. On an earlier occasion, having undertaken to preach in the country, he secured by the false initials an immense congregation; and delivered, as he used to tell the story, a sermon on the "Final Conflagration of all things," which terrified some into fits. Opening one day a letter mis-sent to himself, he found it to be from a pious spinster, asking for a subscription, and requesting an autograph copy of some of J. H. N.'s beautiful verses, to be inserted in her album. He sent the following :—

> "My name's *T.* H. Newman ;
> And sorely grieved I am
> That, like an orphaned lamb,
> I haven't got a dam."

From Magdalen I pass naturally to New College, whence it lineally sprang. Its Warden was Shuttleworth, close friend and ally of the "Noetics," the only Head who in 1834 had courage to vote for the admission of Dissenters to the University; author of a rather dull book on St. Paul's Epistles, but a wit, *raconteur*, caricaturist, mimic. When the queer cupola, extant and inexplicable still, was made to surmount the Theatre, he wrote to Whately—"You ask for news : I have one item only : the Radcliffe has kittened, and they have perched one of the kittens on the top of the Sheldonian." He invented an inclined mahogany railroad, still in use, whereby decanters circulating at the horse-shoe tables in the Common Room could be carried automatically across the interval of the fire-place. A Winchester boy, he made his mark at school as a writer of burlesques; two of his pieces, "Phaethon," and the "Progress of Learning," sent up in 1800 instead of, or together with, the serious poems expected, are preserved in the "Carmina Wiccamica."[1] Here are four lines from the first, where the steeds discover that Phaethon, not Phœbus, sits behind them—

> "For Horses, Poets all agree,
> Have common sense as well as we;
> Nay, Homer tells us they can speak
> Not only common sense, but Greek."

The second opens with the boy leaving home—

> "The fatal morn arrives, and oh!
> To school the blubbering youth must go,"

carries him through school, college, country living, to a Deanery; ends with the predictive lines—

> "As erst to him, O heavenly Maid,
> Learning, to me impart thy aid;
> O teach my feet like his to stray
> Along Preferment's flowery way.
> And, if thy hallowed shrine before
> I still thy ready aid implore,
> Make me, O Sphere-descended Queen,
> A Bishop, or, at least, a Dean."

Episcopal aspirations do not always take shape at eighteen years old; with Shuttleworth they seem to have been continuous; Scott's Homerics satirise him thirty-four years later, as refraining from the Peel and Wellington contest, in order to maintain his expectation of a bishopric from the Whigs—

> Ἀνδρῶν δ' οὐκ ἡγεῖτο περίκλυτος Ἀξιοκερκίς,
> στῆ δ' ἀπάνευθεν ἐών, πεφοβημένος εἵνεκα μίτρης.

A mitre he obtained in 1840, and died sixteen months after his elevation. On going down to his bishopric at Chichester, he was warned by Whately against Manning, an incumbent in his diocese,

[1] Appendix M.

as an undoubted "Tractite"—so Whately always called them. The Archdeaconry of Chichester was vacant, the appointment in the new Bishop's hands. He met Manning at a dinner-party, was impressed with his mien and talk, and they sat together afterwards in the drawing-room mutually charmed. Manning had walked from no great distance; his parsonage lay in the Bishop's way home, and Shuttleworth offered him a seat in his carriage. Set down at his own door, "Good-night, my lord," said Manning; "Good-night, Mr. Archdeacon," said the Bishop.

His Fellows at New College, as at Magdalen, were curiously unequal in merit and distinction. A very few, "the two good Duncans," Bandinel, Tremenheere, Chief Justice Erle, Archdeacon Grant, George Cox, J. E. Sewell, afterwards Warden, William Heathcote, be of them that have left a name behind them; the rest were mostly of very common clay indeed. Until 1838 the College had refused to undergo the public examination for degrees, and was further oppressed by the incubus of founder's kin, which imposed two superannuated dunces from Winchester every year, to the exclusion often of their meritorious seniors. Two centuries earlier the discrediting aphorism, "Golden scholars, silver bachelors, leaden masters," had been popularly applied to the College; and in 1852 it had fallen so low that the undergraduates petitioned for out-college tutors, pleading the incompetence of the resident staff. A wild set were not only the juniors but the seniors far into the Thirties. More than one strange scandal I could recount, of a sort which, like Horace's gold, are best placed when unexhumed. But I can vouch for the following frolic. Some men were going to the Abingdon Ball; and in the Common Room the conversation turned on a highway robbery recently perpetrated near Wheatley. The ball-goers talked valiantly of their own courage, contemptuously of brigand dangers; their fly was announced, and off they drove. Coming home they were stopped in a dark part of Bagley Wood by two masked men, one of whom held the horses' heads, while his mate pointed a pistol into the fly with the conventional highwayman's demand. Meekly our gallant travellers surrendered money, watches, jewellery. One pleaded for a ring which had belonged to his old mother; the deceased lady was consigned to Tartarus, the ring was taken, and the marauders rode away. Great commiseration was shown to the victims when they told their tale, great activity displayed by the police; until, on going into Hall the next afternoon, they saw lying in a heap on the centre of the high table the abstracted valuables, including the maternal ring, while mounting guard over them was a broken candlestick which had done duty as a pistol. The two practical jokers had ridden to the wood, tied their horses to the trees, waited for the revellers, and played the wild Prince and Poins.

A few more men of note I remember, *rari nantes in gurgite*. Public Orator Crowe had lately passed away, farmer-like, uncouth, wearing a long cassock to hide his leather breeches, but a fine Latinist with a magniloquent delivery which found scope each year at the Encænia. The neat Latin inscription on Warden Gauntlett's monument in the antechapel was his; I possess the first draft in his handwriting, endorsed by Routh, to whom he had submitted it. He was known to the outer world by his really fine poem, "Lewesdon Hill"; I remember "Mad" Hoskins, the squire of North Perrott, an enthusiastic Wykehamist, repeating the whole of it as we rode together, in 1846, within sight of that "proud rising." His father was a humble carpenter at Winchester; the son, grown eminent, was standing by the west door of the Cathedral in conversation with the Dean and Warden, when the father, in working dress, his rule projecting from his corduroys, came by, and walked aside from the group in modest avoidance of recognition. Crowe saw him, and called after him in Hampshire Doric, "Here, fayther, if thee baint ashamed of I, I baint ashamed of thee."

Another eccentric of the Thirties, Christopher Erle, brother to the Chief Justice, lived till long afterwards. Like most old-fashioned scholars of an era when philology was not, he knew his Greek and Latin books by heart, pouring out apt quotations with the broad *a* which then marked Wykehamists; was a proficient, too, in Italian, French, and English literature, with his Dante at his fingers' ends. He was a familiar figure at the Athenæum, where one day his Bishop, newly appointed Sam of Oxford, remonstrated with him—very impertinently, since they were on neutral ground—for wearing a black neckcloth. Erle called the club porter. "Porter, do you know this gentleman? This is the Bishop of Oxford.

Get me half-a-dozen white ties, and bring me one whenever this gentleman comes into the club." His living was in the part of Buckinghamshire colonised by Rothschilds—Jerusalem the Golden it was called—and the reigning Baron was his squire. It was Erle's whim to dress carelessly; and the plutocrat, walking one day with a large party and meeting his Rector in the parish, had the bad taste to handle his sleeve and say, "Rather a shabby coat, parson, isn't it?" Erle held it up to him— "Will you buysh? will you buysh?" There ensued an *exitus Israel*, and Erle walked on chuckling and victorious.

Of the same standing, and not less an original, was Lancelot Lee, who, with imposing face and figure, strident voice, assumed ferocity of manner, was a frequent visitor at my father's. He was one of the *Détenus*, Englishmen seized by Napoleon in 1803, and incarcerated till his fall in 1814.[1] They were about ten thousand in number, some previously residents in France, but chiefly visitors or tourists. They included noblemen and gentlemen, clergymen and academics with their servants, workmen, and commercial travellers. All were at first treated as prisoners of war; but this sentence was afterwards limited to English officers, the rest were made prisoners on parole, and lodged in certain fortified towns. Those of higher rank, Lee amongst them, were confined at Verdun, under the charge of a ruffianly General Wirion, who treated them with insolent barbarity. A committee of nine gentlemen was formed to represent the

[1] Page 24.

prisoners and assist the poorer captives, and of this committee Lee was one. Liberated at the peace, he returned to New College, and was presented to the valuable living of Wootton, near Woodstock, where he built an exceedingly handsome parsonage, and ruled his people as a kindly despot, his memory lingering among them affectionately long after his death. Coming out of church one day, he found two disreputable vagabonds in the churchyard. "What are you doing here?" "Oh, sir, we are seeking the Lord." "Seeking the Lord, are you? Do you see those stocks? That is where the Lord will find you, if you stay here another minute." They did not stay. Insulted in his old age by a hulking ruffian, the terror of the village, he gave him a tremendous box on the ear; and the bully, who could easily have thrashed him, slunk off cowed. The degree examination at New College was a farce, and roused his never-failing indignation. Traditions still survive of his furious protests, and Warden Gauntlett's placid insensibility, at each repetition of the sham. It would seem, however, that he was moved by moral disgust rather than by intellectual ardour. Old William Risley, of Deddington, used to relate that he was sitting in Lee's rooms one day when an undergraduate came in with a puzzling equation and a request for help. "Turn over to the next page, sir." "I have done so, sir." "Then turn over to the next"—adding aside to Risley as the discomfited inquirer shut the door, "I hate your d——d clever fellows." He went once with Henry Williams, most cere-

MAGDALEN AND NEW COLLEGE 175

monious and correct of men, to call on Miss Horseman, the delightful old vestal earlier mentioned. She was out. "Who shall I say called, sir?" "Tell her," in a voice which sounded from the High to Canterbury gate, "Tell her it was the man she ought to have married!" He died a bachelor in 1841.

Miss Horseman's name suggests another well-known figure of the Thirties, old Dr. Nares, Professor of Modern History. As a handsome young Fellow of Merton, long before, he had acted in private theatricals at Blenheim, and eloped with Lady Charlotte Spencer Churchill. He was believed to be the author of an amusing book, "Thinks I to Myself," which lay on Miss Horseman's table, but it was also attributed to his grandfather, the Rev. Henry Coles. The old lady and the Professor were fast friends, and she used to repeat to me a piece of clever jargon which he once extemporised to test the power of some bragging memorist. The closing sentence dovetails into Foote's similar improvisation of the Piccalillies and the Great Panjandrum,[1] the confusion probably due to her; the earlier part was, I believe, quite new. I learned it from the old lady's lips, and have retained it unwritten all these years in the receptacle which held Count Smorltork's materials for his great work on England:—

"There was a shovel, and a shackfok, and a one-eyed pikestaff, went to rob a rich poor man of the head of a herring, the brains of a sprat, and a bushel of barley meal. So he got up in

---

[1] Appendix N.

176 REMINISCENCES OF OXFORD

the morning. 'Wife, we're robbed,' says he. 'You lie,' says she. 'Tis true,' says he; 'we must saddle the brown hen and bridle the black staff.' So off they rode till they came to a long wide short narrow lane, and there they met three horse-nails bleeding at both nostrils. So they sent for the Hickmaid of the Hall; she, being a rare stinter of blood, sent them word that Mrs. Jones Tittymouse Tattymouse was brought to bed of a mustard spoon and was very ill, and so she couldn't come. So they sent the boy to Mr. Macklin's, at the corner of St. Martin's Lane, for some plums to make an apple pudding with, but desired they mightn't be wrapped in brown paper, since the last tasted so of cabbage leaves they couldn't eat them. So the baker's boy came in to buy a penny loaf; there being none, they gave him a farthing candle to eat. Presently three bears came by, and one popped its head in, and said, 'What, bless me, no soap!' So the head fell off the block, and beat the powder out of the Lord Chancellor's wig; and he died, and she married the barber; and that's the way that Mrs. Atkins came to lose her apple dumpling."

Ex humili potens might be the motto of New College to-day; its last fifty-seven years exhibit a resurrection as surprising from as profound a depth as is figured in the second part of "Faust." In 1850 the College, with its magnificent equipment, large revenues, scholarly Warden, and distinguished past, had become a hive of drones; its residents few, its mode of life luxurious and expensive, its teaching bald and scanty. Now, in numbers and repute, in the Schools and on the river, New College ranks among the very highest Colleges. Transformation began with the Parliamentary Commission of 1854. It struck off antiquated chains, abolished the too close connection with Winchester, and the mischievous anachronism of founder's kin, increased the number and emoluments of the scholars. The younger men, growing each year in numbers and importance, and imbued with liberal ideas, carried successive reforms in spite of obstruction from their mediæval seniors. The Warden, Sewell, elected in 1860 on the death of Dr. Williams, was conservative by instinct and by habit, with the maxim "*quieta non movere*" ever on his lips. His distaste for the reform was patent, but his respect for the reformers who engineered it was unbounded; reconciled to the measures by the men, he brought caution and sagacity to their assistance. He had his reward, not only in their respect and gratitude, but in the happiness which his new position ministered to a very unusual temperament. "Business," a term incarnated more often than defined, was the breath of his nostrils: to write and answer letters in his beautiful copperplate hand, to sort and docket papers, chronicle collegiate ephemera, draw up reports, supervise and check accounts—all that men are wont to find tedious and remit to secretaries —formed his being's end and aim. If life-tasks such as these are not heroic in themselves, yet, discharged faithfully and well, they make possible the pageantry of life for others: and the destiny which selected him, an unambitious man, to rule an ambitious College, exalted his peculiar gifts, though abstractedly commonplace and ordinary, to become essential factors in a great creation.

And if his life was happy, so also his death was enviable. In expecting his approaching retirement, we all dreaded for him the disruption of his daily work, his exit from the dull back study in which he had laboured through two-and-forty years, from the College in which through four-and-seventy years he was said to have kept every term. He passed away in sleep, the sights and sounds which had made the enjoyment of his life present to him in his latest waking hours. "In such a death," says Cicero in the daintiest of his treatises, "in such a death there is neither pain nor bitterness; but as ripe fruit is lightly and without violence loosened from its branch, so the soul of such departs ungrieving from the body wherein its life's experience hath lain."

CHAPTER XI

ORIEL

"*Summi enim sunt homines tantum.*"
—QUINTILIAN.

Newman—His Character and Career—Had Arnold been at Oxford in his Time!—Vain Speculations—Newman's Life as a Catholic—Hawkins—Charles Marriott—Eden—The Efficacy of the Bible—George Anthony Denison—Tom Hughes—A "Christian Chartist"—His Radicalism—"Tom Brown"—Oxford in Fiction—Charles Neate and John Bright—Neate, Disraeli, and the Angels.

A HUNDRED yards from Miss Horseman's door stands Oriel gateway. What a procession of phantoms meets the inward eye as I approach it! White-haired Provost Hawkins, Newman, Frederick Rogers, Charles Marriott, Eden, Denison, "Donkey" Litton, Low Church leader, inconspicuous in spite of his Double First, of his recognised ability and his two powerful volumes on "Dogmatic Theology," Charles Neate, the only layman of the group, mounting his horse to join the Berkshire hounds. I was living at Iffley during Newman's golden time; knew his mother in her pretty home at Rosebank, turned afterwards into a den of disorderly pupils by poor James Rumsey. I remember the rising of Littlemore church, first among the new Gothic edifices which the "Movement" revived in England; met Newman almost daily striding along the Oxford Road, with large head, prominent nose, tortoiseshell spectacles, emaciated but ruddy face, spare figure whose leanness was exaggerated by the close-fitting tail-coat then worn. The road ceased to know him after a time; he had resigned St. Mary's, and was monachising with a few devotees in his barn-like Littlemore retreat; then, in 1845, Oxford lost him finally—

> " Interque mærentes amicos
> Egregius properabat exul ;"

to the anguish of his disciples left alone, who had made him their pattern to live and to die; to the relief of many more, who thought that Humanism and Science might reassert themselves as subject matter of education against the polemic which had for fifteen years forced Oxford back into the barren word-war of the seventeenth century. By no means a recluse like Pusey, but gregarious, hospitable, seminarising, he was always surrounded by disciples, in his rooms, in Oriel Common Room, in his Littlemore *cœnobitium*. But he would only associate with like-minded men; lived, says, Isaac Williams, with persons younger than himself, who would reflect his own opinions; shrank from healthy friction with avowedly opposed beliefs, broke off relations with his rationalist brother Francis, refused to see Manning, who came out to call on him at Littlemore, in consequence of a sermon he had preached upon the Gunpowder Plot. And so he was not, and is not, in any sense a mystery. While the cryptic element in Pusey's character is deepened by the sacrilegious half-revelations of his biographers, Newman's own "Apologia" and the numerous tributes of his friends have shed a flood of fierce light upon his character. If Mozley's notices of the "Movement" are inaccurate and flippant, Pattison's vindictive, Palmer's tedious, Williams's jejune, Denison's irrelevant, we yet learn something of him from them all; while the entire moral and intellectual epiphanies both of the "Movement" and the man are portrayed severally by Church and Ward.

Surveying him calmly by the light of these, now that his great name and his enthralling presence have become a memory, reading too the expositions of himself which flowed so rapidly from his pen during ten momentous years, we seem to conceive the secret at once of his ascendancy and his shipwreck. It was unfortunate for himself and others that he should have reigned without a rival; his only opponents on the spot, Faussett, Golightly, and the rest, men *impares congressi*. The magic of his personality, the rhetorical sweetness of his sermons—he used to say that he read through Mansfield Park every year, in order to perfect and preserve his style—their dialectic vigour, championship of implicit faith as against evidential reasoning, contagious radiance of intense conviction, far more than the compelling suasion of his arguments and theories, drew all men after him. Had there been in Oxford at the time a commanding representative of liberal theology, with corresponding personal attractiveness, seducing piety, intellectual equipment, argumentative ability and promptitude; had, for instance, Arnold been resident through those years at Oriel, not at Rugby, two camps instead of one would have been formed, Delphi would have been answered by Dodona; Lake would not have been overpowered, Stanley shaken, less by the convincing proofs than by the unconfronted monocracy of the magnificent system which enveloped them; free play would have been proffered to the many minds which came regretfully to avow in later life that Newman exercised a disturbing, not a quickening, influence on their mental and religious growth. Nay, who can tell what consequences might not have issued from the immediate and continued contact of the two great gladiators themselves; how many divergences might have been reconciled by the mutual respect and the recognition of fundamental community which close collision must have produced on two so noble natures, the hurricane of opposing passion hushed by the still small voice of sympathy which vibrates between all good men. Both had their disabilities; both lacked prescience, viewing the present with a short-sighted intensity which could not look ahead: if Arnold's constitutional deficiency was unguardedness and exaggeration, Newman's was impatience and despair. We see his limitations clearly now; of temper, knowledge, mental discipline. We see haste to be despondent in the hero of his valedictory novel, more nakedly in his letters to his sister, until criticism is disarmed by their agony as the crisis becomes inevitable. That his secular knowledge

JOHN HENRY NEWMAN

From a pen-and-ink drawing, 1841

Photographed from the Print by Mrs. Frieda Girdlestone

was limited all his reviews and essays show; ignorant of German as we know him to have been, the historic development of religious reason with its underlying unity of thought lay outside the narrow philosophical basis on which were reared his Anglican conclusions; while Arnold was just the man, *invicem præbens crura sagittis*, to elucidate, correct, counterbalance, these flaws in his temperament and system. And if will governed and narrowed his intellect, so did impatience dominate his piety and self-discipline. Austere in his ideal of Christian life as detached, ascetic, painful, he saw true discipleship only in organised and formal self-surrender, such as he found in the "regulars" of the Roman Church, but missed in English Protestantism. A conviction of his own infallibility underlies his whole mental current; at every succeeding stage *securus judicat*, non-acceptance of his views is censurable in individual opponents, theologically disqualifying to their collective "note of Catholicity." How far years might aid his aspiration, his dreams pass into realities, his tests of Churchmanship find fulfilment in Anglican practice, he would not wait to see. For Teutonic slowness of apprehension he made no allowance, confused the dominant instinct of startled contemporaries with the mature resultant of education and of time. "Had he lived to-day," said to me his old friend Hinds Howell, who passed away but now, "had he lived to-day, he would not have deserted his Church." Had Heads and Bishops tolerated "Tract 90" then, he might have died a Bishop or a Head; but, as Matthew Arnold sang of Clough, "he could not wait their passing."

These are matters of speculation; but it is curious to note how, as a fact, from the moment of his secession his commanding influence ceased. The movement to which he had given birth continued as we know, goes on to-day as a degenerated mechanical survival; that it should have outlived its unique leader is the strongest tribute to his creative force. On the Monday morning when he left Manuel Johnson's house for Oscott, *he* died to his old associates, to the University, to the public. He died to his old associates: Richmond's water-colour portrait of him leant against Pusey's bookshelves; his marble bust, covered with a veil—whether from dust or from reminiscences I never dared to ask—stood in Keble's study; but the three who had been as one in spiritual kinship met only, after many years, to find in an evening of restrained and painful converse that the topics uppermost in the minds of all were topics all must avoid, walking in the house of God as adversaries, not as friends. He died to the University: intellectual and educational changes pursued one another like surging waves in Oxford; but the man who for fifteen years had to all Europe personated Oxford stood aloof from all, unconsulted, uninterposing, because he had fallen into the pit himself had digged, in narrowing the University from its great national, nay worldwide, function to the limits of a divinity school, so that, an alien in this one particular, he became an alien in all. And as from his brethren and from his University, so from the public he stood separate. The days of a Richelieu or an Alberoni are for ever past; but that a Roman Cardinal may popularise and exalt his Church while he endears himself by doing battle in English public life, as a partisan of moral reform, a pleader for social righteousness, a champion of the oppressed and poor against individual and class rapacity, was shown in a series of splendid object lessons by his fellow prelate, a man less great, less single-minded, incomparably less sincere, but more constitutionally altruistic, more observant of the outer world in which he lived. Once only in the forty years did Newman win an audience ranging beyond controversialists and divines, in his famous "Apologia," which will go down, with Blanco White's "Autobiography," Froude's "Nemesis of Faith," and the "Phases of Faith" of his own brother Francis, as graphic self-dissections by men at once acutely and intensely organised of their innermost mental struggles amid distracting spiritual perplexities.

To what task, then, in all these years did Newman's powerful and once restless intellect address itself? No longer to proselytism, to Biblical criticism, to ecclesiastical reform; he gave to old Anglican friends who sought him out, he gave to Denison in 1879, as to Stanley in 1864, the impression of a tragic sadness, of a "wasted life," of fearfulness in the presence of advancing religious thought and speculation, of faded ability to handle questions with which formerly he was the first to grapple, of the piteously recurring cry when looking beyond the bars of his Oratory cage, "O, my mother! Why dost thou leave me all day idle in the market place?"[1] He bent himself, as far as we can see, to the subjective task of dealing with his own soul, working out harmony in his inner nature, gaining certainty as to his relation towards the Unseen, security as to his future acceptance in the indistinct domain which held dead Gerontius expectant on his bed of sorrow. He has long since solved the riddle. Yet, let us admit that his was not the highest aim. The salvation of our own souls, the abstraction of our own natures, is at best a Buddha view of life and of eternity: the consumption of self in active work for others, the disregard of self mounting into Apostolic readiness to be "accursed for our brethren's sake," is the lesson of the life of Christ. Deep respect is due to the man who flung away friends, position, influence, in loyalty to the claim of conscience; deep sympathy with saintliness is an ingredient in all highly strung spiritual natures; but our age more than any calls for a sword rather than a prayer-carpet, a knight-errant rather than an ascetic; a Shaftesbury, a Damien, a Dolling, rather than a Simeon Stylites battering the gates of heaven, however high his pillar, however rapt his insight, however vast his prospect.

Oriel reached its highest eminence under Provosts Eveleigh and Copleston; its decline began with Hawkins. In 1831 he dismissed his three great tutors, Newman, Robert Wilberforce, Froude

---

[1] "Life of Dean Stanley," ii. 342.

whose conception of their duty to undergraduates threatened to establish brothers near the throne. Mark Pattison, an Oriel undergraduate at the time, and Dean Lake, surveying his own past university life, agreed in attributing to Hawkins the dethronement of Oriel from its supremacy among Oxford Colleges. Yet he was no mere fussy despot: Newman in his "Apologia" has told us how much he owed to him: "He taught me to weigh my words and be cautious in my statements; he led me to that mode of limiting and clearing my sense in discussion and controversy which to my surprise has since been considered to savour of the polemic of Rome." That he should have been preferred above Keble for the Headship testifies his extraordinary reputation in the College. He piqued himself on his attitude towards the undergraduates; took pains to know them individually, interviewed each freshman privately before admitting him to the Communion, would mitigate in Collections the wrath expressed against some weak brother by his tutor. One offence he could not overlook; you might hope for leniency in minor peccadilloes, but you must not smell of smoke. I fear that the youthful temperament is more alive to eccentricities than to kindness; the anecdotes which reach me from old Orielites of long ago illustrate chiefly the comic side of Hawkins' rule. He used to give one finger to a Commoner, the whole hand to a Tuft; and was somewhat embarrassed when a certain man went down at the end of Term as Mr. —— and returned as Lord —— of ——. An Oriel undergraduate took to preaching in St. Ebbe's slums.

Hawkins angrily inhibited him. "But, sir, if the Lord, who commanded me to preach, came suddenly to judgment *now*, what should I do?" "I," said Hawkins, "will take the whole responsibility of that upon myself." A man begged leave to absent himself in order to bury his uncle. "You may go," was the reluctant permission, "but I wish it had been a nearer relation." In his high and dry churchmanship he was impartially bitter. Of the Newmania he always spoke in his exegetical sermons as "the late unhappy movement." When Irving's son obtained a First Class as Scholar of Balliol, and wished to stand for an Oriel Fellowship, the Provost refused to receive his name unless he would formally recant his father's opinions. When Jowett was bitten by a Balliol dog, and the quadruped was expelled from the College, the joke went round the University that Hawkins had received and tenderly entertained it. He was monarch of the old Hebdomadal Board, and was amazed when Lake, as Senior Proctor, had the temerity to oppose him. I remember his declaiming once in Congregation on the "very arduous duties of a College Head." Thorold Rogers got up and declared that while he did not exactly know what the Provost's duties were, he would be happy to discharge them for half the Provost's salary. Said Moral Philosophy Wilson, who was sitting by me: "It is the right thing to say, but it wanted a brigand to say it." His mind lacked largeness: a master of detail he was deficient in grasp, and lived amongst minutiæ till his accuracy became pettiness, his conscientiousness scrupulosity, his over exactness destructive of sentiment and warmth. His character was summarised by Charles Neate:

> "His est Prepositus,
> Cunctis oppositus;
> Qui magna gerit,
> Et tempus terit,
> Dum parva quærit.
> Vir reverendus—
> Sed—diligendus."

Of the *minora sidera* which revolved round Newman, Charles Marriott, φιλαίτατος 'Ωρειήλων, was the most notable. Saving every penny for charitable uses, he dressed like a beggar, with a veil over his weak eyes in summer and a dark green shade in winter, draped in a cloak made of two old M.A. gowns unequally yoked together. He often took me for walks, premising always that he had no small talk, and that I must not be offended if he were silent; but it was easy to draw him out, and he would discourse with a kind of dry enthusiasm on some of his philanthropic schemes— economic, social, educational. He contributed several hundred pounds to a co-operative enterprise, called the "Universal Purveyor." The project was commercially sound, but engineered by a sleek French scoundrel, who went off with all poor Marriott's money. I met this adventurer once in his rooms at breakfast; the beast gave his host at parting what he called a "Christian kiss" on either cheek. He turned out to be a spy in the pay of Louis Napoleon. I saw Marriott in his last illness, visiting him at Bonchurch, with R. F. Wilson, Keble's curate at Amp field, Newman's friend and correspondent. As I entered his room he eagerly greeted me, and asked me to tell him the cube root of 1. His brother John hushed him with a "dear Charles," and he became silent, with that queer tightening of the jaw which some of us remember well. But his half-paralysed brain was still active and his sense of fun acute. A new lodging house, ugly, comfortless, uninviting, had been built close by; the owner asked John Marriott what he should call it. Charles suggested the *Redan*—it was the time of our repulse before Sebastopol — " because it would never be taken."

Marriott inherited Newman's rooms, Eden succeeded to his parish. Burgon says of Eden that he strained his friends' affection by conceit and arrogance, meaning probably that he now and then rapped Burgon's knuckles, a feat which might cover a multitude of sins. To my recollection he was supremely agreeable in society. A dinner-party would be assembled in some stiff Head's or Professor's house, no convivial water for the feet or ointment for the head of entering guests, Dons and Donnas dull and silent in the drawing-room like Wordsworth's party in a parlour; when Eden was announced. In he would dart, his droll hare-lipped face radiant with reaction from a hard morning's work and with generous prandial expectancy; would snatch a book from the table or an ornament from the shelf, as text for a vagrant cheery disquisition taking in all the solemn mutes in turn, till a general thaw set in, and we went down to a successful dinner. His manner in church was quaint; the matter of his sermons terse and scholarlike, but the manuscript held close to the candle and read without pretence of oratory, the voice coming and going in fitful gusts now *forte* now *piano*. He could not stand coughers: "if worshippers cannot restrain their coughs, they would better go out," he used to say in eager, snapping tones. He had a great horror, too, of casual lookers-in, migrants, who *taste* successive churches in turn; "Rovers never grow" was his frequent dictum. He had a theory that the letter of the Bible carried sacramental efficacy, that merely to read it to a worldling or a reprobate would drive out devils and sow germinating seeds. He tried it once on poor old Miss Horseman, who was in his parish and supposed to be near her end. She told me that he walked into her drawing-room, said no word, took down and opened her big Bible, read it to her for half-an-hour, and again without farewell departed. He, of course, succeeded only in alarming and disturbing her; to a chapter of the Bible she had no objection, but her formal old-fashioned breeding was outraged by his unceremonious aggression. When he left St. Mary's for the College living of Aberford, a large congregation came to hear his farewell sermon, prepared for an affecting and *larmoyant* valediction. He preached on some ordinary topic; then shut up his sermon case with a slap: "The volume—of the book—of my ministry among you —is closed. It is sealed up—and will be opened at the Judgment Day."

Of George Anthony Denison—picturesque and

exasperating, eccentric and impracticable, stormy petrel in every row, at Oxford as at Eton, during sixty years; restlessly pugnacious as a divine, disappointingly irrelevant as a writer; like Sydney Smith in his estimate of the Church as a social bulwark, like Newman in his assumption of her historic and spiritual claims—I have a word or two to say. He was the best of Hawkins' Tutors; but Mark Pattison, who attended his lectures, speaks of him as deficient in illuminative and stimulating force, gathering all his erudition from the printed notes to the text-book read. And as in scholarship so in theology he was far below the giants of the "Movement"; he had neither Newman's fascination of moral earnestness and literary style, nor Liddon's later doctrinal enthusiasm, nor Pusey's fathomless abyss of learning; he had not even Henry of Exeter's versatile facility in getting up a case and working it with a forensic adroitness which only the initiated could expose. His force was purely gladiatorial, his motive power personal; the side *he* had adopted, the position *he* had taken up, became in his eyes sacramental, opposition to it criminal and blasphemous. When, in 1863, Pusey proposed a compromise to end the Jowett strife, Denison gathered the country clergy in defiance of his old chief, ascending the steps of the semicircle in the Theatre in order to expound to us in Latin the causes "*quia discedo ab amicis meis.*" I remember the roar of displeasure which cut him short, the scream of "*Procacissimi pueri*" with which he descended, the curious subsequent mistake, when Chambers, the Proctor, announced the result of the voting by "*Majori parti placet*"; then, blushing and confused, gave way to his fellow Proctor, Kitchin, who dashed the exultation of Jowett's friends by the amended proclamation, "*Majori parti non placet.*" His sermons were minaciously dogmatic, alienating to large-minded and thoughtful men, grateful only to the prepossession which prefers petulant insistence to sweet reasonableness in argument and appeal. He ruled his clergy in Somersetshire imperiously; I always felt sorry for his Bishop. The only man among them who could stand up to him was Clark, the Vicar of Taunton, a man of temperament much akin to his Archdeacon's, but apt to disregard the *convenances* of gentle breeding which in all his outbreaks governed Denison. Agreeable in society he always was; it was Stanley's delight to place him at the Deanery table among men whom he had just been traducing in the Jerusalem Chamber, and who found their malignant censor transformed into a cheery equal, friendly, anecdotic, convivial. "There are men," he would say to you, as, after vilipending you all the morning, he asked you to take wine with him at luncheon, "there are men whose persons I love and whose opinions I abhor, and there are men whose opinions I honour and whose selves I hate." And this quality redeemed him; without it he would have been a mere firebrand—to some he seemed so all along; but those who saw him in his softer hour—and many such remain—those especially who watched him presiding over his parish water storage and harvest home festivities, still send from the railway windows as they shoot past Brent Knoll a benediction, half humorous, half affectionate; echo regretfully the *Tanden requiescit* of Lord Lyttelton's burlesque epitaph.[1] "Requiescat," they will add, "but not *in pace;* peace would destroy his paradise!"

Associated ever in my mind with Denison, not by similitude, but by graphic contrast, is his junior at Oriel by some fourteen years, Tom Hughes. He came up in 1842; men knew him as an athletic, pleasant fellow, pulling always in fours and eights, eclipsed somewhat by his then more notable brother George. Between George Hughes and Denison there were many points of resemblance, but Tom was everything that Denison was not. Denison was a Don, Tom was a Bohemian; Denison a sacerdotalist in white cravat and Master's hood, Hughes a humanist in flannel shirt and shooting jacket. Denison was an incarnation of lost causes, Hughes the pilot of a beneficent future. Denison rode a painted rocking-horse to tilt with theological windmills, Tom rushed to spike the guns of social selfishness, like his own East in the trenches of the Sutlej forts. The historian of the century, if he recalls Denison at all, will speak of him as the high-bred clerical aristocrat, relic of a class extinct. He will extol Hughes as pioneer of a new and ardent realism, shaping itself to-day under fresh conditions, yet essentially accordant with his creed; as labouring to alleviate the discontent of the many by the self-sacrifice of the few, to extinguish class antagonism and bridge social chasm, to replace an oligarchy of prescriptive privilege, rank, and wealth, by a

[1] Appendix O.

nobler timocracy of eminence in intellectual acquirement and in evangelical generosity of aim. Even as an undergraduate Hughes was a "Christian Chartist," in full sympathy with the passionate discontent which English proletarian misery well justified, yet holding that the party of upheaval must be led by men of property and social rank, if civil war were to be averted by peaceful civic reconstruction. His Radicalism, both at Oxford and elsewhere, was ludicrously composite; Colonel Newcome's electoral programme is hardly a travesty of Hughes: "He was for having every man to vote, every poor man to labour short time and get high wages, every poor curate to be paid double or treble, every bishop to be docked of his salary and dismissed from the House of Lords; but he was a staunch admirer of that assembly and a supporter of the rights of the Crown." And this political confusedness was his strength as a social iconoclast. The unwashed rallied round a gentleman who was for abolishing the very rich and very poor, round a Christian who read Socialism into every page of the New Testament; the aristocracy gave ear of necessity to the well-dressed, well-bred school and University man, who from their own point of view and in their own interest preached reform as alternative to revolution. So for a time the school of Maurice, Kingsley, Hughes, shaped the sentiment and coloured the literature of the country; until, when from the Chartism of the Forties was by degrees evolved the Collectivism of the Eighties, older Radicals shrank back alarmed before the Demos which they had nursed complacently in its childhood.

Of his books, two alone probably will live. The "Scouring of the White Horse," racy but local, interests those only who are familiar with that pleasant, sleepy, peaceful Berkshire vale; his "Memoirs of a Brother" leaves, unintentionally and quite incorrectly, the impression that the muscular representative of the Uffington Hugheses must have been an oppressively pragmatical hero; but theme and treatment combine to make the two "Tom Browns" immortal. I know no more cogent tribute to Arnold's greatness than that Rugby alone of all public schools should have earned world-wide celebrity by an unrivalled biography and an unrivalled epic, both stamped in every page with his pre-inspiring impulse, both lit from the torch of his Idæan fire. Of Rugby, though not of Arnold, Hughes was a better interpreter than Stanley. Dean Lake used to say that Stanley never was a boy; he left school as he entered it, something between girl and man. Hughes was *puerilissimus*, boy in virtues and in foibles; and as, on the one hand, Stanley could not delineate the rough-and-tumble life which moulds nine-tenths of public school boys, could never have appreciated or described the football match, or the fight with Slogger Williams, so, on the other hand, the tribute which Hughes pays to Arnold attests that wonderful schoolmaster's electric influence on unreceptive ordinary natures such as Brown's and East's, no less than on the exceptional temperaments of a Vaughan, a Clough, a Stanley. Of course, in both books Tom is Hughes himself; Arthur, according to Rugby tradition, was a boy named Orlebar; the "young master" was Cotton; East in the one book, Hardy in the other, are probably mere types. And, though continuations are usually disappointing, I should place "Tom Brown at Oxford" not one whit behind its predecessor. Recalling the higher fictions which deal with undergraduate life, "Reginald Dalton," "Vincent Eden," "Peter Priggins," "Loss and Gain," "Verdant Green," the Cambridge chapter in "Alton Locke," the Boniface chapter in "Pendennis," I rank "Tom Brown" before them all for the vigour and the completeness of its portrayal. Every phase of College life as it exuberated seventy years ago— fast and slow, tuft and Bible clerk, reading man and lounger; profligacy and debt, summer term and Commemoration, boat races, wines, University sermons,—passes easily in review, without Kingsley's hysteria, without Newman's priggishness, without Hewlett's vulgarity, without Lockhart's stiltedness, without Cuthbert Bede's burlesque. The New Zealander of A.D. 4000, visiting the tangled morasses of the Upper Thames which once were Oxford, the crumbling chaos of rotting carriages and twisted rails which once was Rugby, will annotate his monumental work on "Ancient England" with Tom Brown's pictures of their ruined sites and Tom Brown's chronicles of their academic humour. They seem to me somehow memorials of a life fuller, more varied, more *youthful*, than is proved to-day by our golden or our gilded juvenility. Stagecoaches, postchaises, peashooters meant more fun than

198 REMINISCENCES OF OXFORD

first-class carriages and railway novels; boys were "fellows" then, now, save the mark! they are "men"; undergraduates who crowded formerly the coffee rooms of the Old and New Hummums, Tavistock, Bedford, melt to-day into a mammoth hotel, gravitate after play and supper to music-halls and casinos, instead of applauding Herr von Joel or shaking hands with Paddy Green at Evans'. I am a fogey, to be sure, and out of date; but, remembering the days when I rode from Southam to Rugby on the "Pig and Whistle," or was dropped at the Mitre by Jack Adams from the box of the Royal Defiance, the days when Cowley Marsh was a rush-grown common, and from Magdalen bridge to Iffley there was not a single roadside house, I feel for those ancient ways and vanished hours what our present youngsters will mayhap feel for their own some ten or twelve lustres hence, and I bless the hand that has preserved the verdure of their antiquity with a pen whose vigour and a heart whose freshness bid antiquity defiance.

I have travelled far from Oriel; I return to find Charles Neate on horseback at the Corpus corner, his face set towards the meet at Brasenose Wood. He began life as a barrister, but was disbarred for horsewhipping—(so says one tradition; for kicking, says another), Bethell, known later as Lord Westbury, then as afterwards the tyrant of the profession, who had insulted him in court. He was cosmopolitan, at home in Paris, a member of London clubs, a mighty hunter. He stood for Oxford City in the Fifties as a Radical, and was elected, but unseated for bribery, negotiated I was told, by one of his committee, and without his knowledge. While in the House he became intimate with John Bright. I have heard him describe their first accost. The smoking-room was crowded; Bright sat upon one chair, and leaned his arm across the back of another. Neate asked him if he required two seats. "Yes, I do; but I'll get you another"—which he did. Neate gave his name, and a friendship soon sprang up. He brought Bright down to Oxford; they came together to a Congregation, where we were voting on some election. The papers, having been counted by the Proctors and the result announced, were burned on a brazier in the room, a custom long since extinct; Bright expressing his amused delight—it was before the Ballot—to find the secret vote enforced in the University of Oxford. Neate was in the Theatre when Dizzy made his famous "angel" speech, at a meeting of the Diocesan Association, S. Oxon in the chair. "What is the question now placed before society with a glib assurance the most astounding? The question is this—Is man an ape or an angel? My lord, I am on the side of the angels." Neate, in a delicious set of Sapphics,[1] inclined rather to range the great posture master on the other side:

> "*Angelo* quis te similem putaret
> Esse, vel divis atavis creatum,
> Cum tuas plane referat dolosas
> *Simius* artes?"

---

[1] Appendix P.

CHAPTER XII

BALLIOL

*"There is a history in all men's lives
Figuring the nature of the times deceased;
The which observed, a man may prophesy,
With a near aim, of the main chance of things
As yet not come to life, which in their seeds
And weak beginnings lie intreasured."*
—SHAKESPEARE.

Two Masters of Balliol—Jenkyns and Jowett—The One who came between—The Succession to Scott—Temple and Jowett—Henry Wall—Dean Lake—"The Serpent"—Lake on Arnold—Jowett and Dr. Johnson—*Obiter Dicta*—A Conversation—Jowett's unfamiliarity with Natural Science—Temple—T. H. Green.

FOR elderly men of to-day the term "Master of Balliol" conjures up two visions. They think of Jenkyns in the Thirties and Forties, of Jowett in the Seventies and Eighties; they do *not* think of Scott, who came between. Overlaid, enveloped, eclipsed by the two luminaries who "went behind him and before," he somehow drops out of sight; his reign is an intervention, and is remembered only with an effort. His was a career of early promise unusual, but unfulfilled. He came from Shrewsbury to Oxford as the best of Butler's pupils, won the Craven and Ireland and the Latin Essay, was First Class man and Fellow of Balliol. His notes to the "Uniomachia" and his Homerics on the Chancellorship showed rare aptness and resource in the exceptional felicities of Greek and Latin scholarship. In 1834, the year after his degree, Talboys, the leading Oxford bookseller, proposed to him to undertake the translation of Passow's German-Greek Lexicon; he consented on condition that with him Liddell might be associated. The Lexicon appeared in 1843; the first edition is now a curious rarity; when shortly before his death Liddell wished to place it in the Christchurch Library, it was long before he could obtain a copy. Their several shares in it cannot be known: Westminster naturally placed Scott below Liddell in its construction. The well-known lines,

> "Two men wrote a Lexicon, Liddell and Scott;
> One half was clever, one half was not.
> Give me the answer, boys, quick, to this riddle,
> Which was by Scott, and which was by Liddell?"

were an epigram sent up by a boy at the "trials" for the Maunday Thursday money, on the thesis "*Scribimus indocti doctique.*" The Rev. W. G. Armitstead, Vicar of Goosetree, writes to me that he was present in school as a boy when the lines were composed, and according to custom were read aloud by Liddell, who complimented their author with the full four-coin meed of fourpenny, threepenny, twopenny, penny silver pieces, awarded to the best composition. A more decided view of the two partners' relative claims emanated from Balliol, in a not very elegant triplet:

> "Part of it's good, and part of it's rot:
> The part that is good was written by Scott:
> By Liddell was written the part that is not."

Scott retired to a College living; and the later editions, changing a tentative into a masterpiece, owed most of their excellence to Liddell, whose desire for its linguistic revision by Max Müller was foiled by Scott's apathy or opposition. In 1854 the old Master died, the College was divided as to his successor. The senior Fellows wished for Temple, an equal number of the juniors wished for Jowett; James Riddell wanted Scott, but would vote for Jowett rather than for Temple. So at the last moment Temple's supporters threw him over for Scott, securing Riddell's vote. For ten years he was an obstructive, wielding his numerical ascendancy to crush all Jowett's schemes of reform. "Your head," said Jowett to a Fellow of another College, "seems to be an astute person, who works by winning confidence; here we have a bare struggle for power"; and when, in 1865, successive elections to Fellowships had given Jowett a majority, Scott's influence in the College waned. Nor was he effective beyond the walls of Balliol. Soon after his appointment he preached a magnificent University sermon on Dives and Lazarus, with application of the "five brethren" episode to the home ties, feelings, scruples, tenderness of undergraduates. When he next occupied the pulpit, St. Mary's was filled from entrance door to organ screen; but the sermon was absolutely dull —on Hezekiah's song—nor did he ever again command an audience; in his Headship as in his earlier career he left, as some one says, a great future behind him. In 1870 Gladstone, at Lowe's entreaty, appointed him to the Deanery of

Rochester in order to make room for Jowett, and he descended into decanal quietude.

Scott's firmest supporter in College had been Henry Wall, Lecturer and Bursar: he figures in the "Grand Logic Sweepstakes" as Barbadoes, having been born in that island. It was he who led the opposition to Max Müller for the "half-a-brick" reason that he was a foreigner. His intellect was clear, logical, penetrating; his temper somewhat arrogant. His lectures, which as Prælector of Logic he delivered publicly in Balliol Hall to all who chose to bring the statutory guinea, were cosmic in their reduction and formularisation of the Aldrich-Aristotle chaos. Keen-eyed, sharp-nosed, vehement in manner and gesture, he fired off questions as he went along at this or that student who caught his eye, with joyous acceptance of a neat response, scornful pounce on a dull or inattentive answerer. He was an undesirable dinner guest, starting questions which he seemed to have prepared beforehand for the pleasure of showing off his dexterity in word fence, rousing temper, and spoiling conversational amenities. He was a great dancer: the waltz of those days was a serious department of life, "to be wooed with incessant thought and patient renunciation of small desires." Readers of "Pelham"—does any one read "Pelham" now?—will remember how Lady Charlotte impressed upon her fashionable son the moral duty of daily practice, with a chair if no partner could be obtained; and to see Wall's thin legs twinkle in the mazy was a memorable experience. He was exceedingly hospitable; giving dances, sometimes on a large scale in Wyatt's Rooms, oftener at his snug little house in New Inn Hall Lane, to the music of old Grimmett's harp and fiddle. With him lived a stout, florid sister, dressed in many-coloured garments, a niece whom pupils knew as "Bet," and a Pomeranian "Fop" who suffered many things when his master's back was turned. He was great in charades, personating now a Radical mob orator, now an ancient crone, now a shy, clumsy, gaping freshman. When well on in years he made a January and May marriage; the bachelor home was recast; poor Bet had died, Fop had borne his mistress company to that equal sky, the jovial sister subsided into small lodgings over a baker's shop in Holywell: *miscentur Mœnia luctu*.

Senior to Scott and Wall was the redoubtable Francis Newman, whose "Phases of Faith" will probably preserve his name. He gained a Double First in 1826, being the first man who ever offered in the Schools the Higher Mathematics analytically treated. Cooke, afterwards Sedleian Reader, pronounced that they could not, according to the Statute, pass beyond the Geometry of Newton; but Walker, Experimental Philosophy Professor, who probably of the three examiners alone knew the subject, persuaded his colleagues to let him examine Newman in the work he offered; and the candidate's answers were so brilliant, that the examiners, not content with awarding his First, presented him with finely bound copies of La Place and La Grange. He once or twice stayed with me at Taunton, sending word beforehand that he was a vegetarian, but eating copiously of fish and eggs. In company he did not so much converse as emit pilulous dogmas from his thin lips in a prim, didactic, authoritative tone;—on Ghosts and Fairy Legends as appropriate to children's minds, on the Teutonic view of the Devil with its humorous tinge, on Almsgiving in the streets, on Horne Tooke and Cobbett, on the position of women in Society, on phonetic spelling, on the *Saturday Review*. I remember too his delivering a fluent, venomous Philippic against Physical Science, in which he had observed me to be deeply interested. He was a slave to total abstinence, to anti-vaccination, to every kind of fad. He would stalk the streets with me, silent and absorbed, in a Tyrolese hat, and a short cloak with long tassels, winning from the street-boys rather formidable attentions:

"Statua taciturnius exit
Plerumque, et risu populum quatit."

Prominent in College work and discipline, and dying at a great age only a few years ago, was Dean Lake. I saw him first in 1842, when Clough, with whom I was reading at the time, took me to breakfast in his rooms. They looked into the quad; and as we stood at the window after breakfast he pointed out a black-haired, smooth-cheeked, ruddy undergraduate, and said, "Notice that man; he will be our Double First this year." It was Temple; and I went with Clough into the Schools to hear his *Viva Voce*. Lake was kind to me after that; one day took me for a walk. We encountered his doctor in Broad Street, and they stopped to talk.

He was looking wretchedly ill, red-nosed, pale, and thin, admitted in answer to questions that he had fasted during Lent; and I listened unnoticed to the wise earnestness with which the doctor, a man greatly respected and beloved, urged upon him the duty of caring for his body as the condition of all useful work. As a fact, the phase of feeling which took shape with him in bodily maceration was a transient one; he had been bitten by the Newmania, but he soon, like Goldsmith's man of Islington, recovered of the bite. He was not liked either as Tutor or as Proctor. His manner was cold, sarcastic, sneering; and a certain slyness earned him the nickname of "Serpent," applied originally at Rugby in reference to his sinuous shuffling walk, and retained by Balliol undergraduates as characterising his methods of College discipline.

It is no less significant of the deviating intellectual vacillations, which in spite of his great abilities disqualified him for leadership, and go far to explain, what has been often cited as unintelligible, his failure to attain conspicuous and commanding eminence. When, in 1849, young Lancaster of Balliol, for playfully fastening up and painting a Tutor's oak, was summoned before a Common Room meeting to receive sentence, the scene was thus rendered by a forgotten wit:—

Incipit "Jinks."

And first out spake "the Master": "The young man must go down,
And when a twelvemonth has elapsed he may resume his gown."

Serpens sequitur.

And the Serpent's brow was calm, and the Serpent's voice was low;
"I'm sorry, Mr. Lancaster, but really you must go.
The fact has come so clearly before the Tutor's knowledge,
And if we once pass over this, what rules can bind the College?"

Lancaster respondet.

Then out spake Harry Lancaster, that man of iron pate:
"I know, ye Dons, I must have gone a mucker soon or late;
But this I say, and swear it too, without or cheek or funk,
The Tutor may have been screwed up, I'm ——— if *I* was drunk."
He left to Mrs. Goddard the packing of his togs,
He paid no ticks, with chums exchanged no farewell dialogues;
But in a fury flinging down
His academic cap and gown,
And striding madly through the town,
Rushed, headlong, to the dogs!

Lake bore, for strictly Balliol consumption, another playful *sobriquet*, an obvious degradation of his name. Walking one day with John Conington, he said, "Do you know, Conington, that the men call you the Sick Vulture?" Conington turned on him his blank, pallid moon-face, and said, "Do you know, Lake, that the men call you Puddle?" There is of the retort yet another rendering, which I cannot bring myself to write. In 1858 he took the College living of Huntspill, then a very valuable incumbency, but a secluded, unhealthy, stagnant village in the Bristol Channel marshes. He was not the man to spend there much of his time: he kept a capable curate, a muscular Christian he half admiringly, half contemptuously, called him; and lived mostly in

London, enjoying club life at the Athenæum, and labouring for a long time on the Duke of Newcastle's Education Commission. I remember standing with him at the Highbridge Station, when one of his principal farmers came up and said, "We don't see much of you at Huntspill, Mr. Lake." "You may depend upon it," said the faithful herdman, "that you won't see more of me than I can help." He was one of the most active members of the Commission, supporting the large recommendations which, novel and startling at the time, were all eventually embodied in Mr. Forster's Act. He told me that the secretary, Fitzjames Stephen, a man in the habit of riding rough-shod over his fellows, tried to dominate and bully the Commissioners. They deputed to Lake the task of extinguishing him, and in rebuke to some instance of unwarrantable interference he went across to the secretary and explained to him with serpentine grace that he was intruding on their prerogative and must confine himself to his proper function. The hint was taken perforce; but one of the reporters said afterwards to Lake, "The expression of Mr. Stephen's countenance when you spoke to him, sir, was truly diabolical." I saw a good deal of him during his visits to Huntspill. He attended educational meetings in which I was interested, an animated, nay violent speaker: arms and coat-tails flew about while he strode hither and thither: for his after-dinner orations we used to clear out of his way the wineglasses and other unstable appurtenances of dessert. Of clerical assemblies he fought shy. Posing at that time as an advanced Liberal and a Broad Churchman, his plea for unfettered admission of Nonconformists to all our schools, and his denunciation of Bishop Gray, just then tramping Somersetshire in his crusade against Colenso, gave deep offence to Philistia. He would have liked to be Regius Professor of Divinity, and was bitterly savage at Payne Smith's appointment. Lord Palmerston consulted Jeune; and Jeune, who while solitary as Vice-Chancellor in the Long Vacation had seen much of Smith, then a sub-librarian at the Bodleian, was impressed by his Oriental erudition and his views on Messianic prophecy, and named him at once. I dare say the Chair lost nothing by his occupancy rather than by Lake's, who was but an amateur theologian; his conception of theology not Biblical criticism, hermeneutics, exegesis, scientific discernment of the spiritual unity underlying all higher forms of religion, but the regulation dogmatism which is in request with Anglican bishops and equips for Anglican Orders.

None the less, at every period of his life, he showed himself extraordinarily capable. His Rugby schooldays placed him in the inner circle of Arnold's best beloved and cherished pupils: as a Balliol Tutor he was among the first to initiate that higher view of the relation between teacher and taught which Jowett carried to perfection. The organisation of the new School of Law and Modern History in 1853 was placed almost entirely in his hands. When he was appointed by the War Office in 1856 on a Commission of Inquiry into the great continental military schools, his two associates, both officers of high rank, bore testimony to the valuable non-professional influence on their counsels of a civilian so highly educated, so tactful, so consummate in practical aptitude. At Durham he used his decanal authority to facilitate the establishment of a Newcastle Science College which Huxley had long been urging. He reanimated the moribund Durham University, raising the number of students from fifty to two hundred; and he restored to dignity and beauty the inadequate services and decaying fabric of the grand Cathedral.

He was not always *facile à vivre:* many persons noted and still recall him as cold, stern, masterful. Shy he may have been—it is the accepted excuse for stiffness—superior to his company he must often have felt himself; and, a Don by constitution and training, he was more likely to exhibit such consciousness than to veil it. But with intimates he was cordial, trustful, staunch, affectionate; and he never forgot old friends. In the company of such he was a very charming talker; his conversation not so much ornate with anecdote, quotation, epigram, as fresh and mobile through its vivid recollection of events, places, men; keenly logical without pedantry, flowing in crisp, well poised, comprehensive sentences, mindful ever of the colloquial rights of others.

He stayed in my house more than once, full always of interesting talk. He gave us one evening a minute description of Dr. Arnold's death. He was a guest in the School House at the time;

the five younger children had gone to Fox How, and all were to follow in a day or two, when the school should have broken up. He and the Doctor strolled till dusk on the Sunday evening in the Head Master's garden overlooking the School Close. Their talk was of the New Testament writers, and he recalled the almost angry vehemence with which Arnold resented a preference of St. Paul to St. John. The great Head Master died early next morning, and Lake went down to Fox How with the tidings. He dwelt on the pathos of the journey, the beauty of the Rothay Valley as he drove along it from the head of Windermere in the early summer dawn, the exquisite peacefulness of the tree-shaded home. It was Arnold's forty-seventh birthday, and the children had prepared to celebrate it; they were waked instead to learn the news, and went back with Lake to see their father's face in death. He went on to talk of his old master, depreciating the value of his influence. Electric and overpowering, it was, he said, more than *boys'* nature could stand; coming on them prematurely, infusing priggishness rather than principle. "Halford Vaughan once agreed with me that it took five years to recover from the mental and moral distortion which it involved." One trait of character, said to have been strongly marked at Oxford, we noticed in him more than once, a sort of superior tuft-hunting: not, of course, the vulgar deference to social rank and wealth, but a rather too exclusive pursuit of and attention to the man of highest note in any company. I met him once at a large dinner party. He found me alone when he entered, and began to talk; presently the Head Master of Winchester was announced, and for him Lake naturally left me. But on the arrival of Eothen Kinglake the Head Master found himself deserted; and when the party was joined by Temple, then in the splendour of his pre-episcopal repute, Eothen in his turn was dropped. Of course, we the rejected ones, combining on the common ground of supersession, discussed our friend's peculiarity with good-humoured impartiality.

He was in his last days every inch a Dean. His tall figure and authoritative diction suited the hieratic consequence of gaiters and apron. His departure left a gap, which, happily for the Cathedral and the University, came to be filled by a successor of attainments not less brilliant and of presence equally imposing. Reckoning him up from his Oxford and his Huntspill days, I should say that he was too self-centred and withdrawn, too aggressively the superior person, to be popular; that, winning an undoubtedly high position, his performance scarcely equalled the expectation men had formed of him; that he remained through life a conspicuous and interesting figure rather than an effectual and influential force.

Of Jowett I shall not say much. The "Jowler myths" served their purpose and are exploded; the facts of his life are told abundantly in the Biography, a book which for my own part I never open without extracting from it gold unalloyed. I was so fortunate once as to meet him in a country house; in such retreats he was always at his best, communicative, receptive, easy. The talk turned on obscure passages in well-known poems—Tennyson's "one clear harp," Newman's "those angel faces"—which their authors when challenged could not or would not explain. He quoted Goldsmith and Johnson's colloquy over the word "slow" in the opening line of "The Traveller." Asked by some one if he meant tardiness of locomotion, Goldsmith said yes. Johnson interposed, "No, sir, you do not mean tardiness of locomotion; you mean that sluggishness of mind which comes upon a man in solitude." He repeated the paragraph exactly, rolling it out with relish. Our host, his old pupil, told us afterwards that he believed Jowett knew his Boswell by heart; no book oftener on his lips or pen. We passed to the "base Judæan" in "Othello." "Herod and Mariamne," Barabas and his daughter in the "Jew of Malta," were proposed as illustrations. The last interested him much, and he asked many questions about the play, which he seemed not to have read; but next morning he said, "I have been thinking it over; it can only mean the Jewish nation and Christ." He went on to condemn Gervinus' Commentary, but found we were all against him. A lady asked him whether Bishop Butler's saying is sound, that, in general no part of our time is more idly spent than the time spent in reading. He roused himself to utter very emphatically, "No." "Mr. Pattison says so." "Mr. Pattison would make all reading difficult, he would have it so perfect and accurate." "Yet one sits at the feet of a great man." "You would not give up your common-sense if you do sit at a great man's feet." She asked his opinion of Greg. He spoke admiringly of his "Enigmas"; went on to describe him as a most curious little man, aged seventy, just married, likely to be always weighing his wife's qualities and to molest her when he found them wanting. Then we discussed old Oxonians. He spoke with absolute reverence of Arnold. Pusey, he thought, had deteriorated; once innocent and a saint, he had become "cunning and almost worldly." Temple, too, had suffered from episcopacy. He pronounced the best Oxford Colleges—it was in 1874—to be Balliol, New College, University, Trinity, Lincoln. He withdrew after breakfast to his Plato, but we had a long walk on Exmoor in the afternoon. As we sat on the hillside, watching the "shadowy main dim-tinted," along which wounded Arthur was borne by weeping queens in dusky barge to Avilion, the blue Atlantic water of the incoming tide pushing itself in great wedges up the brown Severn sea, I picked up and showed him a chunk of old red sandstone at my feet, flecked with minute white spots, which under my Coddington lens became lichens exquisite in shape and chasing. I recall his almost childlike amazement and delight, his regretful confession that to his mind all natural science was a blank, wisdom at one entrance quite shut out. He would have been the first to repudiate the self-consciousness of omniscience suggested by the famous stanza in the "Masque of Balliol,"—

> "I come first, my name is Jowett;
> What there is to know, I know it.
> I'm the Master of this College;
> What I know not is not knowledge,"

which merely recalls a saying of Madame de Staël: "*Monsieur, je comprends tout ce qui mérite d'être compris; ce que je ne comprends n'est rien.*" Much the same thing is said, more audaciously, in a German epigram—

> "Gott weiss viel;
> Doch mehr der Herr Professor:
> Gott weiss alles!
> Doch er—alles besser."

He had, in fact, several times, with a hankering after the unknown, attended meetings of the British Association. In one of these an amusing incident occurred. The meeting was at Newcastle, but on the Sunday men went to Durham, where the fathers of the Cathedral looked askance at the sages in their midst, and appointed Handel's "What tho' I trace" as a significant anthem for the Sunday service. The preacher was Dr. Sanders Evans, a famous Cambridge Scholar, and a Shrewsbury pupil of Butler, but a man eccentric, *distrait*, and very nervous. He had prepared, for the ordinary congregation, a learned sermon on "Essays and Reviews," in which he had assailed the Greek of Jowett's book on St. Paul's Epistles; but his heart failed him when on entering the Cathedral he spied Jowett's white head in a stall. It is one thing to anatomise a book, quite another to vivisect its author, and Evans shrank from the operation. What was to be done? There was present in his place a certain Canon and Archdeacon Bland, who was known to carry a sermon in his pocket wherever he might be. To him was sent a hurried message, and he calmly preached his inappropriate but harmless pocketful. Jowett was not told of the incident, but remarked upon the badness of the sermon.

I told, on p. 205, how, looking from Lake's Balliol windows, I saw Temple in the Quad below. The black-haired, smooth-cheeked, ruddy undergraduate had passed through a Spartan training very unlike that of his comfortably nurtured associates. He had come from a poverty-stricken home, at whose frugal board dry bread was the staple food; had been trained with his brothers and sisters to manual labour; the boys ploughing and gardening, the girls working in the kitchen, house, and dairy:

> "Proles Sabellis docta ligonibus
> Versare glebas, et severæ
> Matris ad arbitrium recisos
> Portare fustes."

Temple's "severa mater" was the founder of his moral, intellectual, and religious character. Knowing not a word of Latin, she taught him his Eton Latin grammar from the first page to the last; took him with the aid of a key through Arithmetic and Algebra, intelligence in each case following upon memory. Her discipline was so judicious that her children seem never to have felt the possibility of being other than obedient. Elected when seventeen years old to a Blundell Scholarship at Balliol, he lived with strictest economy. He drank no wine, in the coldest weather had no fire in his rooms, obtained his Double First entirely without private tuition; a feat performed, it is said, by only one other man in undergraduate annals, the late Bishop Stubbs. His undergraduate career coincided with the crisis of the Oxford Movement: its protagonist at Balliol was his Tutor Ward, whose crushing logical insistency perverted Clough, impelled Newman, baffled Tait, deeply influenced Temple. He told his anxieties to his mother; her quiet response that he should avoid all discussion and think only of his books gave him timely help; he turned from Church reform, the *via media*, and Tract 90, to the stern requirements of the Schools; and his Double First was the result. After a few years as Balliol Tutor he became Principal of Kneller Hall, then, Inspector of Training Colleges; was actively concerned with Canon Brereton and Acland in establishing the Oxford Local Examinations; in 1857 went as Head Master to Rugby. He found it in the trough of the wave; came to it an Arnold Redivivus. The boys received him with distrust; feared from his reforming energy the extinction of their cherished absurdities and inherited rights; were startled by the contrast between Goulburn, placid, affected, cassocked, and his successor's wide shirt-front, rasping voice, martial stride: old Bennett, the patriarchal School *Tonsor*, who had shorn the boys' hair far back into the times of Dr. Wooll, used to relate the consternation with which the new Head Master was surveyed by Town and School, as he *walked* up from the station in a swallow-tailed coat, with a carpet-bag in his hand. But the boys soon learned to love the strong, just, humorous man, to respect the illuminating teacher, to bow before the wonderful Sunday sermons, which recalled to older listeners at once Arnold and Newman; while the discovery that he could walk eighteen miles in three hours, and had privately climbed for amusement all the big elm trees in the School Close, captured them on their athletic side: dislike gave way to appreciation, appreciation to hero-worship. "Temple is all right, mother," wrote home a Sixth Form boy whose parents had expressed alarm as to the political and religious influence of the new Head Master; "Temple is all right; but if he turns Mahometan all the School will turn too." So with the Masters: those already in the School, who had hitherto resembled independent vassals under a mediæval monarch, at once recognised the claims and did homage to the strength of a suzerain who fulfilled Carlyle's conception of the König; the new comers imbibed the influence of his character, and transmitted it to the boys.

Why did he leave Rugby after a reign of only twelve years? Why exchange the freedom, independence, animating environment of a great Head Master for the chains which, however gilded, must shackle an Anglican bishop? By Englishmen generally the step was regarded as something of a descent; outside his new diocese he was not quite the man he had been before. But episcopal trappings did not change him; and the power which had restored Rugby soon renovated Exeter. His predecessor had governed by system and by fear; for machinery Temple substituted life; into system he infused the spirit of service. Confident in his own magnetic will — *velis tantummodo, quæ tua virtus, expugnabis*—he made it his first policy to know and to be known. Not only the popular centres, but the small towns and villages, thinly inhabited moors and scattered tors, whose primitive tenants had never seen a bishop, faced the virile personality, recognised the West Country burr, heard the pleadings, passionate and sometimes tearful, which awoke spiritual consciousness and stirred regenerating resolve. Laymen bowed before a leader who could lead; Dissenters saw a new Wesley in their midst; farmers were subjugated by the strong man who had himself followed the plough; clergy, looking at first distrustfully upon a bishop banned by a clerical Convocation, were shamed, then won, into acceptance and imitation. "Every clergyman," said Dean Cowie after some years had passed, "is doing twice as much as he did before; and they say it is all your doing;" he had not set himself to gain them, but inevitably he gained them, because from the first he came to serve.

He moved to London in 1885; the loud and universal sorrow at his departure reviving a doubt frequently expressed, whether the translation of an approved and popular prelate, except possibly to a Primacy, is not in all cases a mistake. He there strode into the heart of his work, treading on the toes of men more sensitive than were the comparatively Bœotian clergy whom he had left behind in Devonshire. Heroes built like him, "temples without polished corners," come amongst us as his Master came, εἰς κρίσιν, to test capacity of discernment, to attract nobleness, repel superficiality and pettiness. Men priggish, self-complacent, languid, or unreal, disliked him cordially; the House of Lords never to the last accepted him; men high minded, genuine, spiritually akin, found him out and were drawn to him at once. Dr. Gore glorified in receiving from him a not unmerited snub. "We have a *man* here," said Capel Cure, listening to his somewhat stern repulse of irrelevant clerical criticism. "If he sometimes treated us like schoolboys," said another, "we deserved it, and were all the better for being back in school again."

His recorded sayings, pithy or humorous, help out our conception of the man. Such are his—"You cannot grow genius, but you can grow talent;" "it is not knowledge chiefly, but character, that England wants;" "they wish me to formulate a policy; I don't believe in formulated policies;" "one is brought through somehow if one always does one's best;" "help in work is something; I want companionship more." Some of his dicta are in a lighter mood. "I am very pleased, my Lord," began a Very Reverend at a missionary meeting. "You are not," snapped the chairman, who had taught English Grammar in his day; "you are *very much* pleased." "Wherever I go, they give me cold chicken and 'the Church's one foundation,' and I hate both." "My aunt was prevented from sailing in a ship which sank; would you not, my Lord, call that a providential interposition?" "Can't tell, did not know your aunt." A vicar, pointing to a Nonconformist Chapel—"That, my Lord, is where all the people go." Bishop, turning on him—"WHY?" His rough speeches sometimes looked brutal in print, but were not so when tempered by the merry smile which softened them. He had a natural inborn heartiness, Goethe's *Hoftlichkeit des Herzens*, the politeness of helpful benevolent good feeling; he was never ill-natured or cynical; the smooth mask of conventional courtesy he could not wear. "I hate civility, don't you?"

His last public appearance many of us would gladly forget. "That he should have been so dominated by his surpliced legions," wrote to me one of his most devoted friends and colleagues, "as to accept Balfour's Education Bill, and then to be cut short by fatal illness before he poured out his whole soul in favour of making common cause with united Christianity, is the tragedy of his life." Yet to the old among us he stands out as a man nobler than his fellows, laborious, disinterested, self-reliant, with a grand conception of this life, a clear vision of the next; and the character has no less its special meaning for the young. "The air of perpetual Spring blows round his grave; the thought of him speaks reality and hope; and these are the memories which live."

The changes of Oxford life are swift; the water flows fast under Folly Bridge; and to the present generation T. H. Green is little more than a name. Yet before his early death he had attained a repute and wielded an influence in the University which no one has since surpassed. His namesake the historian, coming up to Oxford and invited by him to dinner, sent word that "the shadow would gladly wait upon the substance"; a distinguished statesman still living, who has perhaps by this time outgrown his youthful enthusiam, made a reverential pilgrimage to Green's birthplace; and the philosopher figures in "Robert Elsmere" as the infallible guide and oracle of his day to all who were mentally doubtful, struggling, and distressed.

His outward life was devoid of incident: he represents the history of a *mind*, inert and slow at first, feeding on its own thoughts, not on the thoughts of others; a plant growing, not a brick being moulded. Both as schoolboy and undergraduate he was out of touch with his surroundings; he was influenced at Oxford by Jowett, Conington, Charles Parker, and by no one else; the only authors who inspired him were Wordsworth, Carlyle, Maurice, and Fichte. He cared little for literary scholarship, nothing for academic distinction; his passion was for philosophy and metaphysics, as ministering to the problems of life which alone he deemed worth solving. Rival philosophers professed to see a fundamental incoherence in his thoughts; and the necessary complexities of language which hampered their expression were ridiculed in an amusing verse of the "Masque of Balliol." But he helped to form the highest minds amongst his contemporaries; and those who now read the chapter of his biography called "Religious Principles" will understand the height of habitual exaltation to which he soared; an abiding grasp of the Unseen, of Christianity, of the spiritual life, of human duty, before which the dogmatic materialism of polemic sects and schisms dwindles into littleness.

CHAPTER XIII

TRINITY

",'Tis opportune to look back upon old times: great examples grow thin, and to be fetched from the past world."
—Sir Thomas Brown.

President Ingram — Guillemard — Lord Ward — Isaac Williams — Monsignor Patterson—Fred. Meyrick—Tommy Short.

I WAS one day in company with a distinguished Fellow of Trinity College, Cambridge. Mention happened to be made of an interesting Roman dignitary lately dead, and I recalled him as in my early days a "Fellow of Trinity." The Cambridge Don looked up surprised and doubtful, so I hastened, amid the great amusement of the company, to explain that there exists at Oxford a College which presumes to bear that name, and that to this College Monsignor Patterson had belonged. To be sure, our Trinity cannot hang over its high table portraits of Bacon and Newton, nor have its recent Heads ranked with Whewell for omniscience or for wit with Thompson; but it has played a famous part, and to my own memory it is fragrant. Its President in my early days was Ingram, antiquary, Anglo-Saxon scholar, author of a finely illustrated "Memorials of Oxford." I recall him as a feeble old gentleman, bent nearly double, preserving and relating anecdotes, traditional and personal, of College heroes in the past —of Tom Warton, Budgell, Lisle Bowles, Kett. He succeeded stately Dr. Chapman, whose daughter, my shrewd old neighbour in Holywell, surviving her father more than half a century, with sixty years of Oxford prattle at her fluent tongue's end, was run over and killed by a cricketing brake in the early sixties. Ingram was a Wykehamist, and dined always at our New College Gaudy, invariably in his after-dinner speech making modest allusion to "my little work." Of his Fellows I remember Guillemard, the non-placeting Proctor, along with Church, of 1845; Copeland, earliest disciple and latest friend of Newman; Claughton, tutor to young Lord Ward, whose sister he married, was presented by him to the valuable living of Kidderminster, and became Bishop of Rochester. Lord Ward, afterwards Lord Dudley, was conspicuous by his beautiful face and long waving hair, which the Paris ladies imitated on their own heads by crimping-irons. He used to come to my father's accompanied by an enormous dog, on which one day he perched my brother, afterwards Dr. Tuckwell, then, like the hero of "Boots at the Swan," a "very little boy," and trotted him round the hall. Amongst the Fellows too was Isaac Williams, whose project of "Tracts for the Times," hatched with Hurrell Froude under the trees in Trinity Garden, brought Newman back from Italy and began the Oxford Movement. Williams came up from Harrow with the reputation of a finished Latin scholar, and won the Latin Verse, "Ars Geologica," in 1823. W. G. Cole used to relate that, being Pro-proctor in this year, and keeping one of the Theatre gates at Commemoration, he was annoyed by the pertinacity of a stranger, who insisted on taking the place by storm. Cole gripped him, and asked his name. "My name is Williams, sir; my son has a Prize, and I want to hear him recite his poem." Of course Cole passed him in. Double honours were expected for Isaac; but his health broke down, and by Abernethy's order he was contented with a Pass; recovering, however, to obtain a Trinity Fellowship. He was, under the signature ζ, one of the six writers in the "Lyra Apostolica," and was the author also of Tract 80, on "Reserve in Religious Teaching." I well remember the exciting contest between him and Garbett for the Poetry Professorship in 1841-2. No one denied that he was the better man; but an unwise circular of Pusey's, provoking a dexterous response from Gilbert, gave a theological character to the election. The commotion spread far and wide; the London papers took it up, ranging themselves on what was now first called the "Anti-Tractarian" side. The silent but growing alarm excited by the Tracts found expression in support of Garbett, and a comparison of promised votes showing Williams to be in the minority, he withdrew, married soon after, and left Oxford. A story was told of him later, for the correctness of which I do not vouch. He had an unaccountable antipathy to Jews, and resented the Hebrew Christian name which his sponsors had inflicted on him; his children, at any rate, should bear homely modern *prænomina*. A son was born to him, John Keble was its godfather, and it was baptized John Edward. Nothing, he thought, could be more free from an Israelite taint, though in the first name misgivings might have lurked; until, too late, he discovered that the child's initials would be J. E. W. His autobiography, published after his death, throws a curious sidelight on Newman's character, not found in any other notice of the "Movement." He was a humble, self-distrusting, saintly being, cast in the Keble, not the Newman, type. Of his numerous works in prose and poetry it is likely that one alone will survive, his "Gospel Narrative of our Lord's Passion." In the "Cathedral," the "Christian Scholar," above all in the "Baptistery," are strains of genuine poetry, yet for the most part careless in structure and lacking condensation; but the tenderness, scriptural insight, infusion with the best patristic feeling, of the "Passion" seems to me to leave far behind all other English devotional commentaries.

"Monsignor" Patterson, who left us—absquatulated, as Manuel Johnson used to say—with Manning and others in the second Hegira, was a man learned, genial, musical, and a charming talker. I recall his enraptured face once in New College chapel, when the choristers, at all times *cantare pares*, were led by Miss Hawes, a London vocalist who had come down for an Oxford concert, and who, attending chapel, added her fine soprano to the music. He used to give evening parties in his rooms, to which his friends were warned to bring only "men as can talk and men as can sing," so he used to put it. Some years later I met him in

Dublin; and was touched as I have often been in company with Newman's fugitives, by his pathetically eager recurrence, as of a homesick exile, to Oxford memories and names and incidents. I cannot myself, even now, without a pang recall that ancient time. These men were for the most part the flower of the Anglican as of the Oxford flock; none can estimate their loss to the University, to the Church, to the community; and, through the consequent narrowing of their careers, to themselves. Men of piety, intellect, note, remained; but the heart had gone out of the Movement; it declined, as Liddon used sadly to acknowledge and bewail, from aspirations to observances: its beneficent constructive side, its exuberant energy, unworldly mysticism, studious enthusiasm, leisured erudition, passionate self-devotion, passed into channels not shaped and not available for their distribution. In religion as in politics, the possession of commanding influence is a fearful gift. "Bad men," says a great satirist, "are bad, do the bad, go to the bad; but who shall measure the abiding mischief which a very good man can do?"

Residents at Oxford in the later Forties were frequently aware of a very good-looking junior Don taking his walks abroad with young Lord Robert Cecil, Lord Lothian, his brother Schomberg, and others of the *jeunesse surdorée*, who apparently looked up to him as guide, philosopher, and friend. It was Frederick Meyrick, a lately elected Fellow of Trinity. We thought that a man starting with qualifications so marked, academic, social, personal, must become a shining University light: but he married, became a School Inspector, for a time disappeared, then suddenly came into notice during the *horrida bella* between Newman and Charles Kingsley, as author of a pamphlet bearing the cumbrous title —"But isn't Kingsley right after all?" It was a rather vigorous production, touching with an Ithuriel spear of common sense Newman's dexterous subterfuge and Kingsley's bungling incompetence; and it won Gladstone's admiring approbation. It had no effect upon the public mind; men could not all appreciate reasoning; they could all enjoy the "Apologia" to which the controversy gave rise. Kingsley was entirely discredited, and for several years the sale of his books fell off.

Exchanging his School Inspectorship for a living, Meyrick devoted himself to theological controversy. More than fifty pamphlets stand against his name in the British Museum Catalogue: he contributed also to countless "religious" Journals, and edited seventeenth century Treatises. A wide traveller, an accomplished linguist, a practised disputant, he wrote on the Church of Spain, on the morality of Liguori, on Italian clerical legends, on Vaticanism, on Irish Church Missions. He was a friend and supporter of Döllinger, a vehement opponent of Manning, of Huxley, of Pattison, of Jowett.

How could such a man escape promotion? His youthful friend, afterwards Lord Salisbury, quarrelled with him when in 1865 he voted for Gladstone at Oxford, and his displeasure was possibly permanent. But what was Gladstone about, in his numerous Episcopal creations, to pass over a man so like-minded, so active, and above all so *safe?* Perhaps it was as well for Meyrick: endowment with mitral consequence might not have compensated for deterioration of moral fibre: anyhow, he remained Vicar of Blickling till his death. Dignified, learned, pious, with high College honours and good social position, he preserved the old type of humanistic University training in the past. Intransigent in youth, and sturdy to the end, he remained through life a faithful champion of lost and losing causes. Respecting his fidelity to convictions which he had not idly formed, we appreciate him as type of a class essential probably to the progressive development of its time, extinct and perhaps impossible to-day.

But the prominent representive of Trinity in those days was its Vice-President, "Tommy" Short, who had been College Tutor when the century was in its teens, and was to continue lecturing into the late Sixties. He knew his books by heart, expounding them with fluency and humour; he ranked with the best Oxford whist-players, and kept a spacious cellar of old port wine, including, I remember, a pipe which he had bought from a Dissenting wine merchant, and labelled "Schismatic Binn." But he was especially notable as a conversationalist, the last, perhaps, to represent the colloquial felicities which constituted a fine art in Oxford once, and are to-day recalled sadly as a lost art by superannuates like myself. Talk such as his can hardly be reproduced; unforced, condensed, epigrammatic, crisp, yet at the same time voluble, it becomes vapid when severed from its à propos, loses point unless verbally repeated; lacks above all the twinkling eye and incisive nasal tones of its originator. Yet some of his sayings I remember, and his friend Dr. Plummer has kindly furnished me with not a few besides. Once, when I breakfasted in his rooms with Walter Thursby, known afterwards as the first Englishman to reach the summit of Mount Ararat, he told us that, examining in the Schools the day before, he had asked what mention is made of Marriage in the Articles; to which the scholar "answered briskly, that it is a fond thing vainly invented, without any warrant either in antiquity or Scripture." This scaling of Ararat, by-the-bye, attracted much attention at the time. Thursby, who had just taken his degree, was travelling with another Trinity man, "white" Theobald he was called; and though not practised climbers, they successfully assailed the biblical height. They found the snow in favourable condition, and the *infames scopulos* undeserving of their bad repute; but the marauding tribes haunting the hillside rendered necessary a guard of Kurdish soldiers. "I understand," said Arthur Ridding, when in New College Common Room they told the story of their exploit; "I understand, you took some Curds with you to show the whey."

I return to dear old Short. Cole of Worcester—"Papirius Carbo," Short always called him—went to Short before taking his degree to read aloud the Articles, as was then customary. While he read, Short moved about apparently unheeding, arranged papers and gave instructions to his scout. But he was not inattentive; when Cole read from the Article on the Old Testament about the "commandments which are called moral," Short stopped him to inquire which were the commandments called immoral. He held together with his Fellowship the cure of St. Nicholas, Abingdon. Sanday of Trinity took the duty one day, and came to him for instructions. Said Short, "I feed my flock with hay and straw (prayers and sermon) in the morning, hay only in the afternoon." He used to dine and play a rubber at a house near Oxford. He sat next to a learned lady, whom he knew to be well on the further side of fifty. "Pray, Mr. Short," she said, "when does the human mind reach maturity?" He answered, "Aristotle says, at forty-nine; and what a blue you will be when you reach that age." Arriving late at the same house, he learned that the famous preacher Hugh M'Neile had unexpectedly come upon a visit, and that whist was to be supplanted by a Scripture reading and exposition. Very cross, he sat to endure. Boanerges read a passage from the Acts: "They knew that the island was called Melita." "The d—— they did!" was heard from Short's corner. Dining at another hospitable house, he became sleepy, and let the decanters pass. "Mr. Short," his host remonstrated, "that is Comet Port." [The Comet year, 1811, yielded the finest vintage of the century.] "Oh, is it? then, *comitatis causa*, I will take a glass." When Goulburn, Head Master of Rugby, was expecting the deanery of Exeter, Otter of Corpus naughtily proposed to insert his biography in *The Times*, specifying the number of boys he found at the school, and the loss which his reign had caused. "No," said Short, "that would not be

232 REMINISCENCES OF OXFORD

biography, but boyography." Himself a Master at Rugby under Dr. Wooll, Arnold's predecessor, he was asked by Lord Lyttelton, Rugbean and a Trustee, to furnish a motto for the flogging school. "Great cry and little Wooll," was the answer: Wooll was a diminutive man. Short used to say that at Rugby and at Oxford he had been concerned with more than a thousand pupils; and that for every one foolish boy he had found two foolish parents. The school physician of his time, a Dr. Bucknill, known as "Hip-Hip Bucknill," was a Character. A boy was ill, and to Rugby came the mother in alarm. "Doctor, *is* there any danger?" "There is always danger when there is illness." "But *can* you do anything for him?" "I can't say, Take up your bed and walk." "No, but, Doctor, do tell me how he really is; my husband is so *very* anxious that I should return to him." "So should I be, madam, were I your husband."

"Tommy" Sheppard of Exeter used to ride with Miss Susan ——. Near Godstow one day his horse jibbed and threw him into the water. While the lady sat in her saddle and laughed at his struggles to scramble out, Short passed by. He stopped, and said, "This time the elder is in the water, and Susanna is looking at him." When in his younger days the College living of Oddington fell, Miss Lee, the President's daughter, asked him whether he meant to take it. "Will you go with me?" "No." "Then I shall not take it; but you can't say you never had an offer." When eleven years later Rotherfield Grays was vacant, the lady gave him, and herself, another chance, by repeating the former question. "No," said Short, "as you wouldn't go with me to Oddington, I sha'n't go without you to Rotherfield Grays." Suffering from what Horace calls tumults in the stomach, he went to consult Jephson at Leamington. "Your colon is out of order." "So I guessed, but I want you to prevent it from coming to a full stop." Some one remarked that the child of two unusually ugly parents was a very pretty baby. "Then," said Short, "it must be a bastard on both sides." A scout was dismissed for insolence: he came to Short. "I never thought, Mr. Short, that *you* would take the bread out of a poor man's mouth." "I take the bread out of your mouth? why, you fool, you spat it out." When Plumptre became Vice-Chancellor in 1848, Short stopped him in the street. "Now, Master, you will have to sport a cassock. Make use of the opportunity to wear out your old pairs of black trousers." His own were sometimes shrunken. Crossing the Quad, he overheard two undergraduates commenting on "the brevity of Tommy's trousers." "Yes, you young jackanapes, Tommy's trousers are like you, they want taking down and strapping." He rebuked a youngster for smoking a regalia in the High Street. "Please, Mr. Short, how did *you* know it was a regalia?" "Young man, it is the business of a Tutor to know all wickedness and practise none." A Trinity Scholar who got only a Second Class wrote to Short that he feared it was his duty to resign his Scholarship. "Take my compliments to Mr. ——," Short said to his scout, "and tell him that if he comes into chapel without a surplice I shall fine him a pound." Only Fellows and Scholars wore surplices. Another repartee is somewhat grim, but too characteristic to be omitted. An undergraduate had debauched a girl in humble life, was penitent, wished to marry her, and with singularly bad judgment consulted Short.

> " Cato's a proper person to entrust
> A love-tale with ; "

"if you marry her," said his oracle, "you are a fool; if you don't marry her, you are a blackguard; in either case you will cease to be a member of this College."

Short had a horror of fasting, as ruinous to health. "I remember not many years ago when there were eighteen Tractarian undergraduates in this College. I threw not only cold water, but *dirty* water, on their ascetic practices, and they mostly discontinued them." And he used to tell how Newman's failure in the Schools was due to an idea he had taken up, that the more he reduced his body the better his mind would work. He went in half-starved, and broke down right and left. He had not even read the Third Book of Aldrich, and knew next to nothing of the *Æneid*, while his Mathematical Papers, Ben Symons told Short, were scrawled over unintelligibly; one problem, however, being worked out with remarkable ingenuity. The marvel was that the examiners passed him at all; they placed him as low as they could, in the Second Division of the Second Class, "under the line," as it was then contemptuously called. "My nerves forsook me, and I failed," was his own account of the disaster in writing home. It was a severe blow to his Oxford friends, who had calculated with certainty on his obtaining the highest honours; and they were hardly less startled when only a year afterwards he stood for an Oriel Fellowship, at that time the blue ribbon of University distinction. The moment was singularly unpropitious; in the preceding year Oriel, which prided itself on electing its Fellows according to their prowess and promise in the examination rather than by their previous exploits in the Schools, had chosen a Second Class man, C. J. Plumer, over the head of a First Class man, George Howard, afterwards Lord Morpeth; and had been savagely attacked in the *Edinburgh Review* (by the unsuccessful candidate, as Copleston discovered) for preferring mediocrity to excellence. Copleston and his Fellows could afford to ignore the censure, yet it must tend to make them wary; and their selection of a man whose failure was notorious and recent might seem to justify the vilipendings of the *Edinburgh*. Short, however, who knew what was in his pupil, pressed Newman to stand; he might not succeed, but he would show his power, and retrieve the last year's collapse. Thus fortified, Newman offered himself. "He came to me," Short said, "after the first paper, which was an Essay, and said that he had made of it a complete mess—had broken down entirely. Now I had just seen Tyler, one of the Fellows, who said, 'Tell me something about your man Newman; his is by far the best Essay we have had.' Of course I did not tell this to Newman, but I said to him, 'You go on with the examination, and work through as if you had no chance and were only an unconcerned spectator.'" Short was lunching at the time, and, like the judicious angel visitant to Elijah, made his emaciated pupil eat and drink—"Arise and eat, for the journey is too long for thee"—sending him away strengthened in mind as well as body by a plentiful and savoury meal. It was an object of great importance to Newman at that time to obtain a Fellowship, for his father, a brewer at Alton, had failed. While the examination was proceeding, Short had occasion to call on Copleston, and took the opportunity of telling him that Newman was a highly deserving man, and that the circumstances of his family were such as to make a Fellowship very desirable. The Provost thanked him for the information, saying that such considerations were not altogether without weight in their elections. On the next day Short went into the country; riding back to Oxford soon afterwards, he stopped at Shipstone to bait his horse, and taking up an Oxford paper read, "Yesterday Mr. John Henry Newman of Trinity College was elected Fellow of Oriel." When asked about his old pupil in later days, he used to say, "Newman was a very amenable fellow; he did jib occasionally, but we all liked him very much. He was a wonderful divine in his undergraduate days. I can remember his bringing the Book of Psalms into Collections, and when we asked him to name the prophetical psalms, he started with the second, and went through them all. Oh dear! he used to run you down with his answers. He played the violin, too, very well, and often took a part in quartetts at President Lee's musical parties." Short himself was musical. I recall him one evening in Dr. Bliss's drawing-room, to which he came attired in black pantaloons, grey silk stockings, and silver-buckled shoes, sitting cross-legged at the feet of Mrs. Wingfield, an accomplished pianist, and reproaching her because she played only modern music. The lady pleaded that the age was tired of the old music. "Correct the age," he answered in his nasal tones, and his friend, moving to the piano, played for him a fine piece by Scarlatti.

Once only after Newman's secession he and Short met, when the Cardinal visited Oxford in 1878, and dined at Trinity high table on February 27. Short was too feeble to go into Hall, but Newman went to his rooms. "I asked him whether he remembered lunching with me during the Oriel Examination. 'Yes,' he said, 'and I remember what you had for luncheon; it was lamb cutlets and fried parsley.'" This pleased Short much, and the two agreed that Short had influenced Newman's life more than any man; since, but for Short, Newman would have retired from the examination, while success in that formed the foundation of his whole career. Until his own death Newman said a mass for Short every year.

A touch of soberness falls upon the old Vice-President's closing days. He became blind towards the end, and was led about the streets,

Returning once to Oxford after years of absence, and meeting him in the Turl, I stopped him. "My father's son must shake you by the hand." "Who is it?" "Tuckwell." "Which of them?" "The eldest." "Oh yes, the Master of Taunton school. Well, now, remember that what πολυπραγμοσύνη is to men of business, that is πολυφλογμοσύνη to a schoolmaster." I thought of a printer's error which made Moberly miserable in a published sermon preached by him at St. Mary's just before going to Winchester, whereby the sentence, "We must revive our flagging energies," became, rather too appropriately, "We must revive our flogging energies." T. L. Claughton used to relate that after becoming Bishop of Rochester he met Short one day at the President's. After dinner the two strolled in the garden, and as soon as they were screened from the windows Short went down on his knees, and said, "Claughton, give me your blessing." "I was very much moved," said Claughton, telling the story afterwards to Dr. Plummer. To the same old friend Short said once, "College rooms are very good to live in, but very bad to die in." He died, not in College, but somewhere near Birmingham, in 1879. *Deus sit propitius huic potatori!*

CHAPTER XIV

CORPUS

> " *The Pelican kindly for her tender brood*
> *Tears her own bowels, trilleth out her blood*
> *To heal her young; and in a wondrous sort*
> *Unto her children doth her life disport.*
> *A type of Christ, who, sin-thralled man to free,*
> *Became a captive, and on shameful Tree*
> *Self-guiltless shed his blood, by's wounds to save us,*
> *And heal the wounds th' old serpent firstly gave us.*
> *And so became of meer immortal mortal*
> *Thereby to make frail mortal man immortal."*
> —SYLVESTER's *Du Bartas.*

Bridges—Greswell—Otter—Hext—Coxe—Vaughan Thomas—Blackstone—Furneaux—Tom Faussett.

OF two Corpus men, amusing lunatics both, Frowd and Holme, I made mention on page 27; but my memory, stimulated by an old friend, Professor H. A. Strong, himself in former days a Scholar, has brought before me a further file of worthies from the College of the Pelican.

I remember old President Bridges; his little daughter was my playfellow. Bridges, the Fellow of Corpus, was his nephew. He was a Wykehamist, and had left behind him amongst the Juniors a rather awful memory. He was a keen cricketer, and used to question me about the College and Commoner matches. He gave me the original MS. scores of the first matches played at Lords between Winchester and Harrow. I presented them to T. W. Erle, afterwards Associate in Common Pleas. Bridges—Bridger the boys called him—went to the Bar, and became Attorney General at Hong-Kong. He was very deeply marked with small-pox: when news reached us of his marriage, Arthur Ridding remarked that the lady ought to be *pitied*.

When Dr. Bridges died, the Headship was offered to Greswell. Tommy Greswell he was called: his name was Edward, but the men had re-christened him, as the children re-christened the pig in "The Golden Age." He was a walking library of recondite classics; Macmullen in one generation, Furneaux in another, used to draw him out. Once in his life he was recorded to have made a joke. There was a Gentleman Commoner named Meiklam. Called on by the President at Collections, where it was certain that he would do his Tutors no credit, Greswell said — " Please, Mr. President, leave him to us—*Nos* humilem feriemus agnam; *We* will smite the meek lamb." On his refusal of the Headship Norris was elected President, "a little round fat oily man of God," who kept hunters. Nimrod, in his "Condition of Hunters," mentions the high condition in which Norris' horses were kept. He used to dine with us at New College sometimes, when special Cæcuban was brought out from the College cellars. On becoming President he gave up hunting and sold his horses; his groom came into Quad sobbing out—"I never thought to live to see my master made into an old woman."

Francis Otter, one of the Fellows, who sat for

the Louth Division of Lincolnshire during the Short Parliament, and who married the sister of George Eliot's husband, Mr. Cross, once asked him, as Burgon asked Routh, for a word of wisdom which might be to him a maxim and a guide in the change and chance of life. "I will give you two such, my young friend," said Norris. "First, never make an enemy; and secondly—*never* be drawn into a correspondence."

Otter was famous during the Secession War for his advocacy of the North. It used to be said then that the North had only three champions in England, Queen Victoria, the Duke of Argyle, and the *Spectator* newspaper. Otter made a fourth. The *Spectator* was so unpopular for its advocacy that it lost nearly all its subscribers, but the circulation more than recovered itself after the war. Otter took the chair at a great meeting where I spoke for him at Sleaford in 1890. He talked about the Roman Empire, and never touched his audience. I heard an important land-agent say, "We don't want a d—d Tutor to represent us."

The best known Corpus Tutor of my time was Hext. From a letter which he wrote to me when my book came out, mentioning him as it did in connection with Dr. Frowd, I transcribe the biographical part:—
". . . the pleasure you have given me in reviving so many of *my* reminiscences, which with age are beginning to escape me. In 1836 I got a Scholarship at Corpus, resided till 1858, and then for thirty years never I believe missed a year to look up old friends for a few days. Alas! they are getting scarce now. . . . I treasured Lord Exmouth's port

wine as Frowd had done, never using it but when old Oxford friends came to visit me, opening the last bottle for Evans of Pembroke in 1873. My last visit to Oxford was I think in 1897, to an 'old Corpus' dinner, when I stayed with Furneaux, and met a grand gathering of old friends, most of whom I had not seen for forty or fifty years. I fear I shall never see Oxford again. In 1896 I contributed an article to the *Pelican Record*, on 'Memories of Corpus boating,' in which I gave an account of the seven-oar race, much like your own. Two of the crew, George Hughes and Mackay, were pupils of mine at the time.

"My dearest friend of all time was Harry Coxe. I gave Burgon a few lines about him for his twelve good men. I don't think I have any old *friends* surviving in Oxford except Chase. I see William Ogle occasionally in London. The rest I think are gone.

"I am now retired; gave up my Corpus Living in 1899, and am at last feeling my age. Once more thank you for your Reminiscences: I remember your father well, but I never knew you I'm afraid."

He knew me across the examination table in the Schools. I remember him examining me in the Ethics for Greats in 1852. I knew it "in parts"—I forbear the obvious quotation—and Karslake of Merton my Tutor had imparted to me a variety of dodges by which an Examiner testing one in a weak place might be diverted on to stronger ground. Karslake came in to hear my *Viva Voce;* and on my adroitly and successfully practising his lesson, laughed audibly, and made me smile. Little Hext glared suspiciously; and I was obliged to look serious, a feat which I achieved without difficulty on his asking me a question which I could not answer. He next took me in Horace; set me on, as I thought, in Satire IX., and I gleefully turned to the *Ibam forte*. He corrected me again suspiciously: "I asked for the 9th *Epistle*." But I knew by heart Steele's fine translation of the Septimius missive in the *Spectator*, and restored him to good humour. His letter was written in 1901, when he was eighty-six years old. He died in the same year.

His friend Henry Coxe was Chaplain at Corpus in those days; famous for the pace at which he took the prayers: in amusing contrast to the slow measured reading of President Norris. He was the best mimic I ever met. I once wanted to see Dr. Wolff, the Bokhara missionary and savant; sought him in the Bodleian, and asked Coxe if he was there. Instantly Coxe's handsome face was distorted into Wolff's grotesque phiz, his fingers wreathed themselves in strange twitchings, and Wolff's cavernous voice ascended from his chest. At that moment Wolff himself emerged from one of the cells; gesticulations, face, voice, so exactly as Coxe had rendered them, that I was fain to turn away. He used to render dialogues between old Routh and Burgon; Burgon's piping voice and gushing manner set off by the old President's sedate, soft, measured, half querulous, half sarcastic tones.

Another notable Corpus Chaplain, formerly a Fellow, was Vaughan Thomas, tall, white-haired, red-faced, with sonorous voice. He was the last survivor amongst the men to whom Latin was a mother tongue, pouring forth orations voluble and unprepared. He had been an active University politican; but through some offence given had taken his name off the books. He led the original "Hampden row," as it was called. The protesters against Hampden met in his rooms, and he delivered a fine Latin speech on the historic occasion when the Proctors non-placeted the decree against the Bampton Lectures. His wife was a Miss Williams, daughter to the Botanical professor, who lived in the house overlooking the Gardens at the High Street end of Rose Lane. He lived in Holywell Lodge; but when his wife's sister died, moved into the vacated house. Miss Williams was a character. She inhabited on Sundays an unusually large pew in St. Peter's, which she would allow no one to share. Once, when some preacher drew a crowd, she came late to find her pew filled with undergraduates. I saw her stand at the door and motion them all out, then shut herself in. Vaughan Thomas used a large, old-fashioned, closed carriage, with a handsome pair of horses, in which he and his second wife "took the air" every day. But he was a strict observer of "the Sabbath," and on Sundays left his horses and coachman to their rest, driving to his small living near Oxford in one of May's two-horse flys.

I well knew poor Charles Blackstone. His father held the New College living of Heckfield, and was an intimate friend of Dr. Arnold. He made a figure at the Union, speaking frequently, and giving much time to the preparation of his speeches. He won the Newdigate in 1848—the subject "Columbus," reciting his poem in the Theatre with great force amid loud applause. He was found by his scout one morning lying dead upon his sofa, a discharged pistol in his hand. The conjecture offered at the inquest, and accepted, was to the effect that he had been annoyed by a rat in his room, and had bought the pistol with intent to shoot it: had fallen asleep on his sofa overnight, and, waked by the rat, had somehow entangled the pistol in his dress and lodged the contents in himself.

I come to Henry Furneaux, with whom I was intimate for nearly sixty years. We were juniors together at Winchester in 1842. He was then a very tiny boy, with a large head which used to hang on one side, and great round eyes like those with which a hare gazes at you when you surprise it sitting in its form. He made fun of his diminutive stature, declaring that in a shower he could walk between the drops of rain and not get wet. His astonishing memory first showed itself in the summer of 1844, when he performed in "Standing Up," as it was called, the feat which I have elsewhere commemorated. Later, in the Sixth Form, it was customary in the weekly Horace lesson to construe the whole or part of a Satire or Epistle, then to say by heart what we had translated the week before. One day, our lesson opened at the *Non quia Mæcenas*, which we duly construed, and were prepared to say by heart the Brundusium diary which precedes it. By mistake Moberly set Furneaux on at the piece just construed, which none of us had learned. He went merrily ahead, till Moberly, noting our amused remonstrant faces, saw his mistake, and stopped the performance, adding to Furneaux, after a pause, a few serious words as to the responsibility attaching to his remarkable talent. His forte at that time was original Latin Prose. Many of us were fluent Latinists, but he beat us all. Once a month or so we had to produce a Latin critique on some great classical work of poet, orator, historian : it must occupy twelve pages of a quarto manuscript book. But to our hardness of heart was accorded a blank margin, which lazy boys would sometimes extend till the composition was reduced to a series of slender strips. Furneaux, alone of us all, never deigned to employ any margin; his twelve pages were all covered with black manuscript. His Latin Verse was not particularly good; his English Verse execrable : I remember a poem which he wrote on Gothic Architecture, and which his co-mates criticised so mercilessly that in a passion of tears he tore it up. I myself, in *satira nimis acer*, composed on the occasion a wicked lampoon : but he bore me no spite; malice was not in his nature.

Senior of the School, he fortunately did not go off to New College, the only two vacancies being annexed, according to the vicious practice of that day, by two Founders' kin much his juniors. I say fortunately; for at that time New College absorbed the cream of Winchester and converted it into thinnest milk. He got his

Corpus Scholarship, his First Class, his Fellowship. It was as an undergraduate that he first showed his genius for story telling. He picked up and remembered every *jeu d'esprit* emitted by Thorold Rogers, Blaydes, Bartlett, Tom Faussett, and would retail them with contagious enjoyment of their fun. These passed away from him mostly in after life, until his memory was stirred; then they all came back. In writing my Oxford book I once or twice applied to him to complete some squib of which I remembered only a line or two; and with some effort he usually succeeded. "You certainly are," he wrote to me, "a wonderful person for stimulating my recollection. The verses you want must have slumbered in my memory for I know not how many years. In late years I have not heard of any good thing. I fear the art is extinct, the clever men being too serious, the others too stupid." The most wonderful of his stories was known as "The Cornish Jury." In a case of murder the jury had retired to consider their verdict; and at first beguiled the time with general talk, which Furneaux, a born Cornishman, rendered in the native dialect. Reminded at last by the Foreman that they must "come to a 'cision on this here case," the dikasts delivered their judgments individually, each more amazing than his predecessors. I can recall them, but it would be useless to transcribe them:

"Nam quamvis memori referas mihi pectore cuncta,
Non ta ϛ en interpres tantundem juveris; adde
Vultum habitumque hominis."

248   REMINISCENCES OF OXFORD

Mansel once tried to tell the story in my hearing; he was a professed *raconteur*, but he murdered it dismally.

Furneaux was for some years a School Examiner, but disliked the pressure which the task involved. "They bring you a haystack of Papers at 6 P.M. and expect the marks next morning." And, though a strenuous worker, he loved a leisurely dinner and a good night's rest. He abandoned the practice after a while : it had been, he said, "a youthful folly." He died in 1900, in his seventy-first year.

One old acquaintance more shall close my list, who, like the last, died, *multis flebilis*, before his time, Tom Faussett of Corpus. He held a close scholarship, confined to the county of Oxford. There was only one candidate besides, but as the senior boy at Winchester he was formidable. I remember Faussett's glee when his rival withdrew, preferring unwisely to take his chance of New College. Unwisely—because while New College was decadent, Corpus was a rising College. While at College Faussett was dexterous in epigram and parody; he became afterwards an exceptionally skilful writer of Latin poetry; not the classical poetry of Lord Wellesley and Charles Wordsworth, but the riming mediæval verse, now secular and humorous, now devotional, of Walter de Mapes or of the Paris Breviary. He was an unrivalled punster : his was the quatrain in *Punch* at which all England laughed, when in the Ashantee war King Coffee Calcalli fled from his burning capital—

> "Coomassie's town is burnt to dust,
>   The King, escaped is he:
> So Ash-and-Coffee now remain
>   Of what was Ash-an-tee."

It is not so easy to pun in Latin; but that too he habitually achieved. In some lines sent to Dean Alford at a time when stormy winds did blow he interjects the comment—

> "Contra venti sunt brumales
>   (Audin' quanta vox eis?),
> Si non *æquinoctiales*
>   Saltem *æque noxii*."

An accomplished lawyer and antiquary, he lived and died at Canterbury as Auditor to the Dean and Chapter; died at the early age of forty-eight. While he was an undergraduate, I had heard some one recite from a topical imitation of Gray's "Elegy," which he ascribed to Faussett. The lines kept a hold on me, and ten years afterwards, meeting him in Oxford, I asked him for them. "I don't think a copy is extant," he said with astonishment. "I never even knew that F. had heard of them; but that they should have reached you and remained in your memory is to me wonderful." He recalled and sent me the lines; I reproduce them from his handwriting. It was a letter, written to an absentee comrade at the close of term.

> "Collections o'er—the knell of closing term,
>   The lower herd speed off with eager glee,
> The Dons too homeward trail their steps sedate,
>   And leave the College to the scouts and me.

REMINISCENCES OF OXFORD

Now fades the last portmanteau on my view,
   And o'er the Quad a solemn stillness looms;
Save where young Furneaux coaching still resides,
   And mumbling pupils throng his distant rooms:

Save that from yonder gloom-encircled lodge,
   The porter's boy doth to the porter moan
Of such as issuing from the ancient gate
   Forget the usual terminal half-crown.

Within that number two, that one pair left,
   Where heaves the wall with countless gold-framed views,
All in his snug armchair in silence set,
   Your humble correspondent takes his snooze.

The husky voice of dream-dissolving scout,
   The porter, summoning to the Dean's stern frown,
The bell's shrill tocsin and the echoing clock
   No more disturb him from his morning's down.

For him no more the social breakfast waits,
   Nor smiling Sankey boils the midnight brew,
No mirthful Wadham scatters cheer around,
   No Blaydes applauds the long-divided crew.

Oft did blue devils 'neath their influence fly,
   Their laughter oft his stubborn moods dispelled,
How jovial did they chaff the term away,
   How the Quad echoed as their sides they held!

Ah! let not Christchurch mock their simple life,
   Their homelier joys and less expensive cares,
Nor Merton gaze with a disdainful smile
   On fun too intellectual to be theirs.

The glare of bran new pinks, the pomp of teams,
   The tuft-hunter's success, the gambler's luck,
Alike upon a slippery basis stand;
   A course too rapid endeth in a "muck."

CORPUS

Nor you, ye swells, impute to us a fault
   In fame and memory if to you we yield,
If ours no vulpine brush, no argent vase,
   Proclaim as victors of the flood and field.

Can storied urns or animated "busts"[1]
   Bribe back the mucker which has once been run;
Can knocker wrenched allay proctorial ire,
   Or tails of vermin soothe a clamorous dun?

Yet know, in this our quiet spot have lived
   Hearts close united by affection's tie,
Wit that might shine in Courts as well as Quads,
   And social virtues with which few can vie.

Their names, their deeds, writ in tradition's page,
   Shall sound eternised by her Muse's lyre,
Freshmen to come the fond record shall trace,
   Rejoice in youth, like them, like them in age aspire."

---

[1] *Bust*—slang for a breakdown in character and career, synonymous with "mucker," then first coming into use.

CHAPTER XV

PATTISON, MAURICE, THOMSON, GOULBURN
WILLIAM SEWELL

" *Hast thou seen higher, holier things than these,
And therefore must to these refuse thy heart?
With the true Best, alack, how ill agrees
That best that thou wouldst choose.
The Summum Pulchrum rests in heaven above;
Do thou as best thou may'st, thy duty do:
Amid the things allowed thee live and love:
Some day thou shalt it view.*"
—CLOUGH.

A Contrast to Jowett—Mark Pattison's Character and Career—A Sceptic—And a Cynic—Omni-erudition—His Talk of Books—The Optimist and the Pessimist—Maurice—Archbishop Thomson—Provost of Queen's—Oxford Preachers—Early Recollections—Denison—Hamilton—Adams—Goulburn—Goulburn at Rugby—A Mediæval Saint—Dean of Norwich—William Sewell—More Puseyite than Pusey—His Emotional Theology—His Quaint Lectures—His Translation of Horace—An Epidemic of High Church Novelettes—"Amy Herbert"—"Hawkstone"—St. Columba's College—Singleton—Radley.

THERE remain some *viri illustres* whom I knew, and of whom I have words to say. First of these comes Mark Pattison. To bracket him with Jowett, as is often done, shows superficial knowledge of the pair. Both, no doubt, were clergymen, both missed disappointingly and afterwards exultingly obtained the Headship of their Colleges, both wrote in "Essays and Reviews." Behind these accidents are life equipment, experiences, char-

MARK PATTISON
From a Portrait in the possession of Miss Stirke

PATTISON AND OTHERS 253

acters, temperaments, standing in phenomenal contrast. Pattison's mind was the more comprehensive, instructed, idealistic, its evolution as intermittent and self-torturing as Jowett's was continuous and tranquil. Pattison's life, in its abrupt precipitations and untoward straits, resembled the mountain brook of Wordsworth's Solitary; Jowett's floated even, strong, and full, from the winning of the Balliol scholarship by the little white-haired lad with shrill voice and cherub face, until the Sunday afternoon at Headley Park, when the old man, shrill, white-haired, and cherubic still, bade "farewell to the College," turned his face to the wall, and died.

To a College whose tutors were inefficient and its scholars healthy animals Pattison carried at eighteen years old a mass of undigested reading, an intelligence half awakened, a morbid self-consciousness, a total want of the propriety and tact which a public school instils, but in which home training usually fails. Slowly there dawned in him the idea of intellectual life, the desire to amass learning for the rapture of acquiring it; and to his mental development, with all its aberrations, this idea gave lasting unity. It was broken for a time by Newman's influence, which swept him into the Tractarian whirlpool, arrested the growth of his understanding, diverted him from scholarahip to theology; the reaction which followed Newman's flight told on him with corresponding force. He had missed his First Class through going prematurely into the Schools, and taking in fewer books than were required for the highest honours. The

Examiners had doomed him to a Third, when one of them, Hayward Cox, drew attention to his answers in the Logic and Moral Science Papers, which were gems of thought; and prevailed on his colleagues to place him in the Second Class. He became Fellow of Lincoln, College Tutor and Examiner in the Schools, threw himself zealously into academic discipline and teaching, recovered the bodily health which High Church σωματικὴ γυμνασία had impaired; was useful and ambitious and happy. The Headship of Lincoln fell vacant, and all looked to see him fill it—all except a torpid and obstructive minority amongst the Fellows, affronted by the energy which put their somnolence to shame. Their intrigues succeeded, and he was defeated by Thompson, a man well acquainted with the College estates and business, but not comparable with Pattison in intellectual and teaching power. The disappointment paralysed him, and, broken-hearted, he resigned his Tutorship. Somewhat restored by two years of rambling, fishing, foreign travel, but an altered and embittered man, vindictive, melancholy, taciturn, he fell back on his old ideal of life—the life of a student pure and simple, with no view to literary success, but, as before, for the joy which study brings. Thenceforth for thirty years, with one brief interruption, his life flowed in this single channel. He lived among his books, used his Headship, when it came to him, less in the interests of the College than to enlarge his library and his leisure; produced his monumental "Casaubon," outcome of twenty-five years' reading; flung off from his workshop the chips now mortised into his collected Essays; died, *multa gemens*, as for his reft library, so most of all for this, that his "Life of Scaliger," conceived and shaped in memory and notes, must pass with him into the land where all things are forgotten.

Such a life must needs write wrinkles, not only on cheek and brow, but on heart and brain: it left its mark on Pattison's. It left him sceptic. Puritanism, Anglicanism, Catholicism, had successively widened his religious conceptions, each in turn falling from him like a worn-out garment, till he became Pantheist on the positive side, negatively Agnostic. Religion he esteemed as a good servant but a bad master; the idea of Deity, he told one of his querists, was "defæcated to a pure transparency." Faith he defined as "belief in the unproved"; and what he could not prove, that he would not believe. This discrepancy between esoteric conviction and professional status troubled him not at all. He acknowledged to Thorold Rogers, who had abandoned the Anglican ministry, his own disbelief in what those who hold them call the fundamental verities of Christianity; but said that as a young man he had adopted in good faith the doctrines of the English Church, had shaped his life to meet its demands, was too old now to make a change injurious to himself. It left him cynical. He declined to acknowledge the obligation of self-sacrifice; pronounced Montaigne's dictum, that to abandon self-enjoyment in order to serve others is unnatural and wrong, "a refreshing passage"; quoted with approval Goethe's paradox, "I know not myself, and God forbid I ever should." In his sister Dora's heroism, which, in the light of Miss Lonsdale's book, all England honoured, he saw only self-glorification and misdirected energy. He lectured once at Birmingham while she was combating small-pox at Walsall : she came over to greet him, not having seen him for years. "What, Dora!" was his only salutation, "still cutting off little Tommy's fingers and little Jemmy's toes?" It left him pessimist. As student of history and politics he had seen one after another millennium prevented by the thwarting Spirit which, *sævo læta negotio*, loves unweariedly to spite humanity; Hellenic civilisation in one century, "New Learning" in another, political reform in his younger days, social emancipation in his maturity. He refused to believe in the progressive happiness of mankind, and laughed to scorn the amiable Tennysonian commonplace that good will be the final end of ill. It left him, happily, as it found him, a devotee of knowledge. He was as nearly omni-erudite as man can be in omni-parient days : one who knew him well said of him that you may dig into any portion of his mind with certainty of turning up a nugget. In the book-lined gallery which opened out of his drawing-room he would sit or stand, in the short morning coat which he affected as a dinner dress, the centre of a group of guests, picked men from many walks of thought, scientist, æsthetic, literary : as each proffered his own patented topic Pattison would take it up and handle it with swift, clear, exhaustive analysis, ending always with an apologetic, "But, you know, it's not my subject."

What was his subject? He ranked specially as an expert in moral philosophy, examining therein at one time for the India Civil Service. I asked him once about the relative merits of the candidates as belonging to different Universities. He said that the Oxford man, in shirt front, finger nails, costume generally, was a thing of beauty—and knew nothing; the Cantab, slightly dingy—and knew something; the Caledonian knew little about moral philosophy, much about the Scotchmen who had handled it; the Dublin man was a boor in externals, but knew everything. Yet no one would venture to limit his speciality to philosophy. Apart from literature and philology, fresh chambers were ever opening to one's quest in the basement no less than in the higher stories of his mind. He had a Yorkshireman's love of horses, and cared to know who won the Derby. He narrowly missed the championship of croquet, and could diagnose the mental bias of the players round him by their methods and tactics in the game. In country walks he recognised the note of every bird, and knew or sought to know the name, habit, class, of every uncommon plant or hovering insect. His talk of books was musical in its luminous enthusiasm, and he read aloud the poetry he loved with rare felicity. As a young man he had written hymns for some of the minor Church festivals, but he never enjoyed religious poetry, and would pitilessly dissect the $\mathrm{\mathring{\eta}\theta o\varsigma}$ and the diction of the "Christian Year." He cared little for Tennyson or Browning, though he joined the Browning Society, and once gave a characteristic address on "James Lee's

Wife." Towards Milton he felt as a scholiast rather than as a worshipper. Pope always appealed to him; he recited his poetry with a relishing *cæsuric* swing, was proud of his own commentary on the "Essay," furious at a stereotyped error in the notes which made him quote Milton's "Hymn on the Nativity" as "Ode to Nature." He greatly enjoyed Wordsworth in what he called his higher mood; moral, that is, not lyrical or romantic. Amongst classic writers he placed Æschylus as unapproachable. Anna Swanwick used to relate that she was reading alone in her drawing-room late one night, when there came a ring at the bell and Pattison walked in. "What is the finest poem in the world?" She hesitated. He answered, "The Agamemnon"; turned on his heel, and disappeared. His favourite Latin poet was Virgil; Gray, and perhaps Collins, he pronounced to be the only English poets rivalling the artistic melody of the Augustan age: he loved to read aloud the "Progress of Poesy," as the finest classical ode in the language, always throwing away the book in anger before the copybook bathos of the closing lines. On his last night alive he desired to have read to him the "Ode on Eton College," commenting as he listened with all his old aptness, pregnancy, refinement.

But man cannot live by literary enthusiasm alone; and in Pattison's scheme of life there was a fatal flaw—it lacked benevolence, participation, sympathy:

> "He did love Beauty only, Beauty seen
> In all varieties of form and mind,
> And Knowledge for its beauty;"

and slighted Love avenged itself. His history incarnated the "Palace of Art"; he built for himself a godlike life, but a life of godlike isolation; and so the unseen hand wrote "Mene, Mene," on his palace walls, and the fruit which he plucked so laboriously from the ambrosial tree turned to an apple of Sodom at the last. He was, indeed, in all points the antithesis of Jowett. The one was idealist, the other practical; a Cynic the one, while the other was a Stoic. Pattison brooding, self-centred, morose; Jowett sweet-blooded, altruistic, sociable; Jowett beamingly optimistic, Pattison pessimist to the core. To his old friend's deathbed, so the tale was current at the time, Jowett sent a farewell message: "You have seen so much good in the world that you may be hopeful of the future!" "I have seen so much *wrong* in the world," snarled Diogenes from his pillow, "that I have *no* hope for the future!" *Sunt lacrymæ!* Yet let us remember, while we emphasise the contrast, that to make allowance for the forces which disturb the moral pendulum—heredity, constitution, temperament, environage—is outside our power and our scope. Here, as elsewhere, comes in the weighty "Judge not" of perfect insight and of perfect charity, hushing our presumptuous verdict, alike on the dejected and the buoyant character, alike on the auspicious and the hapless life, in the presence of the all-adjusting grave.

My analysis of Mark Pattison's character in the "Reminiscences" brought me a deeply interesting letter from one of his few very intimate associates, who had been made conversant with the closing incidents of his life. After pleading that I must not take too literally his avowed contempt for Altruism, since his wife's well-known crusade on behalf of working women owed its initial energy to him, while to the last he freely gave both toil and money to the cause of higher female education, my correspondent proceeds: "Your portrait of the Rector is a very fine one; but I could have given you hints which would have coloured your sketch, and rightly so, more to his mind. I mean his true mind; his contempt for dulness often made him play tricks on stupid people. The last thing read to him was not, as you say, Gray's 'Ode to Eton'; though that he frequently called for, but Horace's Archytas Ode, which was repeated by his wish over and over again. During the last hours he made his Apologia, which was, I believe, taken down by his wife, and is extant. It came to this, that his aim had been to live for knowledge; knowledge not for its own sake, but for the joy of acquiring it. His first conception of this joy was given to him, he said, by Newman's writings; though he had come to gain a truer view than did Newman of what knowledge really meant. You ought also to know the truth about Sister Dora. Like many brilliant hysterics, she was a born romancer, driven by the dramatic instinct to impress her company. This was so odious to the Rector, that he never changed his estimate of her. The family did change, when they found she had a following. I must add my admiration of your masterly sketch; I appreciate the power of intellectual discrimination displayed in it." I quoted as original his saying that the idea of Deity was "defæcated to a pure transparency." I have since found it as used originally by Coleridge, and applied by him not to the "idea of Deity," but to "the mist that stands between God and thee," which after all comes to nearly the same thing.

If Pattison and Jowett present a telling contrast, so do Maurice and Pusey: alike in spiritual fervour, occult influence, magical personality; but originating in very different impulses and ending in very different convictions. Pusey ascended to his mission from long deep theologic study; Maurice came down to it from the top of Sinai, a prophet on fire with his message. Pusey's development from the Tractarian starting-point was intelligible and easily traced; Maurice moved in a maze of contradictions and surprises. Though he hated controversy, his life was one long combat; of large charity and deep humility, he tomahawked opponents with savage personal violence; preaching Radical doctrines, he upheld aristocracy and feudalism; was labelled Broad Church by all parties, while holding with devout acceptance the Prayer Book, Catechism, Thirty-Nine Articles, and Athanasian Creed.

Maurice was cradled amid theological strife. His father was a Unitarian minister, his mother a Calvinist, one sister Anglican, another Baptist. The stern tradition of his home forbade the reading of fiction—shut him out from all enjoyment of external nature; it was an atmosphere of thin, cold thought, moral polemic, intellectual puzzlement. He emerged from it with one dominant desire, which shaped all his speculations and determined his ultimate belief—a passionate longing for unity. At Cambridge his mind grew rapidly, under the genial tutorship of Julius Hare, the stimulating society of the "Apostles"—above all, through close intimacy with Sterling. Refusing to purchase a Fellowship by conformity to the Church, he slipped away without a degree for a course of journalism in London, contributing to *The Westminster Review*, and for a time editing *The Athenæum*. Disturbed by mental anxieties and deeming his life a failure, he entered himself at Oxford, in the hope there to attain some moral and religious standpoint. I have told in another chapter (p. 89) how, during a walk with me through Oxford in the Fifties, the late Sir Thomas Acland, his lifelong and admiring friend, stopped before the Martyrs' door of St. Mary Magdalen Church, and said, "Twenty-five years ago Jacobson and I took F. D. Maurice in there to be baptized." He read desperately hard; published a self-revealing novel, "Eustace Conway"; was ordained to a country curacy; became chaplain of Guy's Hospital; and embodied the outcome of a ten years' mental struggle in his "Kingdom of Christ," that book which abides to-day a record of soul-building not less arresting to the psychologist than the *apologiæ* of the brothers Newman, J. A. Froude, and Blanco White. His apprehension of God was intuitional. He would not see design in Nature, infer a *Summun Pulchrum*, deify the ideal human self, accept an authoritative revelation : like a Hebrew prophet, he *saw* the Lord sitting on His throne. Possessed of, and hourly living in, this presence, he deduced from it his view of nature, of humanity, of life. With Augustine, he beheld a City of the World, a welter of individualism, inequality, competition, warfare, selfishness : beheld, too, a City of God, a universal spiritual society, attested in old experience, latent yet discernible in mankind to-day. Behind the pageant of society, the rise and fall of nations, the jar of creeds, the tangle of contemporary politics, he saw the ever-advancing onset of spiritual energies, drawing men together by a comity of righteousness, wherein all bear others' burdens, finding each his own satisfaction in the satisfaction of all. And the constitution of this society was monarchic : it was not a mystical abstraction, but a visible kingdom, ruled by an ever-present King. He saw it in the Catholic Church, its gate of baptism, its Eucharistic guarantee, its witnessing Bible, its consummation in the Athanasian Trinity : found finally—a crowning solecism and surprise to his admirer J. S. Mill—in the English Church a rock on which, after much tossing to and fro, he felt that he could rest. Yet with no party in that Church was he on consenting terms. He controverted Pusey's tract on baptism ; scoffed alike at the Low Church craving for personal salvation, the High Church academic and tradition-bound formality, the Broad Church independence of dogma. Their systems all began with man, his sinfulness, his needs, his aspirations ; Maurice's starting-point was God. The phrase may mean little or much : fully to appreciate its force and its clue to all his action we must read his writings. When once it is grasped, we can co-ordinate all his religious inconsistencies : the thwarting limitations and timidities which sorely tried his colleagues in the social crusade; his horror of democracy; his shrinking from co-operative action; his halting attitude towards Socialism; his anti-Sabbatarianism; his historic denial of eternal punishment; above all, his furious denunciation of Mansel's jaunty agnosticism, humorously characterised by one of his biographers as a theology of Caliban upon Setebos.

One more factor in this strangely compounded nature must be taken into account—the loathing of oppression which hurled him into every fray upon the weaker side; against the tyranny of an unreasoning majority, against unfair popular clamour, against the bray of the religious press, which he honoured with the most truculent of all his hatreds. He defended Ward in 1844—fought for Pusey against the Six Doctors, for Jowett against Pusey, for Colenso against Gray, for Bennett of St. Barnabas' against the Protestant mob.

He lived an isolated life—it was his prayer that he might do so—and he left no followers. Yet, paradoxical and inconsequent as he often was, his message was the message of a prophet; and as a prophet he was received by those who had ears to hear. "The greatest mind since Plato" was the judgment of Archdeacon Hare. Tennyson's admiring lines of tribute "break with the music of waves upon the Channel shore." "The most beautiful human soul," said Kingsley, who, after Sterling, knew and loved him best—"the most beautiful human soul whom I have ever met with upon earth, of all men approaching nearest to my conception of St. John, the Apostle of Love."

The "Essays and Reviews," with Stanley's tremendous article in the *Edinburgh*, provoked a counterblast of conservative theology, in a long-forgotten "Aids to Faith," edited by Archbishop Thomson, then Provost of Queen's, who had himself, amusing to relate, written a paper which missed insertion in the famous volume only by being sent in too late. I knew him as a Fellow long before; we were both on the committee of the "Amateur," and worked together at the programmes. He was an enthusiastic musician, with a superb baritone voice; no one who heard it will forget his singing of the "Boar's Head" chant at the Queen's College Christmas dinner. In his rooms I first received the idea of what came afterwards to be called "culture"; his talk and the books which lay about giving outlook into a wider world than had dawned on the ordinary academic. Educated under Butler at Shrewsbury, he came up to Queen's in 1836, was idle, recovered himself, and became a Michel Fellow of the College. His line as a Tutor was philosophy; his "Laws of Thought" was for many years a valued text-book. His Bampton Lectures on "The Atonement" passed into the limbo retained for these annual apologies of orthodoxy; but his presentation to All Souls, Marylebone, enabled him to attract fashionable crowds, and made him known outside the University. During his residence in College Mr. and Mrs. Skene of Rubislaw, with their family, came to reside in Oxford. We had all read our Lockhart, and looked with deep interest on the white-haired laird, Walter Scott's lifelong friend, accomplished horseman, draughtsman, antiquarian, godfather to the Fourth Canto of "Marmion," to whom Scott owed the conception of the Jews in "Ivanhoe," and of "Quentin Durward." With them was a middle-aged daughter, who sang Handel finely and wrote religious novels, and two young grand-daughters, one pretty, the other clever: let me not be supposed to allege that the pretty sister was dull or the clever sister plain; but so it was, that men used to manœuvre at dinner-parties to take down the clever sister and sit opposite the pretty one. This last—the "Greek Slave" she was called, her mother being a Levantine—was soon surrounded by admirers; from them she selected Thomson, and they were married on his appointment to the London living. In 1855 he was made Provost of Queen's. The election was decided by his vote in favour of himself, and his right to take part in it, being a married Fellow in his year of grace, was challenged; but he persisted, and carried his point, not without abiding friction between himself and the dissenting electors. At Prince Albert's death his name was found prominent on the list of clergymen whom the Prince thought deserving of promotion, and he became at short intervals a Royal Chaplain, Bishop of Gloucester and Bristol, Archbishop of York. The final nomination was said to have been a compromise between the Queen and the Prime Minister. She had marked her old friend Bishop Wilberforce for the see; but Lord Palmerston, between whom and the Bishop there was constant feud, named Waldegrave of Carlisle; and, when neither would give way, threw upon the Queen the responsibility of making the appointment. She was at Coburg, and on receiving Palmerston's letter desired to have the names read over to her. Of several names she said "No—they will not do": at the last, when Thomson's came, she said—"Yes, let it be he; the Prince always thought well of him." As Archbishop, Thomson hardly fulfilled the expectation which dictated and accompanied his rapid rise. Unpopular in London society, it was early understood that he would never succeed to the higher throne of Canterbury. This he had always expected would be his; S. Wilberforce's diary notes on his non-appointment, "Thomson much disappointed." He preached, now and again, extraordinarily eloquent sermons: Dean Stanley, and Thompson, afterwards Master of Trinity, both noted discourses of his in Westminster Abbey as amongst the best which they had ever heard; and his rare appearances on public platforms were marked by addresses of the very highest order; but these efforts were isolated and eruptive; so that, unquestionably in his own time the ablest prelate on the bench, he left no mark either on his Church or on the community. His presence was remarkably imposing, of great bulk and stature, with massive features, sonorous delivery, dignified and stately manners. Imprudently exerting himself when unwell in a December Ordination, the action of his heart failed, and he died on Christmas Day, 1890.

I have said nothing of the early parochial Oxford pulpits. At the opening of the Thirties Evangelicalism was dominant, trumpeted by a tremendous Boanerges named Bulteel, whose powerful but sulphurous sermons filled St. Ebbe's Church. He made a name for himself outside his squalid parish, attacked the Heads of Houses for sloth and unfaithfulness in a violent University sermon, whose impeachments they but feebly answered, practised faith healing successfully in cases where physicians were in vain, ministered in conventicles, found his licence revoked by Bishop Lloyd, whom he thereupon denounced publicly as "an officer of Antichrist," built a chapel of his own, and founded a not long-lived sect of Bulteelites. Reviving High Churchism first echoed in St. Peter's Church, about 1835, from the lips and practice of Edward Denison and his curate Walter Kerr Hamilton, both afterwards Bishops of Salisbury. I remember the beautiful old Norman edifice in my boyhood, neglected and dilapidated: I sat with my mother in a large, high, square pew, into which we locked ourselves on entering, and prayed for their most gracious Majesties King William and Queen Adelaide. A lady in the adjacent pew interested me always by turning eastward and thereby facing us when the Creed was recited; it was explained to me that she was "a very old-fashioned person." In 1836 the church was restored (we worshipping the while in Merton Chapel), an ugly clerk's house in the churchyard swept away, the vast family pews abolished, the services improved to a pitch for that time highly ornate, starveling as it would seem now. Denison was followed by Hamilton; Hamilton by William Adams, author of the once famous "Allegories"; Adams by Stewart Bathurst, who followed Newman to Rome; he by Edmund Hobhouse, not long deceased, at a great age, emeritus Bishop of Nelson. Few churches have ever been so shepherded in a succession so long unbroken. It was believed that a particular set of Merton rooms in which these pastors lived held an occult power of episcopal generation; certainly I have breakfasted there with three occupants who afterwards became bishops.

Good men as all these were, yet, with the exception of Adams, who at his early death left behind him a volume of touching sermons, none of them made the drum ecclesiastic musically resonant. That distinction was reserved for Goulburn in the opening of the Forties. "'Obhouse and 'Ansell are below par," said Mr. Hounslow, the Radical grocer in High Street, to a stranger in quest of Sunday pabulum; "go to 'Olywell and 'ear Goulburn." Always noted as a preacher, Goulburn was a man rather lovable than eminent, a man who sank into the surroundings of the high posts he filled, discharging their duties conscientiously, but affixing to them no stamp of genius. A Balliol Scholar, he was intimate with Lake, Stanley, Brodie, Waldegrave, Golightly; gained a First Class, and became Fellow of Merton. These laurels won, he started on a tour with Stanley, which was terminated by an accident to his leg. Stanley used to tell how, overhearing from his bed the physician, Dr. Bruno—Byron's incapable doctor sixteen years before—express his fear lest suppuration should set in, the invalid called out in his mincing tones, "Sup-pu-ration—I never heard the word before, but it exactly expresses what I feel." Rescued from suppuration and from Bruno, he returned home to take Orders and to become Vicar of the small Holywell parish. His wife was of the Aynhoe Cartwright family; he brought his bride to the pretty little Holywell Cottage, now swept away, and at once made his mark as a preacher. Townspeople and undergraduates swelled his congregations, finding in the frankness, variety, humanism, of his sermons a refreshing contrast to the textiferous platitudes or the dry formalisms emitted respectively from neighbouring Low or High Church pulpits. Nor was the absurd strain wanting which ran ever through his character, actions, talk. Delicious bits of finical rhetoric, set off by his detached, tinkling, monosyllabic delivery, come up to me out of the past; as when, preaching on the Jews of Berea, he began, "It may be predicated of the Bereans that they permitted no extraneous circumstances to counteract the equipoise of their equanimity"; or when, magnifying the wisdom of Providential adaptation in nature, he concreted his illustration by a "min-now," which swam so often into our ken as to be at last greeted with a general titter. His theology, baldly Calvinistic at the outset,

GOULBURN

was afterwards modified by contact with Samuel Wilberforce, when that astute prelate, all things to all men in his diocese, muzzled his Low Church opponents—Litton, Hayward Cox, John Hill, and others—by making their like-minded friend Goulburn one of his examining chaplains. It culminated finally in that dexterously balanced Anglican orthodoxy which, whatever its effect upon their intellectual expansion, earns for its doctrinaires the valuable repute of "soundness," and so "not unfrequently leads to positions of considerable emolument."[1] It led Goulburn to a post for which he was certainly not suited, the Headmastership of Rugby. In the competition his rival was Lake, on all grounds a fitter man. Lake was essentially an educator, Goulburn restrictedly an evangelist. Lake represented all the tendencies and traditions which had made Rugby the first school in England, Goulburn must inevitably thwart them: to the Tory trustees who held the election in their hands, and who later on appointed Hayman, that was Goulburn's strongest recommendation. They chose Goulburn and rejected Lake, causing Arthur Stanley, for once in his placable life, to lose his temper and say hard things.

Goulburn went to Rugby with misgivings, found the work uncongenial, after eight years resigned it with delight. "He was not," writes to me an old pupil who was in his house and loved him well, "he was not intended to be a headmaster. He was a mediæval saint with great social power; simplicity itself, with the pomposity of a D.D. of

[1] Page 124.

those times: he used, for instance, to go out to dinner in his cassock, and never appeared without it among us boys. He preached on excellent theses, but loved Latinised expressions: 'Let the scintillations of your wit be like the coruscations of summer lightning, lambent but innocuous.' He believed in surprises to attract attention; would preach on occasions from the eagle instead of from the pulpit, would choose as a text 'The King of Jericho, one; the King of Ai, one,' and so on, reading out all the thirty-one in order; would conceal a horsewhip under his gown in school, and crack it to help out a passage in Aristophanes. He seldom knew one boy from another: 'Well, little boy, what do you want?' passing his hand over one's head in a fatherly way, but having forgotten all the previous interview. He was fleeced by his servants, who starved us; adored personally by Benson, who saw his goodness; ridiculed by Bradley, who saw his failures: Compton was his relative, and the first attempt at a science master in the school; a good attempt, but badly carried out. When Goulburn left, he tried to keep out Temple in favour of Fanshawe from Bedford, but happily failed. Temple restored discipline by a system of superannuation. Had it not been for Tom Evans, Bradley, Benson, as assistant masters, the teaching would have been as bad a failure as the discipline. And yet he was an ideal gentleman and a Christian."

He returned to the field in which he was an expert, the field of parochial and pastoral work, at Quebec Chapel and St. John's, Paddington;

until he made perhaps the second blunder of his life by accepting the Deanery of Norwich. As Dean he found scope for his preaching power, but was deficient in the secular and practical side of chapter work. At this time were written many of his devotional manuals, and by these his name will be remembered longest. Once or twice he took public action; when Stanley was made Select Preacher at Oxford he protested by resigning the similar office which he held; but the step left untouched their personal friendship, and on Stanley's death he preached a funeral sermon which, since Burgon sternly denounced it, was probably in all ways generous and Christian. He wrote afterwards the Life of that eccentric divine. Few men have offered scope so inviting to a biographer—at once poet, critic, artist, theologian, buffoon, at once indecently scurrilous and riotously comic, he lived and died as if to inspire above all things a brief and brilliant memoir: but Goulburn produced two ponderous volumes as unreadable as the "Guicciardini" of Macaulay's anecdote. After a time his deanery palled on him as his headmastership had done: its quasi-episcopal rubs and worries, exhilarating to a Wilberforce or a Magee, were to him intolerable; he long pined to be rid of it, and at last resigned it. The closing public act of his life was to join with Denison, Liddon, and a few, a very few, besides, in a declaration, called forth by "Lux Mundi," on the "Truth of Holy Scripture," which, defiant of German exegesis, of geological discovery, of universally accepted Darwinism, restated solemnly, sadly, helplessly, the abandoned theories of unadjusted Biblical criticism. There is a double pathos in such spectacles, familiar as they are to times of mental change: pathos in the heartsickness of the seniors, left to stand alone in ancient ways, whence all but they have fled; from which the forces of enlarged conviction have driven the disciples and the friends who once walked with them there; pathos in the half-compassionate reluctance of the younger men to break away, galled by the stigma of desertion, yet submissive to the beckoning of a hand their elders cannot see. Some of us, it may be, can remain apart from and feel sympathy with both; discerning, from our vantage ground outside the conflict, that the old paths and the new, if traversed in obedience to the prick of conscience and of duty, lead to the same goal at last.

I come to the last of my *Papavera*, to William Sewell, subsequent founder of Radley, prominent Fellow of Exeter in the Thirties, a flourishing and conspicuous, yet somehow a questionable, specimen—what botanists call *Papaver dubium*— among the poppies of his day. In fluency of speech, fertility of mind, fascination of manner, he had no contemporary rival; his public teaching, like his private talk, was ever rousing, persuasive, lofty; it seemed that those eloquent lips could open only to emit godlike sentiments and assert uncompromising principles. In truth, they were not often closed: he was Select Preacher and Professor of Moral Philosophy; his lectures on Plato and on Shakespeare filled Exeter College Hall; while in London, as Whitehall Preacher, he drew large crowds, amused to hear leading statesmen of the day denounced under the names of Herod and Pontius Pilate. "More Puseyite than Pusey," his emotional theology attracted a shallower yet scarcely a less numerous class than Newman's inspired sermons. It seemed that a mitre, a Headmastership, or at least the Headship of his College, must descend upon so gifted and so popular an aspirant: yet standing for Winchester in 1835 he was beaten by Moberly; yet when old Collier Jones, the Μαριλαΐδης Ἰωνεύς of Scott's verses, died in 1839, Richards, not Sewell, was elected; and, in spite of the promptings of the *Times*, whose young chief Walter had been his pupil, right reverend Howleys and Blomfields at headquarters were understood to shake doubtful wigs when his name was mentioned for promotion. A taint of superficiality clung to him : "Sewell is very unreal," wrote Newman to Bowden in 1840; "Namby-pamby" Hampden called him ; "Preaches his dreams" was shrewd Shuttleworth's comment on his University sermons ; "Sewell," said Jowett in 1848, "Sewell, talking rashly and positively, . . . has gone far to produce that very doubt and scepticism of which he himself complains." "How silent you have been, Jacobson," said he at the end of a large gathering in his rooms, where, as usual, he had done all the talking ; "you have not said anything worth listening to." "Nor heard," was Jacobson's answer.

So through the Forties he continued Tutor of Exeter—"excessively discursive," says Dean Boyle ;

"would commence a lecture on Aristotle and end with the Athanasian Creed or the beauties of Gothic architecture." "Sewell's last" formed the staple of Exeter breakfast parties. I well remember his cremation of Froude's "Nemesis of Faith," a feat reduced from myth to fact in Max Müller's "Auld Lang Syne." "What is meant by gold, frankincense, myrrh?" he propounded on another day. The regulation answer was given. "Yes; but shall you understand me if I tell you that they also mean logic, rhetoric, and metaphysics?" Many more I could relate, but *ex ungue leonem*. Meanwhile men around him were moving on, and he marked time: opposed in a once famous hysterical sermon the erection of the new Museum; wrote, under the title of "Lord John Russell's Postbag," a series of lampoons, discreditable in their imputations and distortive of his opponents' motives, against the University Commission. He was to learn that ὕβρις has its nemesis no less than faith: a translation of the Odes of Horace from his pen was mercilessly gibbeted in the *Edinburgh* by John Conington, and all England laughed over a review by Conybeare of his "Year's Volume of Sermons." Both articles were, of course, intentionally punitive; the second was good-humoured, and the savagery of the first was justifiable. I have not seen the Horace for fifty years, but some of its absurdities still cling to me. Here is his opening of the *Parentis olim*:

> "If a man upon a time
> Ever has with hand of crime
> Wrenched his sire's aged neck, I ween
> *'Tis that he hath eating been*
> Garlic, deadlier without question

> E'en than hemlock: oh digestion
> Hard as iron of the reaper!
> What is this, that still so deep here,
> Keeps turmoiling in my chest?"

We laughed; but I do not think he lost general repute. He remained the exciting public lecturer and preacher, the supremely fascinating talker, the genial and accomplished host; entertaining in this last capacity the Archæological Society in 1850 at a magnificent entertainment, when the Fellows' pretty garden was illuminated, the great Service tree hung with coloured lamps, the Distin family performing upon their saxhorns in the Hall. Meanwhile his energy had broken out in a new place. One of the cleverest of Oxford skits, "The Grand University Logic Stakes of 1849,"[1] attributed to Landon of Magdalen, and academising with marvellous dexterity the language of the Turf, described the "runners" for the Prælectorship of Logic in 1839 and 1849. Sewell bears the stable name of "Gruel," so richly descriptive of his querulous invalid voice and cataplasmic countenance that it clung to him ever after.

"Gruel continues to make a show in the world, and stands high in public estimation. He has taken to a *novel* line, in which he has come out rather strong. He appears to have left the Turf altogether for the present. After a long season in *Ireland*, where, notwithstanding several influential Backers, he seems to have been a failure, he returned to the Marquis of Exeter's stables. His lordship still drives him in his four-in-hand, giving him an occasional day's work at *Radley Farm*, where he goes to plough and drill on a new system with an Irish horse called *Single-peeper*."

---

[1] Appendix R.

There was in the Forties an epidemic of High Church novelettes. Sewell's name appeared as editor on the title-page of his sister's popular tales, "Amy Herbert" and her successors, and he himself wrote "Hawkstone," a queer, sensational production, but hinting an idea which had for some time taken possession of his mind—the establishment of an educational institution "on a new system," on the lines of our older public schools, but with minute observance of Prayer Book rules. The consequence elsewhere attaching to slowly matured antiquity was here to be ready made, by sumptuous fittings and surroundings, academic dress, a collegiate framework in which the head was to be a "warden," the assistant masters "fellows." St. Columba's College was opened in 1844 at Stackallan, in County Meath. Its warden was Singleton, afterwards head of Radley; its sub-warden Tripp of Worcester, an enthusiastic, amiable, not powerfully minded Wykehamist. It received munificent support from Lord Adare, from the Primate, from William Monsell, and from Dr. Todd of T.C.D.; but friction soon arose, and the site was moved to Rathfarnham on the Dublin mountains, where I believe it still survives. Sewell retired from the enterprise, and in 1847 opened St. Peter's College, Radley, on the same lines, with Singleton as its first warden. For this venture large sums were wanted; Sewell obtained them by his extraordinary genius for enlisting the sympathies and picking the pockets of plutocrats, calling frequently, it was said, at great merchants' counting-houses and coming out with weighty cheques. Soon visitors from Oxford saw cubicled dormitories, a tastefully decorated chapel with a fine Flemish triptych, magnificent carved oak sideboards, tables, cabinets, and, it must be added, very few boys.

Warden Singleton, whom I knew intimately, was one of the noblest of men, self-sacrificing, generous, high-principled, true as truth itself. From considerable private means he had given bounteously to both schools, lending money to Sewell as well. The moral tone of the boys under his rule was perfect, their scholarship respectable, they loved him dearly, he managed economically the current outlay; *but* the numbers did not rise. His manners told unfavourably on Oxford men; over a pipe or on board his yacht he was a genial Irish gentleman, but at the Radley high table, exalting not his person but his office, his stern elevation of manner was repellent. Hascoll, the sub-warden, a half-pay naval captain, who spoke French and was supposed to teach it, had no social qualifications. The assistant masters were gentlemen but not scholars, for the salaries were very low; the only honour man amongst them, Howard of Lincoln, son to Charles Howard, R.A.; afterwards Director-General of Public Instruction at Bombay; spent all his time in plaguing Singleton and agitating for a stronger brew of college beer; for by the statutes the "fellows" were independent of and could control the warden, and three amongst them succeeded in driving Singleton from his post. They chose instead of him William Heathcote of New College, who promptly dismissed the insurrectionary cabal; but, discovering after a time the unsound financial basis of the school, and prevented from obtaining a proper audit of the accounts by Sewell's refusal to explain a certain large and unaccountable deficit, he in his turn threw up the post. Sewell now perforce took the reins himself, with a great name, magnificent conceptions, and a genial acquiescence in Ancient Pistol's motto, "Base is the slave who pays." The school went up with a rush, the "eight" rowed at Henley; entertainments were given on saints' days, the "college plate" on the tables, the senior boy, "Bob" Risley, welcoming the guests in Latin speeches; Sewell proclaiming in terms of pious gratitude that the school was out of debt, at a time when I knew him to owe Singleton £5000, and more than suspected far heavier liabilities behind. In fact, the splendour, like Timon's, "masked an empty coffer." The school had never paid; after the first capital was exhausted reckless purchases had gone on; cases of decorative treasures, including Agra marbles at a guinea a foot, lay still packed in outhouses as they had arrived, to be sold for a trifle when the bubble burst; heavy loans were obtained, heavier debts heaped up; boys were taken for six years' payment in advance at largely reduced fees, which vanished as soon as they were received. Finally, to celebrate the opening of a new gymnasium, which cost *somebody* £1600, a Belshazzar feast was given to all who then or in the past had been connected with St. Columba's or with Radley. A vast assembly came; Sewell, in full Doctor's dress of scarlet and black velvet, welcomed us—as usual, a perfect host. We sat to a splendid banquet; Dan Godfrey's band discoursed sweet music; 600 lb. of strawberries, we were told, covered the tables at dessert, and all went merry as a marriage bell. After dinner, not waiting for the concert, as my wife and I sat expecting our carriage in an unlighted corner, we saw Hubbard of the Bank of England, whom I knew to have made large advances, pacing up and down alone, with anxious face and corroded brow. "The handwriting on the wall," I whispered; and so it was. The reckless extravagance of that evening scared him; a closer inspection of the school affairs revealed secrets of indebtedness which had been hitherto concealed from him. Within a few days he seized the place as principal creditor, sent Sewell right away, repudiated all his debts, cancelled the claims of parents who had paid in advance, sold all unnecessary splendours, placed in charge Norman, one of the masters who was highly popular with the boys, to work the school as his property in reduction of its dues to him. Sewell came into Oxford a broken man, then disappeared; lived for some years on the Continent; returned to England, and died in 1874, at the house of a nephew near Manchester.

CHAPTER XVI

WALK ABOUT ZION

"*Since all that is not heaven must fade,
Light be the hand of Ruin laid
Upon the home I love:
With lulling spell let soft Decay
Steal on, and spare the giant sway,
The crash of tower and grove.*"
—KEBLE.

Venerable Oxford—Ancient Landmarks—The Greyhound—Mother Jeffs—Mother Louse—Mother George—Mother Goose—The Angel—Some Old Establishments—The High—Jubber's and Sadler's—Convivialities—Changes—The Oxford that I love.

THE Psalmist bade his countrymen mark the towers, bulwarks, palaces of their historic city in its prime of queenliness, that they might "tell it to the generations following." What would the Biblical student give for such a Hestiagraph to-day? Many a fragmentary chapter of Jewish story might be well replaced by a brief record, contemporary, personal, picturesque, of the scenes which are now to us mere shadow-names: Solomon's Palace and the Royal Tombs, the Tyropœon megaliths and the Bakers' Street, the pools of Enrogel, Gihon, Siloam, the gilded dome of Zion "towering o'er her marble stairs." Oxford is not, like Jerusalem, a buried city; yet the Oxford of to-day is not the Oxford of the Thirties; ever and again as I recall events and personages they need the background and the setting which enshrined them then, and is now impaired or swept away. The dreaming spires of the sweet city show still from the Cumnor or the Rose Hill heights, as they showed to Matthew Arnold sixty years ago; he could not now go on to say that "she lies steeped in sentiment, spreading her gardens to the moonlight, and whispering from her towers the last enchantments of the Middle Age," for the encroaching nineteenth century has dissolved that still removed charm.[1] Tram-lines mar to-day the pontifical symmetry of Magdalen Bridge; an intruding chasm breaks the perfect High Street curves; St. Mary's spire, tapering from its nest of pinnacles, has been twice deformed by restoration; Vanbrugh's quaint house in Broad Street is sacrificed to a stodgy Indian Institute: Christchurch Meadow with its obstructed river banks tempts me to render railing for railing; the Broad Walk veterans are disarrayed or fallen; a vulgar and discordant pile has banished the civil-suited nymphs of Merton Grove. Visiting extant

---

[1] Let me go back further still, and embalm forgotten lines from Tom Warton's "Triumph of Isis":

> "Ye fretted pinnacles, ye fanes sublime,
> Ye towers that wear the mossy vest of time,
> Ye massy piles of old munificence,
> At once the pride of learning and defence;
> Ye cloisters pale, that length'ning on the sight
> To contemplation, step by step, invite;
> Ye high-arched walks, where oft the whispers clear
> Of harps unseen have swept the poet's ear;
> Ye temples dim, where pious duty pays
> Her holy hymns for ever echoing praise;
> Lo! your loved Isis from the bordering vale
> With all a mother's fondness bids you Hail!"

Oxford, I should explore the venerable haunts, seek the ancient *Termini*, probe the mouldering associations of High and Broad, of Iffley Road, and Cowley Marsh, and Bullingdon all in vain, like Rogers' old man wandering in quest of something. The change had begun when Arnold wept over Thyrsis' urn—"In the two Hinkseys nothing keeps the same"; it is far more devastating to-day. Let me in this last paper recover where I can its erased or vanishing landmarks—*formæ veneres captare fugaces*—as a setting to the recorded incidents and characters which they should illustrate and frame.

In the early Thirties, then, railroads and enclosures had not girdled Oxford proper with a coarse suburban fringe. On the three approaches to the town, the Henley, Banbury, Abingdon Roads, it was cut off, clear as a walled and gated Jericho, from the adjacent country. One side of it there is which I now never dare approach: enclosure Acts and jerry builders and villatic burghers have effaced by "long straggling streets of ricketty cottages" what was once the most harmonious avenue to the most beautiful city in the world. In the days when Tullus was Consul you sped through Nuneham, Sandford, and Littlemore behind the four horses of the *Tantivy* or the *Rival*, until from Rose Hill top you saw and never lost again the long line of pinnacles and spires bosomed in foliage less obscuring than to-day. Past Rose Bank, the home of Newman's mother and her two clever girls, the road ran for a short distance much as it runs now, then opened

WALK ABOUT ZION

houseless and hedgeless all the way, marked only by one towering hawthorn known as the "half-way bush," to the turnpike which barred access to Magdalen Bridge. Far to the right stretched the northern view, across Cowley Marsh, the windows of newly-built Headington Asylum glaring in the western sun, up the Bullingdon ascent, where I have many times shot snipe and gathered Parnassia and butterwort, and so away to Shotover. On the left were the unbroken willow-dotted Isis meadows, rising beyond the gleaming river into Bagley Wood, and to the line of Berkshire hills crowned by Cumnor Hurst and the Gipsy Scholar's Tree. As you neared Oxford, on what is now Christchurch Cricket-ground were unenclosed acres of wheat, decked with poppies, scabious, corn cockle, and blue centaury; on the opposite side towered three vast black hillocks, to and from which all day long passed the Corporation carts laden with coal refuse of a thousand hearths, to be sifted and sold as cinder or as ash. Along the smooth hard road streamed in endless variety the vehicles of pre-railroad days; mail coaches by the score, gigs, tandems, carriages and four, carriers' carts from adjacent villages and towns, mighty *petorrita* of the great London stage-waggoners, lowlier wains heaped high with hay and corn. The bordering gravel path was sprinkled in early morning by troops of fresh-faced girls bearing poised upon their heads high wicker baskets filled with fruit, vegetables, turnip-tops; in the afternoon by academical pedestrians in pairs or triplets, transacting the regulation grind to Iffley, Cowley, or Sandford. Not that the word "grind" was invented then; that and "constitutional" were subsequent terms, the last, I think, first made classical by Miss Cornelia Blimber. Dons were there as well as undergraduates, even one or two Heads of Houses; old Sneyd of All Souls, and tall Plumtre of University, walking daily solitary and solemn, sometimes Gaisford with a handsome daughter, and Macbride with a daughter who was certainly not handsome. There too on most days was to be seen a regiment of boys, commanded by a stern Orbilius clad in spencer and black gaiters, which was known as "Slatter's School." Located at Rose Hill, it was famous far and near; the best Oxford families sent to it all their sons. Amongst my schoolfellows were Le Mesurier, a brilliant scholar of Corpus, who died young; Haggitt, son to Lord Harcourt's Nuneham chaplain mentioned in Madame D'Arblay's diary; and afterwards, as Wegg Prosser, M.P. for Hereford; Stowe, First Class and Fellow of Oriel, who went out as *Times* correspondent to the Crimea and there died; Faussett, till lately the efficient Bursar of Christchurch; and Fred Thistlethwaite, famous in London society for his immense wealth and his manner of spending it: he achieved unique distinction by running away from Eton, Harrow, and Winchester in succession: of the three schools he found Winchester the most intolerable, and resigned it after three days' trial. His father, a Hampshire squire, owned land in what was then the village of Paddington; converted into Westbournia it became golden, and Fred was the *heres dignior*. Slatter was a remarkable man; an accomplished chemist, and one of the best astronomers of his time, having a mighty Herschel's telescope in constant use. He was an admirable teacher; no boys in England were better grounded than ourselves, nor in a greater variety of subjects; but he was disciplinary even in excess of the savage custom then thought necessary in schools. His desk was garnished with a quite curious collection of canes incessantly in use *a posteriori*, and a large wooden tubeless thermometer was reserved for hand-spanking, or, as he called it, "strappado." To the music of these flagellants all our work was set: stimulated by my mother, I kept account during one half-year of my own personal tragedies: they numbered fifty-two, representing on an average more than two in a week, administered for no default of immorality or disobedience, but for syntactical fallacies in construing, or for *Propria Quæ Maribus* incompletely learned. We endured stoically; to cry out was thought pusillanimous; like Dido, we wept in silence, accepting the *baculi ictus* as no less germane to progress than were Grammar and Delectus. And we bore no malice; went back to pay friendly visits to our Busby after we had left; hoped nothing worse for him when consigned to Iffley churchyard than that he might be tended in his repose by cherubs structurally impervious to the discipline, which even in another world he might find impossible to lay aside.

One feature of the Via Appia to the Sacred

City I have not mentioned, old St. Clement's Church, standing in the fork of the Headington and Iffley roads at the entrance on Magdalen Bridge. Andrew Lang in his book on Oxford tells us that visitors approaching it by the eastern entrance would pass the "boiled rabbit" on their right. That is not so; the "boiled rabbit" was built during Newman's curacy in the late Twenties; the old church bore no cuniculous similitude. In the new church, still extant, and notable as one of the few English synagogues where sermons are still emitted in black gown, Newman never officiated; its Pastor for many years was J. W. Hughes, of Trinity, whose family of captivating daughters filled on Sunday the spacious vicarage pew. He took private pupils to read for Matriculation; when two of these had successively married his two eldest girls, he received the name of "the judicious Hooker." He was a handsome, well-dressed man, read the service rhetorically, preached fine parish sermons. He was a hack Saint's-Day preacher at St. Mary's, earning five guineas by the delivery of an old sermon to a church quite empty except for the Vice-Chancellor and Bedels. When Isaac Williams came up to reside as Trinity Tutor, he made a duty of attending all University sermons, to the discomfiture of Hughes, who said to Tommy Short one day, "I wonder what Williams admires in my sermons; he is the only University man who attends them; it is highly complimentary, but puts me to the trouble of looking out sermons appropriate to the days." The system was after-

UNIV. OF CALIFORNIA

THE REVD JOHN GUTCH, F.A.S. M.A.

Registrar of the University of Oxford.

From an Engraving after a Water-Colour belonging to the Family

wards altered: poor Hughes, his daughters, and his sermons, *delevit aetas*.

It was in the old church that J. H. Newman served his first curacy under the octogenarian antiquary John Gutch, Registrar of the University, editor of Anthony Wood, author of "Collectanea Curiosa." Newman in his letters to his sister depicts gratefully the valuable assistance rendered by the old Rector's daughters; Sarah, the youngest, lived to her ninetieth year, the most efficient visitor of the poor in Oxford. For her last ten years she was bedridden when I saw her shortly before her death, in 1882, she told me how the aged Cardinal, visiting Oxford, had climbed to her room and sat long beside her bed, affectionately recalling old times and people. From church and turnpike you passed the bridge, the Physic Garden open on your left; for the residence built by Daubeny had not then risen, and the Professor, Dr. Williams, lived in the house facing Rose Lane. Water-carts were not as yet invented, and in very dry weather the street was irrigated from its five or six fire-plugs—we remember Mr. Bouncer's F.P. 7 ft.—commencing at Magdalen elms. A sheet of canvas with a wooden frame was laid across the gutter, and the water turned on until it swelled into a pool, then with curious dexterity dashed in all directions by a bare-legged Aquarius, with the aid of an enormous wooden shovel. The gate of Magdalen was Jacobæan, of debased style, but more stately and more in harmony with the College than any of its successors; adjoining it was a

T

remnant of the old Magdalen Hall, used as the choristers' school, with a modern cottage inhabited by the College manciple Stephens. He was the most Waltonian of Oxford anglers, my guide on many an occasion to the waters of Cherwell, Upper Isis, Windrush, knowing every spot where a skilfully dropped "gudgin" would capture perch or pike. Where Magdalen schoolroom now stands, was the Greyhound inn. Under one of the trees sat always an apple-faced old woman, Mother Jeffs, selling tarts and fruits, last of a famous sisterhood whose names and effigies survive out of the hoary past. There was Mother Louse, whose portrait by Loggan is a prize to print collectors, the latest woman in England to wear a ruff; Mother George, who at more than a hundred years old would, on payment of a shilling, thread a needle without spectacles; Mother Goose the flower-seller, pictured by Dighton in a coloured drawing which I reproduce; her contemporary Nell Batchelor, pie-woman, an epitaph to whose "pie-house memory" was inscribed by a forgotten wit—

"Here under the dust is the mouldering crust
    Of Eleanor Batchelor shoven,
Well versed in the art of pie, custard, and tart,
    And the lucrative skill of the oven.

When she'd lived long enough, she made her last puff,
    A puff by her husband much praised;
Now here she doth lie, and makes a dirt pie,
    In the hope that *her* crust may be raised."

From Coach and Horse Lane to the Angel stretched a great block of shops, swept away to

MOTHER LOUSE
From the Line Engraving after Loggan

WALK ABOUT ZION

make room for the new Schools. The corner house was tenanted by James, a confectioner, cook of Alban Hall, where the traditional dinner grace ran, "For what James allows us make us truly thankful"; another exhibited the graceful plaster casts of Guidotti, an Italian image-seller, with an extremely handsome English wife. The Angel was the fashionable hotel; the carriages and four of neighbouring seigneurs, Dukes of Marlborough and Buckingham, Lords Macclesfield, Abingdon, Camoys, dashed up to it; there, too, stopped all day post-chaises, travelling chariots, equipages of bridal couples, coaches from the eastern road; all visitors being received at the hall door by the obsequious manager Mr. Bishop, in blue tail-coat gilt-buttoned and velvet-collared, buff waistcoat, light kerseymere pantaloons, silk stockings and pumps, a gold eyeglass pendent from a broad black ribbon; escorted by Wallace, a huge mastiff, who made friends with every guest. All of it has vanished except the spacious coffee-room, which became Cooper's shop. The Old Bank stood where now it stands, already some twenty years old. It was founded by two tradesmen—Thompson, a gunsmith, and Parsons, a draper, the latter brother to Dr. Parsons, Master of Balliol and Bishop of Peterborough. Passing gallantly through the money panic of 1825, when Walter Scott was ruined and half the banks in England broke, it rose into high repute, obtained the deposits of all the Colleges, and retains probably most of them to-day under the grandsons of its founders. Close to it were Vincent's Rooms, the home of the Union, whose debates were held in a hall behind Wyatt's picture shop. In 1835 the house of Wood, the apothecary, at the entrance to Skimmery Hall Lane, was translated into Spiers', now itself extinct, but for nearly sixty years inseparable from Oxford life, better served and more artistic in its merchandise than any shop in England. Its display of papier mâché and of ceramic ware, surrounding a beautiful cardboard model of the Martyrs' Memorial, was one of the features in the 1851 Exhibition.

There were in the High two superior confectioners, Jubber's and Sadler's, where white-hatted Christchurch dandies lounged and ate ices in the afternoons. The principal tailor was Joy, in a large shop opposite Wadham. He was denominated Parson Joy, having been met in the Long Vacation travelling on the Continent with his brother, as Captain and the Rev. —— Joy. He bequeathed his book debts to one of his daughters; they amounted to £4000, and she used to say that every penny was recovered. The two large booksellers were Talboys, in the handsome pillared shop opposite St. Peter's Church, and Joseph Parker, in the Turl, whose management of the Bible Press had converted a heavy debt into £100,000 of profit, and who had lately made a hit by publishing two unassuming and anonymous little volumes, destined, as "The Christian Year"—"The Sunday Puzzle" Sydney Smith called it—to achieve unprecedented popularity. Its success was a surprise both to Keble and his friends. Isaac Williams, to whom he had shown it, did not admire it. Froude feared that

MOTHER GOOSE
From a Coloured Lithograph by Dighton

WALK ABOUT ZION

people reading it would take the author for a Methodist. So careless of it was Keble, that he lost the little red book into which it was written, and it was printed from a copy he had given to Rickards of Oriel. "It will be still-born," said he, as he left the manuscript with Baxter; "I publish it only in obedience to my father's wishes." The chief wine merchant was Latimer, a tall, gentlemanlike, handsome man, with a fine house on Headington Hill. One of his stories deserves recital. A county magnate, notorious for his meanness, had ordered six dozen of a fine brown sherry, which he sent back by-and-by, minus one bottle, with a message that the Duke had tried the wine and disapproved of it. "Put it back," said Latimer to his cellarer, "and we'll call it the Duke's wine." Entertaining a party at luncheon soon after, he narrated the incident, and proposed that they should try the wine. Up came a bottle; the guests smelt, tasted, looked at one another, said nothing, till Latimer's glass was filled. It was toast and water; so was the whole binn : the bottles had been opened, the wine drawn off, the simpler fluid substituted.

Crossing from the Old Bank into Cat Street, you might read in large letters on the All Souls wall "No Bristol Riots," painted there in 1831. Ten years ago it was still visible in certain conditions of sunlight. The squalid cottages in Cat Street had not been long pulled down, and the Radcliffe surrounded with railings. By this last adornment hangs a tale. The outer walls of Brasenose and Lincoln exactly touch one another in Brasenose

Lane; you may walk from the Brasenose gate opposite the Radcliffe to Lincoln gate in the Turl without taking your hand from the masonry. It was in the days when, after dinner, gentlemen became unsteady in their walk; when the joyous closing stave of Maginn's "Ode to a Bottle of Old Port"—

> "How blest are the tipplers whose heads can outlive
> The effects of four bottles of thee;
> But the next dearest blessing that heaven can give
> Is to stagger home muzzy with three"—

was quoted with approval and from experience round many a mahogany tree; and it is easy to understand how opportune to a wine-cheered veteran would be the continuous support and guidance open to him so long as, like Pyramus, he should "draw near the wall." A jovial club, the bibulous champions of either College, dined mutually at Lincoln or at Brasenose on a day in alternate weeks, confidingly hugging the wall as they reeled home from gate to gate. One night it blew a hurricane, and as the Brasenose detachment threaded the opening of the lane just under Bishop Heber's tree, they were met by so furious a gust that they lost hold of the wall and were blown into the open. Struggling in the pitchy darkness to recover their lost stay, they were brought up against the unrailed Radcliffe. Joyously they resumed their progress; occasional suspicion that the way was long floated through their muddy brains; but port wine, deranging reason, leaves faith undisturbed, and on they went. The night was on the wane, and at break of day the early coaches sweeping past beheld a procession of vinous seniors, cap and gown awry, slowly following their leader in single file round and round the Radcliffe. So the railings arose, and repetition of the feat became impossible. Inside Brasenose, in the centre of the Quad, was a curiosity long since removed: the stone figure of a man bestriding a prostrate foe, and raising a mighty jawbone for the death blow. "Cain and Abel" it was called—"Cain taking A-bel's-life, his Sunday Paper," was the current joke; and undergraduates after wines would clamber on to the fratricide's shoulder. Mark Pattison relates how his father, caught there one night by Tutor Hodson, answered his angry challenge by a quotation from Aristophanes, and so Apollo saved him. The Post Office was in Queen Street, removed afterwards to the corner of Bear Lane, to be burned down early one Sunday morning in 1842. I remember the introduction of the Fourpenny Post in 1839, followed by the Penny Post in 1840, with black Queen's head, stamped envelopes having silken threads let into the paper, or Mulready's graceful device.

Restored Balliol and Trinity, with the unharmonious appendage to New College Slipe, are recent alterations. In 1839, the Martyrs' Memorial replaced a picturesque but tottering old house, and the enlargement of St. Mary Magdalen's spoiled a well-proportioned church. Jacob Ley, the Vicar, used to say that a sermon as delivered to the right or left of a certain pillar near the pulpit was absolutely inaudible to worshippers on the corresponding side of it, so that one discourse symmetrically aimed would serve two Sundays. The Taylor

296 REMINISCENCES OF OXFORD

Buildings came a little later, on the site of a lofty edifice, once a mansion, afterwards decayed, and let out in poverty-stricken tenements. The four colossal female statues surmounting its eastern side were declared by an imaginative undergraduate to be effigies of four ladies who lived hard by ; and the myth obtained a more than humorous acceptance. In St. John's gardens, sacred to Capability Brown, still grew a crooked maple tree planted by Archbishop Laud; and the lines in the portrait of Charles I. in the library, inscribing the Psalms of David, were clearly legible with a magnifying glass. Houses were nowhere then numbered, and the names of streets were traditional. Not till 1838 was Coach and Horse Lane nomenclatured into Merton Street, Magpie Lane into Grove Street, Skimmery Hall Lane into Oriel Street, Butcher Row into Queen Street, Pennyfarthing Lane into Pembroke Street, Fish Street into St. Aldate's, Titmouse Lane into Castle Street; while Bridge Street from Magdalen Bridge to East Gate was incorporated into High Street. Only Logic Lane, quoted in the *Spectator*, as commemorating mediæval combats, not always of words alone, between Nominalists and Realists, no one was profane enough to change. The Parks, so called because the Parliamentary cannon were planted there in the siege of Oxford, was a large ploughed field, divided by a gravel walk, bounded on the west by market gardens, on the east by a high broad hedge, beyond which lay the Cherwell meadows ; a haven to nursemaids and their charge, the daily constitutional of elderly, inactive Dons. The earthworks of the siege are marked in Loggan. The lines are clearly traceable to-day in Symonds' field, and the remains of a bastion exist in a small coppice near the Clifton Laboratory.

When the new Museum was opened two houses sprang up just beyond its northern limit, inhabited by Commander Burrows and Goldwin Smith, hence known as Pass and Class. They were vaunt-couriers to a tremendous irruption; to the interminable streets of villadom, converging insatiably protuberant upon distant Wolvercot and Summertown. I cannot frame to pronounce them Oxford; but they suggest to me a momentous query. Nine-tenths of their denizens, I am told, are married Professors, Tutors, Fellows; men who formerly lived in College, resident and celibate and pastoral. The sheep live there still; who shepherds them? Are they successfully autonomous, or controlled by deputy shepherds whose own the sheep are not, or a happy hunting ground for the grim wolf with privy paw? The old monastic Oxford has evaporated into the *Ewigkeit;* as I pace the Norham Gardens and the Bradmore Road, leafy thoroughfares of the bewildering New Jerusalem, I wonder what system has supplanted Zion's, and with what bearing on discipline and morals? I do not prejudge the answer: I question, like Bassanio, in pure innocence; not croaking sinistrous from my Pylian ilex. But as the old glide down the inevitable slope, their present becomes a living over again the life which has gone before, and the future takes the shape of a brief lengthening of the past. To me Oxford, the venerable stones of which I love as

Newman loved the fading willow leaves in Christchurch Meadow, must remain cis-paradisean Oxford, Oxford southward of the Parks, Oxford of the Thirties and the Forties, the Oxford which in these annalistic chronicles I have set myself to recover and re-people. To Oxonians of to-day they will appeal perhaps with something of prehistoric dignity; it may seem suitable that the fading lineaments of a time so different from their own should be portrayed by one, well-nigh the last, of those who drew from them the inspiration of his own youthful dreams and fancies; and some, at least, among the young Patrocli who are there beginning life will join hands filially and affectionately across the chasm of three score and eighteen years with the time-worn commemorative NESTOR who must ere long resign it.

SIT FINIS FANDI.

APPENDICES

A

BRASENOSE ALE

By THOMAS DUNBAR, Fellow of Brasenose, and Keeper of the Ashmolean Museum

(*See p.* 12.)

All ye, who round the buttery hatch
Eager await the opening latch
    Our barrels to assail,
Come, listen, while in pleasing gibe
The rare ingredients I describe
    Which float in Brasenose Ale.

Guiltless alike of malt and hop,
Our buttery is a druggist's shop
    Where quassia's draughts prevail;
Alum the muddy liquor clears,
And mimic wormwood's bitter tears
    Compose our Brasenose Ale.

All ye who physic have professed,
Sir Kit[1] and Poticary West,[2]
    Your practice gone bewail!
The burning mouth, the temple's throb,
Sick stomach, and convulsive sob,
    Are cured by Brasenose Ale.

---

[1] Sir Kit—Sir Christopher Pegge, p. 62.   [2] Poticary West, p. 64.

As poisons other poisons kill,
So, should we with convivial skill
    Old Syms's [1] wine assail,
Or Latimer's immortal tun,
"Herbert" yclept or "Abingdon,"
    We're cured by Brasenose Ale.

The fair Cheltenia's opening salt
Must yield to our factitious malt;
    What double sconce [2] can fail?
But, if you want some tonic stuff,
You readily will find quant: suff:
    A gill of Brasenose Ale.

Mysterious as the Sibyl's leaves
The battels are which each receives;
    But, freshmen, cease to rail!
You're fed and physicked; in your bills
Each week is vinegar of squills,
    Bark, salts, and Brasenose Ale.

Oh that our Bursar would consent
To give the bottled porter vent,
    Porter beloved by Dale; [3]
Smuggled no more by Joey's [3] stealth,
It would improve the College health,
    Well scoured by Brasenose Ale.

---

[1] Syms and Latimer, wine merchants, p. 293.

[2] A double sconce was a fine for improprieties in Hall; the culprit was compelled to drink a gallon of ale.

[3] Rev. Joseph Dale and Joseph Hodgkinson, Fellows of the College addicted to Double X.

APPENDICES

My muse, a half reluctant prude,
In dudgeon vile George Smith[1] pursued,
   Afraid his verse should fail;
When next the annual Ode he woos,
May he invoke a different Meux,
   'T improve our Brasenose Ale.

B

ODE,

RECITED ON THE ANNIVERSARY DINNER OF THE CHESS CLUB, BY THE LAUREATE, THOMAS DUNBAR.

(*See p.* 12.)

From the bright burning lands and rich forests of Ind,
   See the form of Caissa arise;
In the caverns of Brahma no longer confined,
   To the shores of fair Europe she flies.

A figure so fair through the region of light
   All natives with wonder survey,
As her varying mantle now darkens with night,
   Now beams with the silver of day.

Let Whist, like the bat, from such splendour retire,
   A splendour too strong for his eyes;
The Trump and Odd Trick let dull Av'rice admire,
   Entrapped by so paltry a prize.

Can Finesse and the Ten-Ace e'er hope to prevail
   When Reason opposes her weight,
When inviolate Majesty hangs in the scale,
   And Castles yet tremble with fate?

---

[1] He was the College porter.

When the bosom of Beauty the throbbing heart meets,
    And Caissa's the gay Valentine,
What Chessman, who'd tasted such amorous sweets,
    His Mate but with life would resign?

But 'tis o'er—Terebinth [1] the decision approves,
    And Whist has contended in vain;
To the Mansion of Hades the Genius removes,
    Where he gnaws his own counters in pain.

On Philosophy's brow a new lustre unfolds,
    Mild reason exults in the birth;
His creation benign Father Tuckwell beholds,
    And Steph [2] gives the chaplet to Mirth.

C

HENRY MATTHEWS

(Note to page 13.)

Henry Matthews well deserves a notice. His father, Colonel Matthews, was the owner of a beautiful seat called Belmont, on the Wye, in Herefordshire, Colonel of Militia and long M.P. for the county; a sapling planted by him in 1788 is still called Colonel Matthews' oak. In his old age Henry was wont to attend on him to bed each night, where as his head settled into the pillow he repeated always in his Herefordshire dialect the same complacent formula, "I tell yer—'Enery—I thinks—the most comfortablest place in the world is bed—fur—there ye forgets all yer cares." One of the sons, Charles Skynner Matthews, was the intimate Cambridge friend of Byron (Life by Moore,

---

[1] "Terebinth" was a nickname for Lingard; in a later edition it reads "The decision old Lingard approves."
[2] Steph was Stephens, Fellow and Vice-Principal of Brasenose, afterwards Rector of Belgrave, near Leicester.

APPENDICES

vol. i. p. 125), and was drowned in 1812. Another, Arthur, I knew well as a Canon of Hereford and Senior Fellow of Brasenose; Henry was the third. At Eton he was a reckless madcap, driving tandem through the town, and once lighting a bonfire on the floor of Long Chamber. He became a Fellow of King's; his health broke down, he travelled, publishing in 1820 his "Diary of an Invalid," which reached a fifth edition. In 1821 he was appointed Advocate Fiscal of Ceylon, married Emma Blount, of Orleton Manor, Herefordshire, and sailed for India; passing through Oxford on his way to Southampton, and leaving for my father, who was away, a touching letter of farewell, which I possess. He became Judge in 1827, and died on May 20th, 1828. His son is the present Lord Llandaff.

D

THE LETTER H

(See p. 67.)

I insert the original for the sake of comparison. Its authorship was doubted at the time, and it was assigned to Lord Byron. Lady Stanley, in her "Early Married Life," gives Miss Fanshawe's appropriation of it:—"I do give it under my hand and seal this 12th day of February, 1819, that to the best of my belief the Enigma of the Letter H was composed, not by the Right Honourable George Lord Byron, but by me, Catherine Maria Fanshawe."

'Twas in heaven pronounced—it was muttered in hell,
And Echo caught faintly the sound as it fell.
On the confines of earth 'twas permitted to rest,
And the depths of the ocean its presence confessed.

'Twill be found in the sphere when 'tis riven asunder,
Be seen in the lightning, and heard in the thunder;
'Twas allotted to man with his earliest breath,
Attends at his birth and awaits him in death,
Presides o'er his happiness, honour, and health,
Is the prop of his house, and the end of his wealth.
In the heaps of the miser 'tis hoarded with care,
But is sure to be lost on his prodigal heir.
It begins every hope, every wish it must bound,
With the husbandman toils, and with monarchs is crowned.
Without it the soldier, the seaman, may roam,
But woe to the wretch who expels it from home.
In the whispers of conscience its voice will be found,
Nor e'en in the whirlwind of passion is drowned:
It will soften the heart, and, though deaf be the ear,
It will make it acutely and instantly hear.
Yet in shade let it rest like a delicate flower:
Ah! breathe on it softly—it dies in an hour!

E

CHARLES WORDSWORTH

(See p. 87.)

EPITAPH ON HIS WIFE, IN WINCHESTER CHAPEL.

I, nimium dilecta, vocat Deus, I, bona nostræ
    Pars animæ; mœrens altera, disce sequi.

Translated by Lord Derby.

Too dearly loved, thy God hath called thee; go,
    Go, thou best portion of this widowed heart:
And thou, poor remnant lingering here in woe,
    So learn to follow, as no more to part.

CHARLES WORDSWORTH

INSCRIPTION IN THE GRIMSEL HOTEL BOOK

χωρεῖν, καθεύδειν, ἐσθίειν, πίνειν, πάλιν
χωρεῖν, "Βαβαίαξ ὡς καλὸν" κεκραγέναι,
κόντον τρίπηχυν χερσὶν οἰακοστροφεῖν,
Γάλλιστι βάζειν, τοὔνομ' ἐν βίβλῳ γράφειν,
ὀμβρόφορον ὡς τὰ πλεῖστα δυσφημεῖν Δία,
τοιόσδ' ὁ βίοτός ἐστι τῶν ὁδοιπόρων.

Translated :—

> To walk, to sleep, to eat, to drink,
> To cry, "How lovely, don't you think?"
> To wield a six foot alpenstock,
> Talk French, write name in Grimsel book,
> To curse the rain's incessant pour;
> The pleasures these of foreign tour.

F

DRAMATIS PERSONÆ OF THE "BOTHIE"

(*See p.* 98.)

Hobbes was certainly Ward Hunt, afterwards First Lord of the Admiralty.

Lindsay, the "Piper," was F. Johnson of Christchurch, with some touches of W. H. Davies.

Airlie was probably Deacon of Oriel, who joined Clough's reading party in the year following.

Arthur Audley was Herbert Fisher of Christchurch, with, say the Walronds, a touch of Theodore Walrond.

Philip Hewson was Clough himself, with some traits from Winder of Oriel.

Adam was probably not a portrait, but not unlike Clough.

Hope cannot, I fear, be now identified.

G
SEPTEM CONTRA CAMUM
(*See p.* 113.)

i. Vacant.
ii. Robert Menzies, University.
iii. Edward Royds, Brasenose.
iv. William B. Brewster, St. John's.
v. George D. Bourne, Oriel.
vi. John C. Cox, Trinity.
vii. Richard Loundes, Christchurch.
viii. George E. Hughes, Oriel.
Coxswain. Arthur T. W. Shadwell, Balliol.

H
FRAGMENTA E CODICE BAROCCIANO[1]
(*See p* 169.)

"*Insanientem navita Bosphorum.*"
—*Tentabo.* HORAT. Od. III., iv. 30.

EXCUDEBAT W. BAXTER, OXONII

The origin of this clever skit is given on p. 169. Its charm lies in the dexterous rendering into Homeric Greek of Oxford names and witticisms.

MONITUM

Two fragments, of Homeric age apparently, found in the Bodleian.

Fragmenta duo, quæ in nobilissimo Codice apud Bibliothecam Bodleianam evolvendo nuper detexi, religionis duxi non primo quoque tempore publici juris facere. Auctoris nomen desideratur; colorem tamen vere Homericum habent. Adjeci ea quæ inter legendum

[1] Where these *jeux d'esprit* are in a dead language I have appended a translation or short paraphrase.

APPENDICES

mihi occurrebant, tum ex aliis auctoribus, tum e conjectura petita: sed perfunctorie et currente calamo omnia, ut reliquias vere aureas quam citissime cum eruditis communicarem.

Dabam Oxonii, Prid. Cal. Græc. cɪↄ. Iↄ. ccc. xxxiv.
Imprimatur, Wellington, Cancellarius.

I.—E PROŒMIO, UT VIDETUR

Μῆνιν ἄειδε θεὰ φθισίμβροτον, ἣ προίαψεν
ἄνδρας ἀριστῆας περὶ βόσπορον ἶφι μάχεσθαι.
Πάσας δὲ Ψυχὰς, καὶ Ἰάονας ἑλκεχίτωνας,
Μερτῶνας θ᾽ ἑτάρους, Καθέδρην θ᾽ ὅσοι ἀμφινέμονται,   *Gathering Clans.*
τηλεπύλῳ τ᾽ οἰκοῦσ᾽ ἐνὶ Ευστέρῳ, ἔνθα κέλευθοι   5
δύσβατοι ἀνθρώποισιν ὑπ᾽ ἀγνοίης ἀλεγεινῆς,
Σκιμμερίους τ᾽, ἀεὶ γένος ἀστιβὲς Ἀπόλλωνι,
τοὺς δὲ Μετεξετέρους ἔριδι ξυνέηκε μάχεσθαι.

. . . .

II.—CATALOGI FRAGMENTUM

Ἐν δαπέδᾳ δ᾽ ἑκάτερθεν Ἰάονας ἑλκεχίτωνας
Χεῖμαρ ἐκόσμησε στίχεσιν, καὶ Χείματος ἄλλος   10
βριθύτερος, μείζων, στιβαρώτερος ἐν πολέμοισί,
Φίντλεος· οἷς ἑκατὸν πολέμου μήστωρες ἕποντο,
τιμὴν ἀρνύμενοι Ἀρθουρίου ἱππόδαμοιο·
Μερτῶνος δ᾽ ἑτάρους, κρατερῶν στίχας ἀσπιστάων,
ἑξήκοντα βοὴν ἀγαθὸς κόσμησεν Ἔλειος·   15
στῆσε δ᾽ ἄγων ὅθι Πηλείδεω τάξαντο φάλαγγες.
Βαλλιολεῖς δ᾽ ἦγεν θεόφιν Μήστωρ ἀτάλαντος,

3. Ἰάονας, St. John's. ἑλκεχίτωνας, *Hom. Il.* xiii. 685.
5. Ευστέρῳ, Worcester.
8. Μετεξετέρους, Exeter.
10. Χεῖμαρ, Wynter, President of St. John's.
12. Φίντλεος, Wintle, Senior Fellow of St. John's.
15. Ἔλειος, marshy, Marsham, Warden of Merton.
16. Πηλείδεω, supporters of Peel.
17. Μήστωρ, the Master.

Μήστωρ, ὅς μικρὸς μὲν ἔην δέμας, ἀλλὰ μαχητής·
οὔνομα δ' ἔσχεν ἄμετρον, ἀθέσφατον, οὐδ' ὀνομαστόν·
τῷ δ' ἄρ ἕπονθ' ἑκατὸν καὶ πέντε μελαινοχίτωνες.   20

Dr. Fox leads Queen's.
Ἀλλ' οἵοισιν ἄνασσ' ἀρχηγέτις ἐστὶ Φιλίππη
τοισίδε Φόξος ἔην κεφάλη· ἑκατὸν δ' ὑπὸ τούτῳ
ἥρωες κόσμηθεν ἴδ' ὀγδώκοντα Βορεῖοι.

Dr. Bridges leads Corpus.
Ἀλλ' αὖ νῦν, ναίουσιν ὅσοι Τρία Κάππα κάκιστα,
ἥρως ἡγεμόνευ' εἰδὼς πολέμοιο Γεφύρας,   25
ὀγδώκοντ' ἀριθμῷ καὶ ἅπαντας φαιοχιτῶνας,
Ἀλλ' ὅσοι εἰς Καθέδρην περὶ Βόσπορον ἠγερέθοντο
(μακρὴν ἀμφιέποντες ἀταρπιτὸν, οὗ τὰ ῥέεθρα

Dean Gaisford, wielding two mighty lexica, leads Christchurch.
ΧαρΓέλου ἠδ' Ἴσις συμβάλλετον ὄβριμον ὕδωρ)
ἡ διπύλωτος ἄρ' ἐστὶ, διηκόσιοι δ' ἂν' ἑκάστην   30
ἄνερες ἐξοιχνεῦσι λιλαιόμενοι μαχέσασθαι,
Γαισοφόρος κόσμησε, δύω δολιχόσκια πάλλων
λεξικὰ, δυσβάσταχθ', οἷς δάμνησι στίχας ἀνδρῶν
ἡρώων, κριτικῶν· ἅπερ οὐ δύο γ' ἄνδρε ἰδέσθαι
τλαῖεν ἀταρμύκτοισι προσώπασι, σήματα λυγρὰ   35
οἷοι νῦν βροτοί εἰσ', ὁ δέ μιν ῥέα πάλλε καὶ οἷος.

Dr. Macbride leads Magdalen Hall.
Οἳ δ' Ἀπομαγδαλίας κλεινῇ δαίνυνται ἐν Αὐλῇ,
τοῖς μέγα σημαίνων ἀράβησεν ὁ Παρθενοπαῖος·
τῷ δ' ἄρα πεντήκονθ' εἵποντο μελαινοχίτωνες.

Ἔθνεα δ' ἀνθρώπων χαλκέντερα, χαλκοπρόσωπα,   40
Dr. Gilbert leads Brasenose.
διογενὴς Γιλβερτὸς ἄγεν· πολλοὶ δ' ὑπὸ τούτῳ
ὁπλίτας βασιλῆες ἐκόσμεον ἔνθα καὶ ἔνθα·

18. οὔνομα κ. τ. λ., the uncouth name Jenkyns.
21. Φιλίππη, Queen Philippa, Foundress of Queen's.
22. Φόξος, Fox, Provost of Queen's.
23. Βορεῖοι, the Scholars and Fellows of Queen's, mostly from northern counties.
24. Τρία Κάππα, C. C. C., Corpus, κάκιστα, referring to a proverb—the three bad C's—Cappadocians, Cicilians, Cretans.
25. γεφύρας, Bridges, President of Corpus.
33. λεξικὰ, Suidas and Etymologicon Magnum.
35. ἀταρμύκτοισι, unwinking.
38. Παρθενοπαῖος, Macbride. ἀράβησεν—he was Professor of Arabic.
41. Γιλβερτὸς, Gilbert, Head of Brasenose.

APPENDICES

Μύκτηρ οις φέρεται Χαλκοῦς δείνοιο πελώρου,
(σῆμα βρότοις ἔριδος, Γοργείου κρατὸς ἀπορρώξ)
ὀρθὸς ἐπ' ἐγχείης, περὶ σαυρωτῆρα πυλασθείς·   45
τῶνδε διηκόσιοι πολεμόνδε καὶ εἴκοσι βαῖνον.

Σνευδέι δ' εἰπόμενοι λευκαύχενι, δουλιχοδείρῳ,   Mr. Sneyd lea
ἕπτ' ἴσαν ἡρώων δεκάδες, διὰ φύλοπιν αἰνήν,   All Souls.
Πασῶν ἐκ Ψυχῶν ἰφθιμότατοι καὶ ἄριστοι,
σηρικὰ σείοντες καρακάλλια, τετραφάληροι.   50

Ἐκ δὲ Καπηλείου Κραμήριος ὦρτο Νέοιο,   Dr. Cramer lea
τοῦ καὶ ἀπὸ γλώσσης μέλιτος γλυκίων ῥέεν αὐδὴ   New Inn H
τῇ πέρυσι δήμοιο πανηγύρει ἀκριτομύθῳ.
μοῦνος ἔην δ' ἑτάρων, παῦρός τε οἱ ἕσπετο λαός.

Τοὺς δὲ Μετεξετέρους ὁ Μαριλαΐδης ἀγ' Ἰωνεύς   55   Dr. Collier Jo
μειδιόων βλοσυροῖσι προσώπασιν ἱπποκόμοιο   leads Exet
κακκεφαλῆς· ὅς χθίζ' ἀνὰ Βόσπορον ἀνθυπατεύων   preceded
σκῆπτρ' ἔχεν, Ἡφαίστου τεχνάσματα, θέσκελα ἔργα,   five "Poker
ὧν τρία μὲν χρυσᾶ, τρία δ' ἀργυρόηλα τέτυκτο,
δῶκε δὲ Βοσπορίοις βασιλεῦσιν ὁ Κυλλοποδίων   60
πολλοῖσι νήεσσι καὶ ἄστει παντὶ ἀνάσσειν.
τοὺς μὲν ἄγεν πολεμόνδ'· ἄλλους δ' οἴκοι κατέλειπε
τείχεα φρουροῦντας καὶ ἐπάλξιας οἰκοδομοῦντας·
ἥμισυ γὰρ τετέλεστο, τὸ δ' ἥμισυ γυμνὸν ἐλείφθη.   64

    43. Μύκτηρ Χαλκοῦς πελώρου, the brazen nose over the gate.
    47. Σνευδέι, Sneyd, Warden of All Souls, noted for his long neck and corresponding white tie.
    51. Κραμήριος, Cramer, Principal of New Inn Hall.
    55. Μαριλαΐδης Ἰωνεύς, *Collier* Jones, Rector of Exeter.
    58. σλῆπτρα, the bedel's staves; he was Vice-Chancellor.
    60. Κυλλοποδίων, lame-foot, Vulcan.
    64. Buildings must have been going on at Exeter, probably the Turl front.

The following lines about Shuttleworth were apparently never printed, but handed round in *writing* with copies of the printed piece.   Dr. Shuttl
                                                 worth (p.
                                                 with his
Ἀνδρῶν δ' οὐκ ἡγεῖτο περικλυτὸς Ἀξιοκερκίς·   on a bishop
στῇ δ' ἀπάνευθ' ἑτάρων, πεφοβημένος εἵνεκα μίτρης.   stands apar

I
OXFORD[1]
(See p. 145.)

O'er Oxford's halls the dewy hand of night
Sows the still heavens with gems of lustrous light,
Earth sinks to rest, and earthly passions cease,
And all is love, and poesy, and peace.
How soft o'er Wykeham's aisle and Waynflete's tower
Falls the mild magic of the midnight hour;
How calm the classic city takes her rest,
Like a hushed infant on its mother's breast!
How pure, how sweet, the moonbeam's silver smile
Serenely sleeps on fair St. Mary's aisle,
And lends each sculptured saint a chastened glow,
Like the calm glory of their lives below.
Now, stilled the various labours of the day,
Student and Don the drowsy charm obey,
E'en Pusey owns the soft approach of sleep,
Long as his sermons, as his learning deep:
Peaceful he rests from Hebraistic lore,
And finds that calm he gave so oft before.
Lo! where on peaceful Pembroke beams the moon,
Delusive visions lull the brains of Jeune;
Slowly he finds in sleep's serene surprise
The mitred honours which the world denies;
Dreams of a see from earthly care withdrawn,
And one long sabbath of eternal lawn.

[Lacuna valde deflenda, sed ne in antiquissimo quidem codice suppleta.]

[1] Composed by W. W. Merry, Alfred Blomfield, Charles Bowen, and J. W. Shephard, all of Balliol.
Given to Mr. Madan in 1885 by J. R. King of Oriel, who was present at the composition, and himself contributed a few words. To Mr. Madan's kindness I owe this copy, and other valuable help.

See fresh from Eton sent, the highborn dunce,
So late a boy, now grown a man at once :
Proud, he asserts his new-found liberty,
And slopes in triumph down the astonished High.
Mark the stiff wall of collar at his neck,
More fit to choke the wearer than to deck;
And the long coat which, dangling at his heels,[1]
His "bags" of varied colour scarce reveals.
So, when the infant hails the birthday grant
Of gracious grandmother or awful aunt,
Forth from the ark of childhood, one by one,
The peagreen patriarch leads each stalwart son;
O'er Noah's knees descends the garment's hem,
And clothes in solid folds the shins of Shem,
His ligneous legs in modesty conceals,
And two stout stumps alone to view reveals.
Pleased with the sight, the infant screams no more,
And groups his great forefathers on the floor;
Sucks piety and paint from broad-brimmed Ham,
But thinks that even Japhet yields to jam.

J

ON CHANTREY'S CHILDREN IN LICHFIELD CATHEDRAL

(*See p.* 153.)

OSBORNE GORDON.

Ἀ Μοῖρα ἀ κρυερὰ τὼ καλὼ παῖδ' Ἀφροδίτης
ἥρπασε· τῶν καλῶν τίς κόρος ἐσθ' Ἄιδᾳ;
Ἀλλὰ σύ γ' Ἀγγελία, τὸν ἀηδέα μῦθον ἔχουσα,
Βάσκε, μελαντειχῆ πρὸς δόμον ἐλθὲ θεοῦ.

---

[1] The long ulster-like coats which came in just then (in 1856) are alluded to.

312 REMINISCENCES OF OXFORD

Λέξον δ', ὦ δαῖμον, τὰν καλὰν ὤλεσας ἄγραν,
οὐ γὰρ τὰς ψυχὰς, οὐδὲ τὰ σώματ' ἔχεις.
Αἱ μὲν γὰρ ψυχὰι μετέβησαν ἐς οὐρανὸν εὐρύν,
σώματα δ' ἐν γαίᾳ νήγρετον ὕπνον ἔχει.

May be thus translated, faithfully, not adequately:

Love's fairest twins cold Fate has rapt from earth:
    Death craves each loveliest birth.
Go, thou, whose lore insculps the unpleasing word,
    Go to the dark-realmed Lord.
Forbid him triumph;—his the power to slay,
    Not his to hold the prey.
Their forms unwaking sleep beneath the sod,
    Their souls rest aye with God.

I transcribe from a copy given to me at the time of its composition. In the "Anthologia Oxonensis" is an altered reading of line 4, Βάσκ', ἴθι, παγκοίταν εἰς 'Αἴδαο δόμον, probably the latest correction of the author. Both epithets are finely classical—μελαντειχῆ Pindaric, παγκοίταν Sophoclean. I append a translation, the best I can render: it is quite inadequate as transmitting the old-world feeling of the original, but it is nearly literal. Ἀγγελία, line 3, I have taken to mean the sad message of death inscribed in the sculptured forms. The Dean of Durham thinks that the somewhat tame last line (last but one in the translation) shows inability on Gordon's part to "get in" the thought he had—"the souls rest in heaven, the bodies are immortalised in stone."

APPENDICES

K

CARMEN[1]

IN THEATRO SHELDONIANO
NON RECITATUM
VII. DIE JUNII, MDCCCLIII.

(*See p.* 154, *in which the poem is paraphrased.*)

Quem Virum aut Heroa lyra vel acri
Tibia sumis celebrare, Clio?
Scilicet quem te voluere Patres
        Hebdomadales.

Te decet jussum properare carmen,
Ficta nam Phœbus patitur, tuisque
Laudis indignæ fidibus canoris
        Dedecus aufert.

Jamque dicatur gravis et decorus,
Et sibi constans memoretur idem,
Ille, qui multis superare possit
        Protea formis.

Quin et insignem paribus catervam
Laudibus tollas, quibus, heu fatendum,
Ista de nobis hodie paratur
        Pompa triumphi.

Plura si tangas, tacuisse velles;
Vix enim linguæ tulit eloquentis
Præmium, verbis relevare doctus
        Præmia magnis.

---

[1] By Osborne Gordon; on the Installation of Lord Derby as Chancellor.

Nec magis palmam meruit decoram
Sævus in mitem, nimiumque vincens
Dulce ridentem Samuelis iram
        Voce cruenta.[1]

His tamen constat decus omne nostri,
Hic Duci magno Comes advocatur,
Talibus flentes premimus tropæis
        Grande sepulchrum.

Deditis ergo gravis ille nobis
Partium tristem trahit huc ruinam,
Et rates obstat reparare quassas
        Isidis unda.

Gaudeant istis pueri et puellæ:
Mente diversa notat, et Theatri
Excipit vani sonitum maligno
        Patria risu.

---

[1] This refers to a passage between Lord Derby and Samuel, Bishop of Oxford, during a debate on the Canada Clergy Reserves in the House of Lords. The Bishop advocated their surrender; "Fiat justitia, ruat cælum," he said. Provoked by his arguments, and by the aggravating smile with which he met his own indignant attack, Lord Derby quoted the line from Hamlet, "A man may smile, and smile, and be a villain" (see p. 154).

APPENDICES

L

FACSIMILE OF THE "THUNNUS" PARODY

(See p. 155.)

IN A CONGREGATION to be holden on Saturday, the 31st instant, at Two o'Clock, the following form of Statute will be promulgated.

F. JUNIUS,
Vice-Can.

UNIVERSITY CATACOMBS,
Nov. 3, 1860.

Placuit Universitati 2009.
In Epitaphio Thunni in Musæo Academico depositi hæc verba

THUNNUS QUEM VIDES
MENSE JANUARII A. S. MDCCCLVII
AB HENRICO W. ACLAND TUNC TEMPORIS ANATOMIAE IN AEDE XTI. PRAELECTORE
EX MADEIRA INSULA
QUO HENRICUM G. LIDDELL AEDIS XTI. DECANUM
INFIRMA VALETUDINE LABORANTEM DEDUXERAT
PRAETER OMNEM SPEM OXONIAM ADPORTATUS EST.
TYNA ENIM NAVE VAPORARIA IN QUA REDIBAT PRAELECTOR
AD SCTI. ALBANI PROMONTORIUM IN COMITATU DORSETIAE EJECTA,
QUUM IPSE VIX SOSPES E FLUCTIBUS EVASIT,
HIC PISCIS IN NAVE RELICTUS PER VOLUNTATEM NAUTARUM AD TERRAM ADVECTUS EST,
DEINDE IN MUSAEO AEDIS XTI. POSITUS
PER ARTEM CAROLI ROBERTSON 'ΕΣΚΕΛΕΤΕΤΘΗ.

abrogare, et in eorum locum quæ sequuntur subrogare:—

THUNNUS QUEM RIDES
MENSE JUNII A. S. MDCCCLX
AB HENRICO W. ACLAND NUNC TEMPORIS MEDICINAE IN ACAD. OXON. PROFESSORE REGIO
EX MUSAEO ANATOMICO
DE QUO HENRICUM G. LIDDELL AEDIS XTI. DECANUM
AETERNA MANSUETUDINE PERORANS SEDUXERAT
PRAETER OMNIUM SPEM OXONIENSIUM HUC ADPORTATUS EST.
ORATIONE ENIM VAPORARIA IN QUA GAUDEBAT PROFESSOR
AD SCTI. ACLANDI GLORIAM IN CONGREGATIONEM DOCTISSIME INJECTA,
QUUM MUSAEUM IPSUM VIX SOSPES EX HOSTIBUS EVASIT,
HAEC AREA IGNAVE REFECTA PER SEGNITATEM MAGISTRORUM AD FINEM PROVECTA EST,
QUAE IN MEDIO AEDIFICIO POSITA
PER ARTEM BENJAMINI WOODWARD ΙΣΚΙΔΜΩΡηλη.

M

THE STORY OF PHAETHON

By P. N. Shuttleworth

(See p. 169.)

Once upon a time, so goes the tale,
The driver of a country mail,
One Phœbus, had a hare-brained son,
Called from his uncle Phaethon.
This boy, quite spoilt with over care
As many other children are,
All day, it seems, would cry and sputter
For gingerbread or toast and butter;
And sure no father would deny
Such trifles to so sweet a boy.
But that which rules all earthly things
And coachmen warms as well as kings,
Ambition, soon began to reign
Sole tyrant in this youngster's brain;
And, as we find in every state
The low will emulate the great,
As ofttimes servants drink and game
Because their lords have done the same,
The boy, now hardly turned of ten,
Would fain be imitating men;
Till what, at last, must youngster do,
But drive the mail a day or two.
In vain with all a father's care
Old Phœbus tries to soothe his heir,
In vain the arduous task explains
To ply the lash and guide the reins,
Tells him the roads are deep and miry,
Old Dobbin's blind and Pyeball fiery;

At length he yields, though somewhat loath,
And seals his promise with an oath;
The oath re-echoing as he sware
Like thunder shook his elbow chair,
Made every rafter tremble o'er him,
And spilt the ale that stood before him.
All then prepared in order due,
The coach brought out, the horses too,
Glad Phaethon with youthful heat
Climbs up the box and takes his seat,
And, scarce each passenger got in,
Drives boldly off through thick and thin.
Now whether he got on as well
The sequel of my tale will tell:
Scarce gone a mile the horses find
Their wonted driver left behind:
For horses, poets all agree,
Have common sense as well as we:
Nay, Homer tells us they can speak
Not only common sense, but Greek.
In vain our hero, half afraid,
Calls all his learning to his aid,
And runs his Houyhnhnm jargon through
Just as he'd heard his father do—
As "Gently Dobbin, Pyeball stay,
Keep back there Bobtail, softly, way!"
The more he raved and bawled and swore,
They pranced and kicked and run the more
Till, driver and themselves to cool,
They lodged all safely in a pool.
Hence then, ye highborn bards, beware,
Nor spin *your* Pegasus too far,
From Phaethon's mischance be humble,
Go gently—or the jade will stumble.

P. N. SHUTTLEWORTH.

Winchester College, 1800.

N

(*See p.* 175.)

This is said to have been repeated impromptu by Foote in order to puzzle Macklin, who boasted that he could re-word any tale after once hearing it:—

"The baker's wife went into the garden for a cabbage leaf to make an apple pie. A great she bear walking down the street put its head into the shop: 'What, no soap?' So he died, and she very imprudently married the barber. And there were present at the wedding the Piccalillies, the Joblillies, the Gargulies, and the great Panjandrum himself with the little round button on the top; and they all played at Catch-who-catch-can till the gunpowder ran out of the heels of their boots."

O

(*See p.* 194.)

Hic tandem invitus requiescit
GEORGIUS ILLE ARCHIDIACONUS DE TAUNTON
Qui vulgo
GEORGIUS SINE DRACONE
Audiebat,
Amicorum dum vivebat Deliciæ,
Whiggorum,
Radicalium,
Rationalistarum.
Gladstonophilorum.
Flagrum Indefessum, Acerrimum.
In Clericorum Convocatione
Facundissimus, Facetissimus.
In Baronibus

Seu humanis et Hagleiocolis
Sive bovinis
Demoliendis,
In Feriis Autumnalibus apud East Brent
Conveniendis,
In denegando
De Ecclesia, De Republica,
De omnibus rebus et quibusdam aliis,
In piscium venatione,
Nulli secundus.
Se ipso judice,
Erroris Expers,
Per Vices Rerum Quantaslibet
Immutatus et Immutabilis.

LYTTELTON Baro fecit. *Jan.*, 1868.   A.D. 1910.

Here rests at last against his will
G. A. D.,
Known commonly as George-without-the-drag-on.
In life the delight of his friends;
Of Whigs, Radicals, Gladstonians,
The unwearied scourge.
Eloquent in Convocation,
Unrivalled in social charm,
Keen Angler, universal Gainsayer,
In his own opinion faultless,
Unchangeable amid surrounding change.

BY LORD LYTTELTON, 1868.

P

DIZZY AND THE ANGELS

By Charles Neate

(*Note* 1, *p.* 199.)

At a meeting of the Oxford Diocesan Society in the Theatre, November 25th, 1864, Bishop Wilberforce presiding, Mr. Disraeli said : "What is the question now placed before society with a glib assurance the most astounding ? The question is this—Is man an ape or an angel ? My lord, I am on the side of the angels."

<small>ngel? No, Ape.</small>
    Angelo quis te similem putaret
    Esse, vel divis atavis creatum,
    Cum tuas plane referat dolosus
        Simius artes ?

<small>limbimg to the tree-top, and flinging the fruit at his enemies.</small>
    Sive cum palma latitans in alta,
    Dente quos frustra tetigit superbo
    Dejicit fructus, nuceam procellam,
        Tutus in hostem;

<small>ith feigned gravity emitting claptrap.</small>
    Sive cum fictæ gravitatis ore
    Comico torquet dehonesta rictu
    Turba quod risu, nimium jocosa,
        Plaudat inepto.

<small>ith feigned sorrow beating a gorilla breast.</small>
    Sive (quod monstrum tua novit ætas),
    Cum furens intus rabie, feroque
    Imminens bello, similis dolenti
        Pectora plangit.

<small>e religious and devout? tell it to his brother Jew, Apelles.</small>
    Scilicet veræ pietatis ardor
    Non tulit pressis cohibere labris
    Fervidam vocem—tuus ille forsan
        Credat Apella.

APPENDICES

Credidit certe pius ille noster
Ore qui blando data verba reddit,
Non prius nobis ita visus esse
    Credulus Oxon.

Our "Sam" feigns belief, but his tongue is in his saintly cheek.

Q

Facsimile of letter to Charles Girdlestone ("Commentary" Girdlestone he was called), accompanying a copy of the "Suggestions for an Association," written by Palmer of Worcester, revised by Newman, and corrected by Ogilvie. Girdlestone, whose answer follows, was a leading Evangelical, and had recommended Newman as a kindred spirit to his first curacy at St. Clement's. These two letters are not published in Mr. Mozley's book. They illustrate: (1) The wide extent of Newman's initial propaganda, amongst extreme Low Churchmen no less than in directions not inevitably hostile to the movement; (2) the confident, excited temper, and defiant objurgatory language with which he embarked on his crusade; (3) the deep instinct of opposition felt from the first by weighty theologians of the Clapham School, spreading and increasing as the Tracts went on, though not culminating till the publication of Tract 90.

Oriel Coll. Nov. 1. 1833

Dear Gladstone,

Thank you for your account of your proceedings at Liverpool. I heartily wish it were in my power to help you in finding a minister for the new Church. I have mentioned it to several men, but without success hitherto. The accompanying suggestions have brought out a feeling which will not soon (please God) be put down. We are in motion from the Isle of Wight to Durham & from Cornwall to Kent. Surely the Church will shortly be to be delivered from its captivity under wicked men who are worse than Jeroboam— Rehoboam or the Philistines. We proclaim aloud that heterogeneous un-ecclesiastical Parliament, and will not submit to its dictation. I do not know how far these sentiments will approve themselves to you; we shall be truly glad of your cooperation, as of one who really fears God & wishes to serve him— but if you will not, we will march past you. We have been joined by persons of the most opposite sentiments, & I trust may do something toward uniting opposite parties in the Church. Among our supporters are Archdeacons Watson, Froude, Bailey, Shepshanks & Lyall, the Dean of Ripon, Lord Colchester, Dr Buddicom, Richards, the Wilberforces, etc etc.— If we do nothing after all, still we shall have discharged a duty, and may sleep on quietly. We are publishing Tracts. Do you think there is any chance of Mr Moore of Birmingham joining us?

Yours very truly

John H. Newman

P.S. We do not mean to form an organized society...

C. GIRDLESTONE'S ANSWER TO J. H. NEWMAN'S LETTER

SEDGELY VICARAGE, DUDLEY,
6th Nov. 1833.

DEAR NEWMAN,—It gives me very great pain indeed to differ so widely as I fear I do from you in the matter to which your printed circular and written letter refer. Nor do I like to say no to your application without assigning one or two of the reasons which chiefly weigh with me.

1. Your objects are indistinctly defined. "Maintain inviolate" looks very like to an Anti-Church-reform Society; though your definition goes no further than I should gladly go with you, being extremely averse to any change which "involves the denial or suppression of doctrine" (sound doctrine I conclude you mean) or "a departure," &c., &c. I honestly assure you I could not be certain whether it is your intent to promote any change at all, though I guess from the tenor of the whole paper that almost any change would be counted innovation.

2. Besides this indistinctness as to your principles, I am at a loss to understand in what way they are to be practically applied: whether the publication of a periodical, the influencing elections for M.P.'s, the putting yourselves under the direction of a committee in all matters connected with your first object, or the mere circulation of tracts.

3. I cannot approve of the feeling which pervades your document, nor assent to the presumed data on which it proceeds. The spirit of the times does not appear to me in the same light as it does to you. And, the worse it is, I am the more desirous that in the Church at least a good spirit should be cultivated. Now, this whole paper breathes a censorious, querulous, discontented spirit, a spirit of defiance, unless I am much mistaken, to the party predominant at present in the State, a spirit which is the most likely

of all others to bring the Church into contempt with that party, and, what is worse, a spirit which is thoroughly opposite to the Christian rule of overcoming evil with good.

I have written the more freely because I cannot but think it new and strange to you to write as you have written about the Parliament, &c., and I hope you may be disposed to weigh the grounds on which I have come to conclusions so opposite to yours. I regard the men at present in power as no worse Christians than their predecessors, counting no doctrine worse than that which sacrifices the morality of the people on the shrine of finance and expediency. (See Beer bill, appointment of Philpotts to be Bishop, defence of the venality of votes in elections, multiplication of oaths at Custom House, &c., &c.) I count them to be entitled to our respect because they are in power; and, without being as I trust a Vicar of Bray, I cannot comprehend how you reconcile the names you call the Parliament with the prayer you daily use for its prosperity. The many grievous faults which as a Christian I cannot help seeing in many of their measures (not more than in those of their predecessors) make me the more anxious to conciliate their affection to the Church, and through the Church to the Gospel of Jesus Christ, by manifesting in our politico-ecclesiastical conduct that zeal against abuses, that self-denial, humility, and charity, which we preach up in private life.

And, lastly, I have hope that much good will come of their schemes for Church reform, even if ill meant by them (which I trust they were not), for I count as the greatest enemies of the Church, even those to whom her present perils will hereafter be ascribed, the men who have winked at every scandalous abuse and resisted every attempt at reasonable amendment.[1] There now! I take out the word "reform," for fear you should dislike it, though the root was thought a good one at the time of the Reformation. But call it amendment. Who for a word would quarrel with

---

[1] Altered from "moderate reform."

a friend? Not I, if I could help it. And earnestly I hope that you will not quarrel with me for this letter. I do not think you will, or I should scarcely have said so much. Yet some whom I used to know well, and still love as well as ever, look now askance when they meet me in their path, for no other reason that I know of than that I thought ten pound voters better than close boroughs, and have also publicly maintained that a Dissenter may get to Heaven, and ought to be treated as a brother Christian whilst on earth. Do, dear Newman, well consider where you are going in this business, and do not, as you threaten, march past me, unless you are quite sure that you will not hereafter wish to march back again.

Many thanks for your help in searching for an incumbent for my church at Sedgley. I have as yet made no appointment. It is by the conscientious discharge of our duties in our cures, by the due disposal of our patronage, and by the exercise of self-denial in preferment offered to ourselves, that I hope we may silence the gainsayers, or, if not, yet justify the Church. I would gladly enter into an association for these objects, if we were not by our vows as ministers and as Christians already members of just such a society. Ever Yours, C. GIRDLESTONE.

Rev. J. H. NEWMAN, Oriel College.

R

THE GRAND UNIVERSITY LOGIC STAKES

(*See p.* 267.)

Late in the Summer Term of 1849 we noticed lying in Vincent's and Macpherson's windows a slim anonymous pamphlet labelled " Grand University Logic Stakes." It was one of the two most brilliant topical *jeux d'esprit* which the century produced in Oxford, the other being Jackson and Sinclair's *Uniomachia* of 1833. It described a recent contest for the Prælectorship of Logic, which, founded in 1839, had been held during ten years by Richard Michell, and was to be filled again by election to a second decennial occupancy. It was written, unavowedly, by Landon, Fellow of Magdalen, and Examiner in the Great-Go Schools: its felicitous personal characterisations of men notable then and since were heightened by their dexterous adaptation to the language of the Turf; for Landon, a Yorkshireman born, was, like Henry Blount in "Marmion," a sworn horse-courser, and an adept in stable slang. The skit is now extremely scarce, and the rust of time has settled on the original polish of its allusive wit and fun; but, as having been coeval and conversant with its actors, I have appended a *Notularum Spicilegium*.

It unfolds and advertises the

"GRAND UNIVERSITY LOGIC STAKES of 250 sovs., for Horses of all ages above three years, without restriction as to weight or breeding. Ten-mile course. Gentlemen riders. Second Decennial Meeting to come off June 14, 1849.

"The following are the entrances up to present date :—

1. Mr. Bailly Jenks's b. c. Barbadoes, 17 yrs. . . . B. Jowett.
2. Mr. St. John's bl. c. Mainsail, 6 yrs. . . . . . Higgs.
3. Lord Oriel's ch. c. Christmas, 8 yrs. . . . . . Buggon.
4. Her Majesty's br. c. Tom Towzer, 16 yrs. . . . Barrott.

This great and important race, which afforded so much sport to the academical world in 1839, is now on the eve of being contested for the second time since its institution by that sporting chief, the illustrious Gilbert. The stakes are raised by capping the junior members of the University to the amount of sixpence a head, which yields a fund of nearly 250 sovs., liable to a heavy deduction for expense of collection, which may, however, possibly be reduced to a more reasonable percentage.

"Previously to entering on the merits of the competition, it may not be uninteresting to take a brief survey of the subsequent history and performances of the horses engaged in the memorable struggle of 1839. For that race, it may be remembered, eight horses were entered: *St. Michael, Gruel, The White Horse Bob, Lancastrian, Reformation, Barrister, Stockbroker,* and *Barbadoes.*

"*St. Michael,* the winner on that occasion, has proved by his late successes that his merits had not been over-rated, and it may be mentioned, as a proof of the steady confidence of his admirers, that he has been a prime Favourite as well as a successful runner for the different races he has since contested. He won the Rhetorical Sweeps in a common canter; and as far as credit was to be derived from such an event, put in a most respectable appearance for the Bampton Stakes, which is generally a slow race for aged horses and heavy weights, rarely accomplished under the hour; the nominations being often confined to somewhat inferior cattle. St. Michael has lately been purchased by an elderly gentleman at a very high figure. He is located in a very snug stable, and is already the sire of some very promising stock.

"*Gruel* continues to make a show in the world, and stands high in public estimation. He has taken to a novel line, in which he has come out rather strong. He appears to have left the Turf altogether for the present. After a long season in Ireland, where, notwithstanding several influential backers, he appears to have been a failure, he returned to the Marquis of Exeter's stables. His Lordship still drives him in his four-in-hand, giving him an occasional day's work at Radley Farm, where he goes to plough and drill on a new system with an Irish horse called Single-Peeper.

"The *White Horse Bob* has been shipped off to the

Antipodes to improve the breed in Her Majesty's Colonies. He is already said to have attracted considerable notice among judges in those quarters.

"*Lancastrian*, though now an aged horse, has of late displayed evidences of more than ordinary vigour.

"*Reformation*. This fine old horse still works his coach with his usual regularity. On the death of his late master he fell into the hands of a deputation from the Parent Society, by whom, we are happy to hear, he is driven gently and kindly treated.

"*Barrister*. Little has been heard of this horse since the meeting of 1839. He may possibly have been at work in the Metropolitan Conveyance department. He is undoubtedly a superior animal if he would work steadily. He walked over the other day for one of Her Majesty's Plates, which will entail upon him a good deal of public running, from which much is anticipated.

"*Stockbroker*. Turned out to grass at the expense of the University, which had no other provision for him. He has lately had a sack or two of corn sent down, to keep up his spirits.

"*Barbadoes* is the last horse on the old list, and the first on the new one. He is the only one of the old lot who has had pluck enough to run again. Not long after the last race he changed owners, Mr. Bailly Jenks having purchased him from A. Hall, Esq., for 300 sovs. and half his future earnings. It is gratifying to find that he has fallen into such good hands, as Mr. Jenks is one of the most sporting men in the University. His annual meeting in November for the Foal Stakes is always well attended, honestly run, and better contested than any similiar race in the University. He is no less wide awake in drafting off an unsound or suspicious animal than in getting hold of good ones to begin with. Three winners out of four in the last University Trial Stakes are no small proof of the excellence of Mr. Bailly Jenks's

APPENDICES

training establishment. A little more sweating of the young ones on the Catechetical Course is the only decided improvement that might be made, as they have been on several occasions very much distressed for want of this kind of exercise. Some persons fancy it does not signify, because they see horses who have quite shut up at this part of the course go ahead before the end of the race. Be that as it may, it gives a respectable finish to the style of the cleverest winner. The great merit of Barbadoes is his age and steadiness. There is no danger of his bolting over the ropes or causing any disturbance on the course; and there is little doubt but that Mr. Jenks's well-known colours, the yellow body and pink sleeves, will be seen well forward in the race. There are rather heavy books against Christmas, Tom Towzer, and Mainsail. Barbadoes is free from this disadvantage; but on the other hand, many sportsmen prefer to see a good book made up before they back a horse to any great amount.

"We have now to make a few remarks on the three new horses who are to come before the public on the present occasion, namely the following :—

"*Her Majesty's brown colt Tom Towzer*, a dark horse, but one who has a great many friends on the ground of his careful training for this particular event. He ran for the University Trial Stakes in 1840, and came out only a third. Some persons were of opinion that he was amiss at the time, but whether it was so or not, he has had ample opportunity since then to mend his pace and improve his action. It may be a question whether his style is not too high and too much of the canter for a University Logic Race. Mr. Samuel Cudsdon, whose attachment to everything connected with royalty would naturally ensure his support to her Majesty's horse, has backed him strongly, and is supposed to have a pot of money depending on the event.

"*Mr. St. John's Mainsail.* A cocky little horse, full of fun and frolic, but warranted free from vice. His performances have hitherto been first rate, and he is strongly backed by that eminent sportsman, Sir William Hamilton. He is a horse of undeniable merit and lasting power: has been known, even in hot weather, to work a coach for twelve hours a day, without delay or disappointment to the passengers. He is admirably supported by his owner, who backs him in the most spirited manner. His jockey is sure to do him justice, if we may judge from the way in which he put along that slow old horse, Grey Roundabout, for the Members' Plate. N.B. Mainsail's friends are respectfully informed that the proceedings of the day will be concluded by a first-rate ordinary at the Lamb and Flag.

"*Lord Oriel's Christmas.* A very fine colt, got by the Provost out of Brascinia. Like Tom Towzer's, his action is perhaps a touch too high, but he is one of the right sort for this kind of race. Some had objected to his rider as too heavy, and a trifle long in the leg; but he carried him uncommonly well on the way from Worcester right into Lord Oriel's stable, running bang over a poor fellow of the name of Smith, who happened to be in the way. 'Tap the Physic,' and 'The Shady Cloud,' have somewhat shaken public confidence in this stable by their recent performances; and there have been other melancholy instances of unsoundness amongst Lord Oriel's horses, arising possibly from over-training. His Lordship has done all that man could do to keep them on their legs; and in refusing a warranty to the Marquis of Exeter, when he purchased Shady Cloud a few seasons back, gave ample proofs of the correctness of his judgment and the honesty of his conduct. Many sporting men of high reputation would be glad to see Christmas a winner, but the general impression is that the race will be among the other three.

"The following is the latest quotation of the odds:—

"3 to 2 against Barbadoes.
2 to 1 against Mainsail.
4 to 1 against Tom Towzer.
15 to 1 against Christmas.

"Gentlemen proposing to be present at the race are informed that everything has been arranged with a view to their comfort and convenience by the Vice-Chancellor and the Proctors, under the able superintendence of Mr. P. Bliss, the much respected Clerk of the Course. On entering the Grand Stand they are earnestly requested not to push one another more than is absolutely necessary, as there is plenty of accommodation for all.

"The thanks of the University are due to the owners of St. Michael for not starting him on the present occasion, as, in case of his appearance, this exciting race might have shared the fate of the Lady Margaret Stakes, and degenerated into a dull, periodical walk over.

"*Postscript.*

"Friday morning, June 15. The following is the result of the race, decided yesterday:—

"Mr. Bailly Jenks's br. c. Barbadoes, 17 years (B. Jowett), I.
Mr. St. John's b. c. Mainsail, 6 years (Higgs), II.
Her Majesty's br. c. Tom Towzer, 16 years (Barrott), III.
Lord Oriel's ch. c. Christmas, 8 years (Buggon), drawn."

Here ended Landon's *jeu d'esprit*. It remains to explain the allusions. The 1849 candidates were *Barbadoes, Mainsail, Christmas, Tom Towzer*.

The brown colt *Barbadoes* was Henry Wall of Balliol, born in that island. Jenks was the irreverent sobriquet of Dr. Jenkyns, Master of Balliol. Wall was proposed by Jowett. The black colt *Mainsail* was H. L. Mansel of St. John's, afterwards Dean of St. Paul's, proposed by Dr. Higgs of the same College. The chestnut colt

Christmas was C. P. Chretien of Oriel, proposed by Burgon. Her Majesty's brown colt *Tom Towzer* was Thomas Bowser Thompson of Queen's. His proposer was Barrow of Queen's, Principal of St. Edmund's Hall, a learned cheery little man, but a strong Tractarian; while the Hall, long under the influence of Daniel Wilson, had become a nursery of Evangelicals. He soon resigned, went abroad, and died a Jesuit. The years represent each man's years of residence.

The "sporting chief" was Ashurst Turner Gilbert, Principal of Brasenose, in whose Vice-Chancellorship the "Readership," as it was originally called, came into existence. He was made Bishop of Chichester in 1842. The salary of £250 was to be provided by a small payment from every member of the University, servitors excepted, under the degree of M.A. The arrangement did not answer, was abandoned, and is here ridiculed.

The eight horses for the 1839 race had been *St. Michael, Gruel, The White Horse Bob, Lancastrian, Reformation, Stockbroker, Barbadoes.*

St. Michael was Richard Michell, Reader in Logic during the ten previous years. The "Rhetorical Sweeps" was the post of Public Orator, which he had for some time held. While delivering the Crewe Oration from the rostrum at Commemoration he used to gesticulate with his cap. I remember once his extending it with an animated flourish, when an undergraduate in the gallery just above him dropped a halfpenny into it. By the "Bampton Stakes" was meant, of course, the Bampton Lectureship, which he held in 1849. His sermons, which I dutifully attended, were extraordinarily tedious. The elderly gentleman was Macbride, Principal of Magdalen Hall. He was very learned, very ugly, and the only Head besides Marsham of Merton who was not in Orders. When Gandell, the Chaplain, was late for or absent from Chapel, the old man, though a layman, used to read the entire service himself. He had made Michell Vice-Principal in succession to Jacobson, who became Regius Professor of Divinity.

Gruel was an amusingly apt name for William Sewell of Exeter. The "novel line" refers to his editing his sister Elizabeth's religious novels, "Amy Herbert," "Margaret Percival," and the rest, eagerly read once, now, I fear, forgotten. He wrote also himself a hysterical novel called "Hawkstone." His "season in Ireland" was spent in the foundation of St. Columba's College; the "influential backers" were Lord Adare, the Primate Lord John Beresford, and Dr. Todd of Trinity College, Dublin. He broke away from this enterprise, nobody quite knew why, and transferred his energies to Radley. Single-Peeper was Singleton, its first Warden.

The *White Horse Bob* was Bob Lowe of Magdalen, an Albino with snowy hair. He was a popular Class Coach, but left Oxford for Australia, returning after a distinguished career to become a member of Mr. Gladstone's Government, and to be made Lord Sherbrook. His first wife was a Miss Orrid. It was said to be an "'Orrid Low match."

Lancastrian was T. W. Lancaster, formerly Fellow of Queen's, who lived in Oxford, an elderly man with an elderly wife, for a time Usher of the Magdalen Choristers, and frequently Examiner in the Little-Go Schools. The "evidence of more than ordinary vigour" refers to a sermon he had preached before the University, in which he had spoken of Hampden as "that atrocious Professor." He was severely censured by his College, and published a lengthy pamphlet in self-defence.

Reformation was John Hill, Vice-President of St. Edmund's Hall. His "late master" was Principal Grayson, who died in 1843; a ponderous being with a handsome wife much younger than himself. He is mentioned contumeliously in "Black Gowns and Red Coats." The "deputation from the Parent Society" was W. Thompson of

Queen's, who succeeded Grayson at the Hall, and was an ardent supporter of the Church Missionary Society. Herein Hill was strongly in accord with his chief, being always appointed to receive the Society's deputation at the Oxford meetings. He was the recognised leader of the Low Church party, giving tea-parties to like-minded undergraduates once or twice a week at his house in the High, where pietistic talk, prayer, exposition, and hymnody were lightened by the presence of his four charming daughters.

Barrister was Henry Halford Vaughan, Fellow of Oriel. He had left Oxford to practice at the Chancery Bar, the "Metropolitan Conveyance." "Her Majesty's Plate" was the Regius Professorship of Modern History, to which Vaughan was appointed in 1848. His high reputation drew at first large audiences to the Theatre, but his lectures were too condensed and close in texture to be followed easily by the casually-minded undergraduate, nor was there at that time any Modern History School to stimulate serious study.

Stockbroker was Dr. C. W. Stocker of St. John's. He had been "turned out to grass" on a country living in the gift of Convocation. The "sack of corn" was a grant of money bestowed on him by the University for some parochial purpose.

Barbadoes, as we have said, was Henry Wall. By his "change of owners" is meant his election to a Bursary and Fellowship at Balliol from St. Alban Hall, of which he was Vice-Principal. The "Foal Stakes" was, of course, the annual contest for the Balliol Scholarships. The "drafting off" meant expulsion from the College; two recent instances gave point to the passage. The "three winners out of four" were James Hornby, afterwards Head Master of Eton, Henry Smith, Professor, and Curator of the Museum, and William Warburton, now Canon of Winchester. The "Catechetical Course" was the *viva voce* examination in Divinity for Greats; in this several Balliol men had shown weakness. Jenks's colours, "yellow body and pink sleeves," commemorate the nickname "Yellow Belly" borne by Dr. Jenkyns's butler, almost as notable a character as his master, and arrayed always in a protuberant canary-coloured waistcoat.

Tom Towzer was Thomas Bowser Thompson of Queen's, a "dark horse," because, being idle in his younger days, he obtained only a third in Greats. Samuel Cudsdon was Bishop Wilberforce, who energetically supported Thompson. Those who remember Mansel will appreciate the description of *Mainsail*. He was the exponent in Oxford of Sir William Hamilton's philosophy. His coaching for twelve hours a day was one of the *ben trovato* myths which sprang up round him and Jowett. When Fearon of Balliol, afterwards H. M. Inspector of Schools, was within six or seven weeks of the Schools, he went to Wall with his Logic. Wall examined and dismissed him, "could not in so short a time make up for previous neglect." Jowett heard of it and sent for him. "I hear Mr. Wall gives you up; I will undertake you, if you like. I am engaged always till 12 at night, but if you like to come to me from 12 till 1, I will do the best I can." For six weeks the midnight work went on; then said Jowett, "I think you may face the examiners now"—and Fearon got his First. A "Jowler myth" most likely, but showing the estimation in which he was held. Mansel's "owner" was President Wynter; his "jockey" was little Dr. Higgs, who had been an active canvasser for Charles Grey Round, "Grey Roundabout," a parliamentary candidate for Oxford University in 1847. The "Lamb and Flag" were the armorial bearings of St. John's; a big dinner was given in Hall after the voting to all the St. John's supporters of Mansel.

G. P. Chretien of Oriel, *Christmas*, had been elected to a Fellowship from Brasenose (Brascinia). His rider was Burgon, whose queer person was supported by two unusually "long legs." He had been elected from Worcester to an Oriel Fellowship over the head of Goldwin Smith; is it not written, acrimoniously, in Mark Pattison's "Memories"? "Tap the Physic" was Clough, a play on Toper-na-Fuosich. "Shady Cloud" was Froude, whose "Shadows of the Clouds by Zeta" had been published in 1847. He afterwards suppressed it. The "instances of unsoundness" refers to the Newmanian secessions. Hawkins refused a testimonial, or "warranty," to Froude when he stood for, and was elected to, a Fellowship at Exeter.

The "Clerk of the Course" was Dr. Philip Bliss, University Registrar. The "Grand Stand" was the Divinity School, where the voting arrangements were outrageously inconvenient. I remember once, when we were struggling to record our votes, Archdeacon Bartholomew, at the far end of the room, shouting a pathetic appeal to the Vice-Chancellor, Dr. Williams, who answered that unless the gentleman should hold his peace, he would send a bedel to remove him.

The "Lady Margaret Stakes" was the Margaret Professorship of Divinity, then a biennial appointment, but renewed as a matter of course. It had long been held by Dr. Fausset.

S

THE WHITEHALL PREACHERSHIPS

For this interesting history of an extinct but once famous institution I am indebted, as for much besides, to Dr. Farrar of Durham.

Oxford being disloyal to the House of Hanover, Walpole advised George II. to summon Oxford divines to preach before him, as an endeavour to conciliate the University. It being pointed out that this would be looked upon as a slight to Cambridge, it was determined to take from each University twelve resident College Fellows, each in turn to preach once a fortnight, and their appointment to be permanent so long as their residence continued. It was found, however, after a time that the abler Fellows, passing away from the Universities, ceased to hold their office; while men unmarried and unpromoted stayed on obsolete and senile. One of these was Griffith. Howley, when Bishop of London, hearing complaints of his preaching, went to hear him, and found him worse than he had thought possible. After service he followed him into the vestry. "Mr. Griffith, I want to speak to you about your sermon." Bowing low, Griffith replied: "I beg that your Lordship will not do so: it is a sufficient compliment to me that you should be present; I cannot bear to hear your commendation of the sermon." Howley went away discomfited; and ascending to Canterbury soon after, bequeathed the difficulty to his successor Blomfield. He attempted interference, and was in his turn foiled by Mo.; but as the Whitehall Chapel Royal, in which the sermons were delivered, needed extensive repair, he took the opportunity of dismissing all the preachers; and when two years later the Chapel was reopened, obtained the Queen's consent to a change of system, appointing two resident Fellows, one from each University, to preach month by month for two years only, with a salary of £300 a year from the Queen's privy purse. Of course, Mo. was not reappointed: he used to come to the Chapel, seat himself in some corner which the preacher's voice ordinarily failed to reach, and say aloud from time to time—"I cannot hear a word."

INDEX

A

Abernethy, 65
Acland, Sir H. (Dr.), 33, 37, 45, &c., 52, 58, 142, 154, 315
Acland, Sir T., sen., 89, 91
Acland, Sir T., jun., 84, 85, 86, 88, &c., 217, 262
Adams, W., 85, 169
Adare, Lord, 278
Adelaide, Queen, 4
Albert, Prince, 267
Aldrich, Dean, 71
Alford, Dean, 249
Allbutt, Professor, 111
Allen (of Holland House), 142
Angelo (fencer), 107
Argyll, Duke of, 241
Armitstead, W. G., 201
Arnold, Dr., 182, 183, 193, 195, 210, 211, 218, 231
Arnold, Matthew, 97, 110, 121, 184, 283, 284
Atterbury, Charles, 145

B

Badcock, 15
Baden Powell, Professor, 18, 42, 49
Baden Powell, Mrs., 17
Bagot, Bishop, 129
Baker, G. W., 35
Balfour, Professor, 58
Bandinel, Dr., 161, 170
Banks, Sir J., 36
Barnes, Dr., 129
Bartlett, R. E., 109, 247
Batchelor, Eleanor, 290
Bathurst, Stewart, 269
Bathurst, W., 19
Baxters (gardeners), 34
Baxter (printer), 293
Bayliss, Judge, 72
Bayly, E. G., of Pembroke, 153
Bennett (St. Paul's, Knightsbridge), 143
Bennett (Rugby Tonsor), 217
Benson, Archbishop, 272
Beresford, Lord J., 278
Besant, Walter, 111
Bethell (Lord Westbury), 198
Bishop, Sir Henry, 73, 81
Bishop (of the Angel), 291
Blachford, Lord, 153
Blackstone, Charles, 244
Blagrave (Magdalen), 163
Blagrove (violinist), 76
Blanco White, 185, 262
Bland, Archdeacon, 216
Blaydes. *See* Calverley
Bliss, Dr., 152, 162
Blomfield, Bishop, 27, 275, 337
Blomfield, A., 310
Bloxam, Dr., 170
Bloxam, Matthew, 84, 165
Blyth (organist), 77
Böckh, Professor, 126
Bode (Christchurch), 150, 155
Boone, Shergold, 115
Bothie, 98, 120, 305, and *see* Clough

340 INDEX

Bourne, Dr., 63
Bouverie, 137
Bowen, Ch., 310
Boyle, Dean, 275
Boxall, Miss, 7
Bradley, Dean, 272
Brancker, Tom, 174, &c.
Brasenose Ale, 94
Bree, Archdeacon, 28
Brereton, Canon, 89, 217
Bridges, President, 239, 308
Bridges (Fellow of Corpus), 239, &c.
Bright, John, 199
Brodie, Sir B., sen., 56, 65
Brodie, Sir B., jun., 57, 58, 98
Brookfield (Cambridge), 86
Browning, 2
Bruno, Dr., 270
Buckland, Dr., 36, &c., 48, 49, 141
Buckland, Mrs., 38
Buckland, Frank, 37, 38, 39, 41, 106, &c.
Buckley, 108
Bucknill, "Hip-hip," 232
Bull, Dr., 26, &c.
Buller, Charles, 86
Bulteel, 268
Bulwer Lytton, 69
Bunsen, Baron, 90, 147
Burgon, 54, 190, 233, 241, 243, 273
Burne-Jones, 51
Burney, Miss, 9, 72
Burrows, Commander, 296
Burrows, Sir G., 65
Burton, "Jack and Tom," 7
Butler (of Shrewsbury), 206, 215
Butler, Bishop, 213, 265
Byron, 127, 303

C

Cain and Abel, 252
Calverley, 109, &c., 247

Canning, G., 7, 69
Canning, Lord, 36, 185
Cardwell, Mrs., 52
Cardwell, M. R., 95
Carlyle, 56, 92, 222
Carroll, Lewis, 155, &c.
Cecil, Lord R., 227
Chamberlain, "Tom," 108
Chambers (Magdalen), 164
Chambers (Proctor), 192
Chapman, President, 224
Chapman (naturalist), 42
Charles I., 163, 296
Charlotte, Queen, 131
Chase, Dr., 126, 242
Chretien (Oriel), 134
Church, Dean, 85, 153, 224
Clarence, Duke of, 102
Clark (Taunton), 193
Claughton, Bishop, 84, 224, 238
Clementi (violinist), 76
Clifton (Brasenose), 72
Clough, 97, &c., 126, 184, 196, 205, 212
Cole, W. G., 224, 225
Cole (Papirius Carbo), 225, 230
Colenso, Bishop, 209
Coleridge, S. T., 2, 117
Coleridge, Herbert, 117, &c.
Coleridge, Sara, 117
Coles, Henry, 175
Collins (the poet), 258
Combe (of the Clarendon), 49
Compton (Rugby master), 272
Congreve (Wadham), 121
Conington, John, 104, 105, 206, 207, 222, 276
Conybeare, 276
Copeland, 29, 224
Copleston, Provost, 16, 17, 121, &c.
Corfe, Dr., 77
Corfe, Mrs., 51, 77
Corfe, Charles, 51

INDEX

Costar, 4, 145
Cotton (Rugby master), 197
Cotton, Dr., *frontispiece*
Cotton, Archdeacon, 127
Cowie, Dean, 219
Cox, George, 114, 170
Cox, Hayward, 254, 271
Cox, John, 114
Cox, Valentine, 118, 243
Coxe, Henry, 163, 242, 243
Crabbe, 2
Cramer, Dr., 116, 309
Cross, 241
Crotch, Dr., 73
Crowe (Orator), 171, 172
Cure, Capel, 220

D

Dale, J., 300
Dalhousie, Lord, 85
Dalton, Reginald, 60
Damien, Father, 186
Darnel (of Corpus), 16
Darwin fight, 52, 56, 139
Daubeny, Dr., 31, &c., 49, 54, 57, 163, 164, 289
Davies, "Tom," 21
Davison, 17
Davy, Sir H., 41
Deane, Sir T., 56
Deichmann, 148
Delane, 51
Denison, Archdeacon, 179, 181, 191, &c., 318
Denison, Bishop, 268, 269
Derby, Lord, 49, 102, 154, 304, 314
Détenus, 24, 173
Dibdin, T. F., 12
Dickens, 2
Dickinson (novelist), 85
Dindorf, 125

Disraeli, 199, 320
Dolby, Madame, 155
Dolling, Father, 186
Döllinger, 228
Donkin, Professor, 72, 98
Dons, 19
Douglas, Helen, 127
Doyle, Sir F., 86
Draper, Professor, 54
Driffield (musical amateur), 72
Dunbar, 12, &c., 116, 299
Duncans, the brothers, 115, 170
Duncan, Phil., 35, 175,

E

Eastwick, 23
Eden (Oriel), 63, 179, 190, &c.
Egerton, Sir P., 37
Elgin, Lord, 85
Ellerton, Dr., 22
Elvey, George, 74
Elvey, Stephen, 73
Eothen. *See* Kinglake
Erle, Christopher, 6, 122, 123, 172
Erle, Sir W., 5, 17
Erle, T. W., 240
Evans, Dr. S., 215, 272
Evans (Pembroke), 242
Eveleigh, Provost, 186
Everett, U.S. minister, 151
Exmouth, Lord, 24, 241

F

Faber, Frank, 116, 160, 164, 165
Faber, "Waterlily," 116, 169
Fanshawe, Catherine, 67, 99, 303
Fanshawe, Frederick, 272
Faussett, R., 286
Faussett, T., 247, &c.
Fichte, 222
Fitzroy, Admiral, 55

Foote, 175
Foulkes, Dr., 7
Foulkes, Mrs., 7
Foulkes, E. S., 101
Fox (Queen's), 308
Freeman, J. A., 102, 105
Freytag, Professor, 135
Froude, H., 116, 121, 142, 186, 292
Froude, J. A., 185, 262, 276
Frowd, Dr., 12, 24, &c., 241
Furneaux, Henry, 48, 99, 120, 240, 245, &c., 286

G

Gabriel, Dr., 15
Gaisford, Dean, 37, 71, 106, 116, 123, &c.
Gaisford, Miss, 126
Garbett, Professor, 152, 225
Gardiner, S., 126
George, "Mother," 290
Gilbert, Dr., 14, 98, 225, 308
Giles, Archdeacon, 94
Girdlestone, Charles, 321
Gladstone, 60, 61, 85, 86, 115, 202, 228
Goethe, 221, 255
Goldsmith, 213
Goodenough (Christchurch), 128
Goodsir, Professor, 46
Goose, "Mother," 290
Gordon, Osborne, 53, 120, 127, 155, &c., 311, 313
Gore, Bishop, 214
Goss, Dr., 81
Goulburn, Dean, 141, 217, 231, 269, &c.
Grant, Archdeacon, 170
Grantham, G., 75
Granville, Lady, 7
Gray, 258, 260
Green, T. H., 118, 221, &c.

Green, "Paddy," 198
Greg, 214
Gregorians, 76
Gregorie, David, 66
Grenville, Lord, 37
Greswell, E., 7, 240
Greswell, R., 54
Griffith, Mo., 12, 27, &c., 336
Griffiths (Wadham), 49
Grote, 133
Guidotti, 291
Guillemard (Proctor), 153, 244
Gutch, J., 289
Gutch, Sarah, 289

H

Hacker, Marshall, 8, 162
Haggitt (Wegg Prosser), 286
Hallam, A., 84, 86, 121
Hallé, 72
Hamilton, Bishop, 28, 85, 86, 268, 289
Hammond (Merton), 7
Hampden, Bishop, 18, 100, 244, 275
Hancock (Christchurch porter), 126
Hardy, Gathorne, 60, 61
Hare, Archdeacon, 264
Harington (Brasenose), 123
Hascoll, Captain, 279
Hawes, Miss, 226
Hawkins, Provost, 18, 126, 179, 186, &c., 192
Heathcote, W. B., 50, 175
Henderson, Dean, 165
Hendry, Abel, 17
Henslow, Professor, 34, 53, 57
Herbert, Algernon, 139
Herbert, Edward, 138
Herostratus, 162
Hewlett (chorister), 75, 82
Hewlett (novelist), 85
Hext (Corpus), 25, 241, &c.

INDEX

Hibbert, Julian, 136
Hill, J., 96, 271
Hinds, Howell, 18, 182
Hobhouse, Bishop, 269
Hobhouse, Lord, 98
Hodgkinson, J., 300
Hodson, Frodsham, 201
Holland, Lady, 142
Holland, J. M., 81
Holme (Corpus), 27
Hooker, Sir J., 56
Hope (Museum), 48, 58, 59
Hope, Scott, 85, 89
Horseman, Miss, 9, &c., 66, 175, 179, 191
Hoskins, "Mad," 172
Hounslow, 269
Howard, G., 235
Howard (of Radley), 278
Howe, Lord, 5
Howley, Archbishop, 27, 37, 275, 336
Hubbard, 281
Hughes (artist), 52
Hughes, George, 114, 194, 196, 242
Hughes, Tom, 114, 194, &c.
Hughes, J. W., 287
Hullah, 76
Hunt, Holman, 49
Hussey, R., 126, 150
Huxley, 53, &c., 210, 228

I

Ingram, President, 116, 223, 224
Ireland, Dr., 63, 64
Irving, of Balliol, 119, 188

J

Jackson, Cyril, 124, 125
Jackson, of the Uniomachia, 94
Jacobson, Dr., 167, 275

James (confectioner), 291
Jeffs, "Mother," 290
Jelf, Dr., 130
Jelf, W. E., 76, 132, 150, &c.
Jenkyns, Dr., 116, 200
Jenner (Magdalen), 162
Jephson, Dr., 233
Jeune, Dr., 51, 144, 310
Johnson, Dr., 24, 140, 144, 166, 213
Johnson, Manuel, 49, 184
Jones, Collier, 275, 309
Jowett, 54, 98, 121, 188, 202, 212, 222, 228, 253, &c., 259, 261
Joy, " Parson," 292
Jubber, 292
Jullien, 76

K

Karslake, W. H., 29, 242
Keble, J., 2, 17, 37, 184, 225, 292, 293
Kett, "Horse," 15, &c., 224
Kidd, Dr., 16, 47, 62, 63
Kidd, Misses, 63
King, J. R., 310
Kinglake, A. W., 80, 212
Kingsley, Charles, 148, 195
Kingsley, Henry, 119
Kitchin, Dean, 150, 312

L

Lake, Dean, 182, 185, 187, 188, 196, 205, &c., 269, 271
Lancaster, Harry, 206
Lancaster (of Queen's), 158
Landon (Magdalen), 277, 296
Landor, Savage, 16
Lang, A., 287
Latimer (wine merchant), 293, 300
Laud's tree, 296

INDEX

Le Mesurier, 286
Lee, Harriett, 67
Lee, Lancelot, 173, 174
Lee, President, 237
Lee, Miss, 232
Leonard, 65
Levett (Christchurch), 128
Lewis (Jesus), 151
Ley, Jacob, 150, 253
Liddell, 37, 85, 117, 145, 154, 160, 201, 202, 315
Liddon, 134
Linwood, Miss, 150
Linwood, Professor, 150
Litton, "Donkey," 271
Liverpool, Lord, 125
Lloyd, Bishop, 128, 136, 268
Lloyd, Mrs. and the Misses, 129
Lloyd, Foster, 150
Lockhart, 62, 65
Logic Stakes, 326
Lonsdale, J., 98
Lonsdale, Miss, 256
Lothian, Lord, 227
Louse, "Mother," 290
Lowe, "Bob," 94, 202
Lowndes (oarsman), 114
Lyttelton, Lord, 232, 318

M

Macaulay, 111, 273
Macbride, 63, 115, 286, 308
Maclaren, 108
Maclean, Donald, 5
Macmullen (Corpus), 240
M'Neile, 231
Maconochie, 134
Macray, Dr., 164
Madan (of Bodleian), 12, 310
Malan, G. C., 95, &c.

Malmesbury, Lord, 87
Manning, 86, 88, 169, 170, 180, 228
Mansel, Dean, 60, 248, 264
Marriott, Charles, 95, 133, 152, 179, 189, &c.
Marriott, John, sen., 17
Marriott, John, jun., 190
Marsham, Dr., 307
Martyrs' Memorial, 295
Massey, M. P., 92
Massie (Uniomachia), 94
Matthews, Arthur, 302
Matthews, Colonel, 302
Matthews, Henry, 13, 302
Maude (of Queen's), 24
Maurice, F. D., 89, 195, 222, 261, &c.
Maurice, Dr. Peter, 74
Mayow (Uniomachia), 95
Menzies, Fletcher, 113
Menzies (Brasenose), 72
Merivale, Dean, 86
Merry, W. W., 310
Meyrick, F., 227, &c.
Michell, R., 59
Microscopic Society, 56
Mill, J. S., 263
Millais, 49
Milton, 258
Moberly, Dr., 98, 236, 246, 275
Monro, 52
Moon (oarsman), 74
Morris, W., 5, 53
Morris, "Jack," 151, 243
Mozley, J., 169, 184
Mozley, T., 17, 181
Müller, Max, 48, 72, 80, 90, 146, &c., 202, 203, 276
Mundella, Rt. Hon., 101
Mundy (Magdalen porter), 35
Murray, G. W., 76
Museum, 46, &c.

INDEX

N

Nares, Dr., 175
Neate, Charles, 37, 174, 189, 198
Ness, Charlotte, 14
Nestor, 1, 82, 298
Neve, Mrs., 7
Newman, Francis, 180, 185, 204, &c.
Newman, J. H., 2, 17, 71, 100, 116, 135, 142, 163, 179, &c., 190, 192, 197, 217, 218, 224, 226, 227, 228, 234, &c., 260, 262, 275, 287, 289, 322
Newman, T. H., 166, &c.
Newman, Mrs., 179, 284
Nicol, Professor, 133
Noetics, The, 17, 173
Norman (of Radley), 281
Norris, President, 240

O

Oakley, Sir H., 51, 77
Ogle, Dr., 47, 63
Ogle, Octavius, 167
Orlebar (Rugby), 197
Otter (Corpus), 120, 231, 241
Ouseley, Sir F., 73, 77, 78, 81, 82, &c., 148
Owen, Professor, 37, 52
Oxford, Bishop of, *see* Wilberforce
Oxford Novels, 85, 197
Oxford Spy, 64, 116

P

Palmer, Roundell, 84, 95
Palmer, William, 84, 181
Palmerston, Lord, 267
Parker, Charles, 222
Parker, Joseph, 17, 292
Parnell (St. John's), 152
Parr, Dr., 15, 161

Parrott (organist), 82
Parsons, Bishop, 15, 291
Parsons (Old Bank), 219
Patterson, Monsignor, 226, &c.
Pattison, M. J., 295
Pattison, Mark, 37, 95, 121, 133, 136, 181, 187, 192, 213, 216, 223, 228, 252, &c., 295
Pattison, Dora, 256, 260
Pearse, Mrs., 7
Peckwater, 129
Peel, Sir Robert, 117, 125, 183
Pegge, Sir Christopher, 13, 45, 62, 299
Phillips, Professor, 32, 44, 49
Piozzi, Mrs., 73
Plato, 87, 156, 214, 275
Plumer, C. J., 235
Plummer, Dr., 230, 238
Plumtre, Dr., 233, and *frontispiece*
Pollen, Hungerford, 50, 52
Pope, 7, 31, 54, 105, 145, 258
Powell, *see* Baden
Price, Mrs. B., 52
Prinsep (artist), 52
Prout (Christchurch), 155
Pugin, 158
Pusey, Dr., 36, 134, 136, &c., 151, 180, 184, 214, 225, 261, 263, 264, 275, 310
Pusey, Lady Lucy, 131
Pusey, Philip, sen., 90, 133, 143
Pusey, Philip, jun., 138
Pyne, Louisa, 77

Q

Quick, Edward, 23

R

Radnor, Lord, 183
Randall, "Tom," 114

INDEX

Reade, Charles, 165
Reid, Wemyss, 84
Reinagle (musician), 76
Reynolds (Proctor), 153
Richards (Exeter), 275
Richardson (flute player), 76
Rickards (Oriel), 293
Riddell, James, 202
Ridding, Arthur, 112, 230, 240
Rigaud, John, 26, 163, 166
Risley, W., 174
Risley, "Bob," 280
Robertson, Charles, 16, 64, 154
Rogers (artist), 53
Rogers, Thorold, 100, &c., 133, 188, 219, 247, 255
Rolleston, Dr., 32, 58, 140
Rose, Hugh James, 136
Rossetti, 52, 53
Rothschild, 173
Routh, Dr., 116, 159, &c., 172
Routh, Mrs., 30, 159
Rowden, G., 72
Royds (oarsman), 113
Rudd (Oriel), 23
Ruskin, 33, 52, 98
Russell, Lord J., 276
Rutland, Duke of, 89

S

Sadler (confectioner), 292
Salisbury, Lord, 228
Sanctuary (Exeter), 129
Sarratt (chess player), 66
Sawell, J., 74, 167
Schlippenbach, Countess, 130
Scott, Dr., 94, 125, 169, 200, 212, &c.
Scott, Walter, 2, 143, 260, 266, 291
Sellon, Miss, 134
Selwyn (Winchester boy), 110

Senior Fellows, 21
Septem contra Camum, 113, 306
Sewell, J. E. (New College), 52, 170, 177, &c.
Sewell, R. (Magdalen), 169
Sewell, W. (Exeter), 49, 274, &c.
Shaftesbury, Lord, 186
Shaw, Dr., 125, 126
Shea, the brothers, 52
Sheppard, J. W., 310
Sheppard, "Tommy," 232
Short, "Tommy," 18, 84, 229, &c., 287
Shuttleworth, Warden, 22, 23, 37, 147, 168, 275, 309, 316
Sibthorp (Magdalen), 164
Sinclair, W., 94
Singleton (Radley), 278, 279, 280
Skene, of Rubislaw, 225, 266
Skey, Dr., 65
Skidmore, 52, 160
Slatter (schoolmaster), 286, &c.
Smith, Cecilia, 123
Smith, Dean, 123
Smith, Goldwin, 104, 105, 297
Smith, Henry, 61
Smith, Payne, 209
Smith, Sydney, 17, 18, 47, 193, 292
Smythe, Miss, 51
Sneyd, Warden, 309
Spedding (Cambridge), 86
Spiers, 249
Stainer, Sir J., 82
Stanhope (artist), 52
Stanley, A. P., 79, 97, 98, 121, 182, 185, 196, 198, 267, 269, 271, 273
Stanley, Bishop, 79
Stanley, Lady, 303
Stanley, Lord, 79
Stephen, Fitzjames, 208
Stephens (angler), 290
Sterling, J., 86, 262

INDEX 347

Stowe (Oriel), 286
Streets, names of, 296
Strong, Captain, 49
Strong, Professor, 229
Stzrelecki, Count, 92
Sunderland (Cambridge), 84
Swanwick, Anna, 258
Symons, "Ben," 109, 152, 204, and *frontispiece*
Symonds, Charles, 297

T

Tait, Archbishop, 37, 95, 217
Talboys, 201, 292
Tatham, Dr., 147
Taunton, Lord, 36, 90
Temple, Archbishop, 105, 212, 214, 216, &c., 272
Tennyson, 86, 121, 213, 251, 257, 264
Thackeray, 76
Thalberg, 76
Theobald, "White," 230
Thistlethwayte, F., 286
Thistlethwayte, Mrs., 92
Thomas (naturalist), 43
Thomas, Vaughan, 243, &c.
Thompson (Trinity, Cambridge), 86, 223, 267
Thompson (Lincoln), 26, 218, 254
Thomson, Archbishop, 37, 77, 136, 265, &c.
Throgmorton, Sir R., 133
Thunny, the, 155, 315
Thursby, Walter, 230
Ticknor (American), 92
Todd, Dr., 278
Tremenheere (New College), 170
Tripp, H., 278
Tuckwell, 62, &c., 302
Tuckwell, Dr., 224
Tyler (Oriel), 235

U

Uniomachia, 93, 200

V

Vaughan, Halford, 85, 106, 211
Venables (curate, St. Paul's), 50
Victoria, Queen, 2, 5, 241

W

Waldegrave, Bishop, 267, 269
Walker, Professor, 43, 204
Wall, Dr., 62, 63
Wall, Henry, 99, 203, &c.
Wall, Miss, 204
Ward, Lord, 224
Ward, W. G., 95, 100, 217, 264
Warton, T., 162, 224, 283
Weatherby (Balliol), 110
Wellesley, Dr., 20
Wellesley, Lord, 248
Wellington, Duke of, 2, 113, 125, 133, 141
West (apothecary), 64, 299
Westbury, Lord, 198
Westwood, Professor, 20, 58, &c.
Whately, Archbishop, 17, 37, 121, 168
Whewell, Dr., 223
White, *see* Blanco
Whorwood (Magdalen), 166, &c.
Whorwood, Madame, 166
Wilberforce, R., 186
Wilberforce, Samuel, 50, 53, 54, 154, 172, 199, 267, 314, 320
Wilkins, Harry, 35, 110, 117
Williams (botanical professor), 32, 289
Williams, Henry, 174
Williams, Isaac, 180, 181, 224, &c., 287, 292

Printed in the United States
118629LV00007B/127/A